Suffer the Children

Suffer the Children

How We Can Help Improve the Lives of the World's Impoverished Children

GARY SCOTT SMITH
JANE MARIE SMITH

CASCADE *Books* • Eugene, Oregon

SUFFER THE CHILDREN
How We Can Help Improve the Lives of the World's Impoverished Children

Cascade Books
An Imprint of Wipf and Stock Publishers
199 W. 8th Ave., Suite 3
Eugene, OR 97401

www.wipfandstock.com

PAPERBACK ISBN: 978-1-5326-0071-5
HARDCOVER ISBN: 978-1-5326-0073-9
EBOOK ISBN: 978-1-5326-0072-2

Cataloguing-in-Publication data:

Names: Smith, Gary Scott. | Smith, Jane Marie

Title: Suffer the children : how we can help improve the lives of the world's impoverished children / Gary Scott Smith and Jane Marie Smith.

Description: Eugene, OR: Cascade Books, 2017 | Includes bibliographical references.

Identifiers: ISBN 978-1-5326-0071-5 (paperback) | ISBN 978-1-5326-0073-9 (hardcover) | ISBN 978-1-5326-0072-2 (ebook)

Subjects: LCSH: Poor children—care. | Poverty. | Children—Social conditions

Classification: HQ792 S6 2017 (paperback) | HQ792 (ebook)

Manufactured in the U.S.A.

We dedicate this book to our grandchildren:

Xander, Keira, Aveson, Patrick, Stella, Brenna, Ilianna, Gideon, Lydia, and Mirakai.

We pray that our work will, in some small way, improve the world we leave to them.

Contents

Preface

It takes a whole village to raise a child.

Igbo and Yoruba (Nigeria) Proverb

This proverb applies to our book in two ways. First, it will take the diligent efforts of people throughout the world to enable children to have clean water, more food, better shelter, education, health, greater safety and opportunities, and a brighter future. Second, this book rests upon the work of a village of scholars, activists, and practitioners. We utilize the expertise of hundreds of academicians and tell the stories of numerous educators, pastors, missionaries, business leaders, criminal justice personnel, NGO staff, government officials, and individuals who have overcome tremendous adversities, some of whom we have interviewed. People from Seattle, Washington to Wilmington, North Carolina and from Kenya to India have told us inspiring stories, shared helpful insights, and offered practical solutions for the problems that plague impoverished children.

Because many people "just don't know the facts," declares Peter Edelman, a Georgetown University Law Center professor who has worked on issues related to destitution for more than fifty years, "we need to tell the stories of poverty."[1] "We're invariably more moved by individual stories than by data," argues *New York Times* columnist Nicholas Kristof.[2] "Against-all-odds stories resonate deeply within us and keep us mindful of the power of the human spirit to overcome challenges and adversity."[3] "Great storytelling

1. "Poor Are Still with Us."
2. Kristof and WuDunn, *Path*, 192.
3. Maholmes, *Why Hope Still Matters*, 2.

can be a powerful catalyst for change," asserts Stephen Friedman, the president of MTV.[4]

A young boy descends into the dark pit of a coal mine where he labors long hours every day and where his mother and father have worked for many years. He lives in a village of makeshift huts in northeast India, which few residents ever leave. They stay because they need to feed their families and this is the only life they have ever known. To reach the bottom of the pit, this boy makes a dangerous descent every day on a ladder built into the side of the chasm. At the bottom he crawls through spaces so small he can barely fit—with only a headlamp for light. When he reaches a previously untouched wall, he chips out coal with his pick. Despite his deplorable circumstances, he dreams that someday he will have a different life. Millions of voiceless, vulnerable, victimized children around the world live in similar circumstances. How can we help them fulfill their dreams? What can we do to make life better for them?

While we discuss it briefly, we assume that our readers understand and accept the scriptural basis for assisting the impoverished and working to end poverty. Our focus is on identifying what causes and sustains destitution and practical ways we can work to abolish it.

In his song "Do Something" Matthew West, expresses his disgust that millions live in poverty and children are sold into slavery.

> So, I shook my fist at Heaven
> Said, "God, why don't You do something?"
> He said, "I did, I created you."

God has given us the talents and resources to end poverty. Together we can do it.

4. Quoted in Kristof, "TV Lowers Birthrate."

Acknowledgments

In addition to the individuals we interviewed for this book, we wish to thank many others who helped with research or provided constructive criticism of chapters. The work of Grove City College alumna Claire Vetter who served as a student researcher for two years was especially helpful. Grove City College students Sarah Markley and Luke Leone assisted with the appendix and the bibliography. Conni Shaw procured dozens of books for us through Grove City College's interlibrary loan services. Several Grove City College colleagues—Tim Mech, Tim Sweet, Gina Blackburn, Lois Johnson, Jarrett Chapman, Phyllis Genareo, and Lisa Hosack—offered beneficial suggestions about sources and helped us refine our arguments and conclusions. Jane's daughters Erin Tooley and Cheryl McWilliams and alumna Rebecca Torre read chapters and provided helpful feedback. Members of a social justice Bible study group in which my wife and I participated—Melissa Danielson, Brian Danielson, Jodi Brown, Brian Brown, and Patrick McElroy—also supplied valuable insights. We also thank Thomas McWhertor of World Renew and Pamela Gifford of International Justice Mission for their thoughtful analysis of chapters. My mother Arlene Smith and Grove City College seniors Sarah Gibbs and Alexia Skoriak painstakingly proofread our book. We thank Chris Spinks, Ian Creeger, Brian Palmer, Mary Roth, and Matt Wimer of Cascade Books for their assistance in publishing our book. The contributions of all these people immeasurably improved our book, and we are deeply grateful for their help.

1

Introduction

The test of the morality of a society is what it does for its children.

DIETRICH BONHOEFFER

There can be no keener revelation of a society's soul
than the way in which it treats its children.

NELSON MANDELA

In many ways we are typical Americans. Jane is a retired reference librarian who worked for twenty-five years primarily at Butler County Community College and Slippery Rock University. I have taught history, humanities, and sociology at Grove City College, a Christian liberal arts college north of Pittsburgh, since 1978. I am also an ordained Presbyterian Church, USA minister and have served five congregations as an interim or stated supply pastor. We are proud parents and grandparents who enjoy hiking, reading, and travel.

Our personal experiences in dealing with poor children, however, are numerous and diverse. For ten years I served as the part-time pastor of a church in a small city and had numerous encounters with indigent residents. For the past five years, we have served on the board of the Christian

Assistance Network (CAN), an organization that helps individuals and families in our area with financial emergencies. CAN has aided hundreds of people, including many children, by paying for medications, car repairs, and home repairs. It has also kept many families from being evicted from their apartments or from having their heat and lights shut off. As a result, we have learned much about the problems, frustrations, and hopes of poor parents and children. CAN has assisted many individuals who are homeless, unemployed, retired, divorced, or have been previously incarcerated. Most of our clients, however, have been the working poor who either have a full-time job that pays too little ($7.25 to $9 an hour) to cover their basic expenses or who work part-time and receive no health benefits. Many of these individuals work diligently, pay their bills regularly, and care deeply about their children. Their life stories are often heart-breaking. We have worked cooperatively with churches, the Salvation Army, a local food pantry, two thrift stores, a ministry to women who have been recently released from prison, and welfare system staff.

My first encounter with poverty occurred when I was eight and a family on welfare moved into a ramshackle house across the road from us in rural western Pennsylvania. Their twelfth child was born soon after they arrived. Repelled by the children's tattered clothes, lack of social skills, rank odors (the house had no running water), and poor performance in school, I and the other neighborhood children avoided them as much as possible. Adults reacted similarly. During the six years they lived there, my mother was the only one who showed them any kindness. After the family moved away, my grandparents, who lived next door to them, reacted as many other Americans with sufficient means might have: they bought the dilapidated house at a sheriff's sale and had it torn down so that no other indigent family could occupy it.

I spent the summer after my sophomore year of college working with a mission organization in Colombia. There I had my first experience with the grinding poverty that plagued much of the developing world in the 1970s. Trips to visit impoverished rural Christians, the slums of Medellin and Bogota, and a week with an Indian tribe living near the Panama border were deeply disturbing.

As a college student, I helped found a ministry at George Junior Republic (GJR), a residential facility for male juvenile delinquents located in Grove City. "New Life" initially sponsored Bible studies and discipleship groups and a big brother program that enabled about seventy-five college students to take GJR residents off campus for a couple hours each week. Since 1988 I have served as the faculty advisor to this organization. Each academic year about 125 students hold weekly Bible studies and spend time with these teenage males in various settings. Hailing from across the United States, these boys are at GJR because of their use of illegal drugs, theft, truancy, and other law-breaking activities. Many of these students come from impoverished homes, usually single-parent ones in inner-cities, and have a parent who has been or is incarcerated. Their relationships with Grove City College students has led many of them to become Christians, grow in their faith, and participate in a church after leaving the institution.

For several years Jane served as a volunteer court-appointed special advocate (CASA) in our county. She worked closely with children under state care and served as their voice in the courts. These interactions opened her eyes to the struggles these children face as well as to the problems of our underfunded and understaffed child welfare system.

We both became certified as foster parents. Our longest placement was with African-American siblings: a five-year-old girl and her four-year-old brother. This experience taught us about the challenges and joys of fostering. We struggled to understand and nurture them and to cope with cultural differences, help these precious children who had been deeply wounded by neglect and abuse, and provide appropriate childcare while we both worked full time.

For the last decade, we have actively participated in a bi-racial Presbyterian congregation in New Castle, a small city in western Pennsylvania. Among its other ministries, our church sponsors a free lunch every other Saturday for indigent community members.

Other personal experiences have given us insights into the plight of poor children around the world. For several years we participated in a group whose members read books about and discussed social justice issues, especially global poverty. For almost twenty years, I taught a Social Problems course that examined world hunger, destitution, disease, and violence. Jane has worked to fight human trafficking for the past fifteen years as a researcher for Stop Child Trafficking Now in New York City and as an activist. She has written op-eds, done radio interviews, given talks to church and community groups, spoken with legislators in Harrisburg and Washington, and created a local organization to combat contemporary slavery. We have participated in short-term mission trips at home and abroad—to inner-city Pittsburgh and Philadelphia; Mississippi (after

Hurricane Katrina); Greenville, North Carolina; Romania; and Belize. In addition, for thirty years, we have been members of Bread for the World, an organization that lobbies Congress to provide greater assistance to the poor at home and abroad.

We have also learned much about the poverty children experience through our family and friends. My brother and his wife have worked for more than thirty years in two ministries in the Phoenix area to help Native American children. The son of a couple in our Bible study group founded a school in Kenya, and we have closely followed its amazing progress. Friends from our church served as foster parents of a young brother and sister for three years and eventually adopted them. One of my colleagues at Grove City College started a ministry in 2008 to share the gospel and aid the impoverished in south Asia. Several of our friends have adopted children either domestically or from Africa or South Korea.

Unfortunately, for many Americans, poverty in the United States is invisible. Most middle- and upper-class Americans rarely interact with the poor who typically live in the inner city, mobile home parks on the edge of communities, dilapidated apartments scattered throughout cities and towns, or rural areas. Despite living in our town of 8,000 residents for more than three decades, we had little understanding of the nature or scope of our area's poverty until we began working with the Christian Assistance Network in 2011. Now we wonder how we could have been so blind. In *A Path Appears*, Nicholas Kristof and Sheryl WuDunn discuss the pathologies and problems that plague Breathitt County, Kentucky, in the heart of Appalachia. Strikingly, every problem they describe—the drug and alcohol abuse, dysfunctional families, school dropouts, difficulty finding jobs that pay livable wages, and hopelessness—is present in our community. Even though you may have little contact with them, the poor undoubtedly live in your community or area.

Global poverty is much easier to see. Because of television, the Internet, print media, and the wonderful work of many humanitarian organizations, we all know about it. We see images or read about the hunger, disease, and squalor that afflicts billions around the world. Pictures abound of children sleeping on sidewalks and begging in the streets. We know that in war-torn areas thousands of young boys are forced to serve as soldiers and many young girls are raped. We often, however, feel overwhelmed by the extent of and confused about the causes of global poverty. We do not feel responsible to help alleviate it. After all, what can one individual do?

Trying to aid the hundreds of millions of poor children around the world often seems fruitless, akin to putting a Band-Aid on a gaping wound. Many people help distressed individuals if they get to know them personally, think their intervention can make a difference, and believe their endeavors will be successful. Few people, however, feel compelled to combat social ills when they have no personal contact, the problems seem massive, and success seems unlikely, which is how millions of Americans view global poverty and injustice.[1]

The Biblical Basis

Our personal experiences prompted us to write this book to describe the immense problems of impoverished children around the world and to discuss potential solutions for them. Christians can obviously support dozens of worthy causes. We can help fund and participate in evangelistic enterprises and endeavors. Christians can engage with and work to enrich culture by financing colleges, buying books and magazines, and viewing websites, musical performances, movies, plays, and works of art. All of these ventures compete for our time, energy, and money. Why should we give priority to aiding the indigent?

Near the end of his public ministry, Jesus told a parable about sheep and goats to accentuate God's concern for the poor. Nowhere does Scripture explicitly declare that we will be evaluated on Judgment Day by how faithfully we read the Bible or how well we understood it, by how often we attended church or witnessed to nonbelievers, how often we prayed, or by the depth of our theological understanding. Jesus clearly states, however, that we will be assessed by how we have treated the "least of these"—the impoverished (the hungry, naked, and thirsty), the stranger, and the imprisoned.

How we respond to the most vulnerable and marginalized members of our society and the world is very important to God. More than one thousand biblical verses accentuate God's passionate concern for justice and exhort us to provide just political, economic, and social arrangements and practices. Although Christians disagree about many aspects of public policy and social welfare (including the best ways to help the poor), that we should aid the indigent is undebatable.[2]

1. Kristof and WuDunn, *Path*, 194.

2. Sider and Unruh, "Poor Children," 136. See also Sider, *Just Generosity*; Sider, *Good News*; Stearns, *Hole in Our Gospel*; Keller, *Generous Justice*; DeYoung and Gilbert,

We have other powerful incentives for helping poor children. Doing so lessens suffering, enables children to develop their God-given potential, and costs nations much less in the long run. The lower economic output resulting from inadequately prepared workers and the higher welfare payments and the criminal justice expenses connected with destitution are much more expensive than eradicating child poverty. The Children's Defense Fund estimates that reducing child poverty by sixty percent would require only one-sixth of the $500 billion that child poverty costs the United States each year.[3] Moreover, altruism has many psychological and physical benefits.[4]

Suffer the Children

When the disciples rebuked people who tried to bring children to Jesus, he indignantly declared, "Let the little children come to me, and do not hinder them, for the kingdom of God belongs to such as these" (Mark 10:14).[5] Jesus explained that only those who received the Kingdom of God in the unassuming way children did could enter it. Then Jesus took children into his arms and blessed them. We have chosen the language the King James Version uses in this verse, "suffer the children," as the title of our book. The word play on Jesus' invitation to the children to meet with him emphasizes the tragic reality that many children in today's world are suffering because of their poverty and its concomitants of hunger, disease, threadbare clothing, and substandard shelter.

Because Jesus valued children so highly, he was furious when some disciples tried to prohibit them from conversing with him. Jesus highlighted the importance of children in other ways. When his disciples argued about who among them was the greatest, Jesus used a child to illustrate the humble attitude they should instead have. He also warned that anyone who

Mission of the Church; Stearns, *Unfinished*; Chester, *Good News*; Bradley and Lindsley, *Least of These*; Wydick, "Best Ways to Help the Poor."

3. Edelman, "Child Poverty." This is based on the calculation that child poverty costs $170 billion in later lost productivity, $170 billion in increased expenses combating crime, and $160 billion connected with worse health. See also Holzer et al., "Childhood Poverty," 41–61.

4. E.g., Smith and Davidson, *Paradox of Generosity*.

5. Unless otherwise indicated, all biblical references are to the New International Version.

caused children to stumble would be better off having a millstone placed around his neck and being drowned in the sea (Matt 18:1–6).

Jesus' treatment of children contrasted sharply with the practices of his day. Infanticide, abandonment, and child abuse were all common throughout the Roman Empire. Children were considered to be the property of their parents.[6] Given Jesus' treatment of children, Wess Stafford, former CEO of Compassion International, argues, we might have expected the disciples to develop a theology that puts "children at the center of the work of the church." By affirming their value, Stafford contends, Jesus urges his followers to aid children who are victims of the slave trade, pornography, war, and poverty.[7]

In 2015, Pope Francis visited the Philippines where 35 percent of children live in poverty and more than a million children are homeless. A twelve-year-old girl, who had long slept on the streets, asked him why God allowed so many children to become prostitutes and use drugs. "Why," she protested, "are children allowed to suffer." Visibly moved, the pope urged his audience to ask themselves, "Have I learned . . . how to cry when I see a hungry child, a child on the street who uses drugs, a homeless child, an abandoned child, an abused child, a child that society uses as a slave?" Do we cry when children suffer and then work to end their agony?[8]

The Scope of the Problem

Both global and domestic poverty adversely affect children. Extreme poverty has been the perennial condition of the vast majority of humanity. Today 795 million people suffer from chronic hunger, and about 160 million children under the age of five are stunted in their physical development.[9] More than a billion people, including more than one-third of Africans, do not have clean water, and 2.5 billion lack basic sanitation facilities. Poor people in developing countries spend about seventy percent of their income on food, leaving little money for life's other necessities.[10] A mere one

6. Laes, *Children in the Roman Empire*, 222–77.

7. Stafford, *Too Small to Ignore*, 176–80; quotation from 177.

8. Whaley and Ramzy, "Outpouring for Francis" (first quotation); Tufft, "Pope Francis" (second quotations).

9. "Accelerating Progress to Overcome Malnutrition," http://www.ifpri.org/event/accelerating-progress-overcome-malnutrition.

10. Daigle, "World's Poorest Kids"; *Progress for Children*, www.unicef.org/publications/index_82231.html.

percent of the world's people owns almost half of the world's wealth. Their collective wealth is sixty-five times greater than the total assets of the poorest half of the world's population.[11]

Major progress, however, is occurring. In 1980 half the people in the developing world lived in extreme poverty; today only 20 percent of them do. The illiteracy of adults worldwide has dropped from more than 50 percent in 1950 to 16 percent today.[12] Fewer children are starving to death or dying of disease now than ever before, and a significantly higher percentage of children are attending school.[13] Deworming is common throughout much of the world. Most countries have malaria under control. AIDS is declining. Even in Haiti more than four out of five children receive some childhood immunizations.[14] Worldwide, maternal deaths during childbirth were almost cut in half between 1990 and 2015.[15] Even in the planet's poorest region, sub-Saharan Africa, conditions are improving.[16] World Bank officials argue that the world has the resources to eliminate extreme poverty by 2030.[17]

In the United States, 22 percent of children live in poverty—14 percent of white children, 33 percent of Hispanic children, 37 percent of Native American children, and 39 percent of African-American children.[18] Moreover, 1.7 million households barely survive on a cash income of less than $2 a person a day—the kind of desperate poverty experienced by the indigent in developing nations.[19] About 600,000 Americans are homeless, including one in thirty children.[20] That 14.7 million poor children and 6.5 million extremely poor children live in the United States is "unnecessary, costly and the greatest threat to our future national, economic and military security."[21] An African-American boy born in 2001 has a one in three

11. Hjelmgaard, "Richest 1%."

12. Kristof and WuDunn, *Path*, 307–8; "Remarkable Declines in Global Poverty."

13. See Editorial Board, "Race to Improve Global Health."

14. Kristof, "Scrooges."

15. "Maternal Mortality," http://www.who.int/mediacentre/factsheets/fs348/en/.

16. Radelet, *Emerging Africa*.

17. "World Can End Extreme Poverty."

18. "Kids Count," http://www.aecf.org/m/databook/aecf-2015kidscountdatabook-2015-em.pdf.

19. Lowrey, "War on Poverty."

20. "State of Homelessness 2016," http://www.endhomelessness.org/library/entry/SOH2016.

21. Edelman, "Child Poverty."

chance of being incarcerated during his lifetime and a Latino boy born the same year has a one in six chance.[22]

Moreover, two of five American children live in families whose income is at most 50 percent higher than the poverty line. These families face many financial difficulties. A parent who has two children and works full time at the federal minimum wage of $7.25 an hour earns $4,700 less than the poverty level. While poverty line income varies by family size and location, on average a family of four needs a member working full-time for at least $10 an hour to be above it.[23] As a result, about one-third of all American workers do not earn a living wage.[24] Strikingly, by the age of seventy-five, three-fourths of Americans have lived at least temporarily below 150 percent of the poverty line.[25] Among the thirty-five Organization for Economic Cooperation and Development countries, America ranks 34th in relative child poverty, ahead only of Romania.[26]

The United States' economic recovery since 2009 has had few positive consequences for its poorest citizens. The number of people eligible for food stamps remains at a record high of 46.5 million, while the amount of cash assistance has been reduced.[27] Almost 20 percent of American children live in households that experience food insecurity, and the figure is 34 percent for children residing in female-headed households.[28] Speaking for millions, Erika McCurdy, a nurse's aide in Chattanooga, says, "There's just no way, making $9 an hour as a single parent with two children, that I can live without assistance."[29]

22. Edelman, "Who Are We?"

23. Jacobs, "Minimum Wage."

24. Mandelbaum, "Trying to Understand." HUD recommends that no more than 30 percent of a household's income should be used to pay rent or a mortgage, which amounts to only $377 a month for a full-time minimum wage earner. Little housing at this price exists anywhere in the United States. See "Housing Wage Calculator," http://nlihc.org/library/wagecalc.

25. Rank, *One Nation*.

26. Edelman, "Child Poverty."

27. Bittman, "State of Food."

28. "Hunger and Poverty Facts"; Gundersen and Ziliak, "Childhood Food Insecurity."

29. Greenhouse, "Low-Wage Workers."

The Impact of Poverty

Growing up in poverty has a very negative physical, intellectual, and psychological impact on children. Abundant research shows that the disadvantages poor children experience have many harmful life-long consequences.[30] As Beth Lindsay Templeton argues, "poverty is more than a lack of money. It becomes a way of thinking, reacting and making decisions."[31] Stafford maintains that "a lack of money" produces "a lack of options, which is perhaps a more accurate definition of poverty."[32] Poverty affects how responsive children's parents are to their needs, how much education they receive at home, the quality of children's physical environment, the amount and type of food they eat, how frequently they change residences and schools, and their self-image and emotional well-being. The lack of proper nutrition between birth and age three often causes physical and intellectual impairment. Sadly, but understandably, many mothers and fathers who received little positive attention as young children never learn how to properly take care of their children.[33]

Anxiety, unhappiness, and dependency are common feelings among those who grow up in a destitute household. Poverty frequently leads to a lack of self-discipline and low self-esteem and reduces children's trust and empathy. Destitute children often feel angry, depressed, and insecure. Many of them view life as hopeless, pointless, and fruitless. This gloomy, pessimistic perspective prompts many of them to put forth little effort to get good grades, plan for the future, or improve their lives. "More than any other emotion," Stafford argues, "the poor feel overwhelmed." Having limited financial resources, education, or skills to improve their situation, many of them "succumb to the downward spiral" that ends in "hopelessness and despair."[34] Their sense of shame and stigmatization often leads poor children to withdraw socially, make reckless decisions, and misbehave.[35]

30. See Maholmes and King, *Oxford Handbook of Poverty*.

31. Templeton, *Understanding Poverty*, 20.

32. Stafford, *Too Small to Ignore*, 176–80; quotation from 177.

33. Alexander and Olson, "Urban Poverty." See also Alexander, Olson, and Entwisle, *Long Shadow*.

34. Stafford, *Too Small to Ignore*, 184.

35. See Brooks-Gunn and Duncan, "Effects of Poverty," 58, 80.

Myths about Poverty

Misunderstandings of poverty abound. Many assume that only a relatively small number of Americans are impoverished, that people usually remain poor for many years, that the indigent receive substantial welfare assistance, and that poverty generally results from not working hard enough. All of these assumptions, however, are false. Almost 40 percent of Americans will spend at least one year below the official poverty line ($24,250 in 2016 for a family of four) while they are between the ages of twenty-five and sixty. Moreover, at some point in their lives 80 percent of Americans will receive welfare payments, be unemployed, or live in or near poverty. The average time people are poor is rather short—one to two years—although some have more than one stint in poverty. One of two American children will live in a household that uses food stamps for part of her childhood. Our nation spends less of its GDP percentage-wise than any other post-industrial country to pull families out of poverty and protect them from falling into it. Unlike most other highly developed nations, the United States does not supply universal health care, affordable childcare, or moderately priced housing for low-income citizens. As a result, the American poverty rate is about twice as high as the average of European nations. A high percentage of the poor have worked or are working substantial hours. Our political, economic, and educational structures and policies, rather than individual laziness, accounts for most poverty.[36]

A 2014 Pew Center poll found that more than 55 percent of America's most financially secure residents think that "poor people today have it easy because they can get government benefits without doing anything in return."[37] In reality, the poor face many challenges. In addition to worrying about how to pay their bills, many of them struggle with low self-esteem and sense of purpose. Financial institutions refuse to serve many indigent Americans who are "nearly eaten alive by exorbitant fees," especially the ones to cash payroll checks and buy money orders. The poor also often cannot get credit, have to purchase used cars at outrageous interest rates, and are fined by police departments to raise revenue.[38]

36. Rank, "Poverty in America." See also Rank, Hirschl, and Foster, *American Dream*.

37. "Financial Insecurity."

38. Blow, "How Expensive It Is to Be Poor."

Why Are People Poor?

Many affluent individuals are reluctant to help the poor because they believe these myths and blame the indigent for their plight. The wealthy often see poverty as a moral failure and think that anyone who studies and works hard, sacrifices for the future, and obeys the law can succeed.[39] Many agree with conservative pundit Bill O'Reilly that people are destitute because of their "irresponsible personal" conduct, especially their "addictive behavior, laziness and apathy."[40] The poor are allegedly indolent, imprudent, present-oriented hedonists who make poor choices, including drinking excessively, using harmful drugs, and having children they cannot afford to raise. Conservatives and liberals agree that poor people are more likely than middle and upper-class individuals to engage in harmful behaviors and to focus more on instant gratification and less likely to exercise self-control and plan for the future. Conservatives typically argue that these behaviors cause poverty, while liberals generally maintain that poverty causes these behaviors.[41]

Surely, we can all agree that children do not deserve to be poor. Their poverty results from their parents' conduct and choices, not their own self-destructive acts, faulty decisions, or irresponsible behavior. Being wealthy and successful or poor and distressed is determined not simply (or even primarily) by people's virtue, hard work, and self-discipline, but "by an inextricable mix of luck, brain chemistry, child rearing, genetics, and outside help."[42] Numerous factors contribute to poverty at home and abroad: socialization patterns, mental and physical handicaps, lack of education, opportunity, and social networks, and social injustice.

Most of the parents of poor children were also raised in homes by adults (often only mothers) who had many emotional problems and neglected or abused them or gave them little loving nurture or educational enrichment.[43]

Some attribute the much higher poverty rates of African Americans, Native Americans, and Hispanic Americans to cultural attitudes

39. Kristof and Wudunn, *Path*, 14. When asked, "Which is more to blame if a person is poor," 35 percent of respondents to a January 2014 Pew Research Center/USA Today said "lack of effort on his or her part" while 50 percent said it was "circumstances beyond his or her control." See "Inequality Growing."

40. Pavlich, "True Poverty."

41. Rosenberg, "Cycle of Scarcity." See also Katz, *The Undeserving Poor*.

42. Kristof and WuDunn, *Path*, 15.

43. Velasquez-Manoff, "Status and Stress."

and child-rearing practices that produce limited aspirations and failure to plan for the future. Others blame discrimination, restricted opportunities, pessimism, and feelings of resignation born out of frustration and bitter personal experiences.[44] The median income of a black household is only 60 percent that of whites.[45] One contributing factor to this disparity is growing up in a single-parent home, which typically involves lower income, less parental involvement, and greater tension, and is much more common among African Americans (67 percent) and Native Americans (53 percent) than whites (25 percent).[46] Many studies report that the absence of a stable father especially has "adverse consequences for boys' psychosocial development and educational achievement."[47]

Hunger also fuels poverty. About seven million American households include an individual who skips meals so that other members have enough to eat.[48] Consequently, many impoverished children eat less nutritious food, which contributes to lethargy, obesity, chronic illnesses, and other health problems.[49]

Many economists contend that the most important reason for poverty in America is the poor state of the labor market for low-wage workers and the nation's escalating inequality. Prior to 1970, Americans could find manufacturing jobs that paid a decent wage. Since 1970 automation, foreign competition, and outsourcing have cost our nation 30 million manufacturing positions. Although blue-collar workers have generally become better educated and more skilled during the last thirty years, their income has declined.[50] Today instead of making steel, cars, or electronics, many Americans flip burgers at McDonald's, stock shelves at Walmart, or sell clothing at The Gap for low wages.[51] Technological changes and globalization, coupled with the waning of labor unions and the diminishing value of the minimum wage, have produced higher levels of unemployment and reduced upward mobility and income. This, in turn, has contributed to fewer

44. E.g., Wilson, *Truly Disadvantaged.*

45. Cohen, "Public-Sector Jobs Vanish."

46. "Kids Count." See, for example, Hymowitz, "Single Motherhood," and Hymowitz, *Marriage and Caste.*

47. Edsall, "What Makes People Poor?"

48. Kinsman, "Ongoing Struggle."

49. "'Wealth Gap' Seen in American Diet"; Tanner, "Americans' Eating Habits."

50. Lowrey, "War on Poverty."

51. See Cherlin, *Labor's Love Lost.*

marriages, more out-of-wedlock births, high rates of transitory cohabitation, increased poverty, and greater dependence on government support.[52]

Pervasive poverty exists in the world's richest country. In the United States "the life prospects of the young are" more "determined by the income and education of their parents" than in most other post-industrial nations. During the past 35 years, the income of people with only a high school diploma has declined 13 percent.[53] "The six Walmart heirs are worth as much as the bottom 41 percent of American households put together."[54] This "widening and deepening inequality" affects people's quality and length of life and their access to jobs, food, education, and healthcare.[55]

Our Approach

Suffer the Children analyzes the major problems children face in today's world. We examine hunger, the lack of clean water, disease, substandard housing, deficient parenting, inadequate education, insecure property rights, police corruption, ineffective and unjust judicial systems, gangs, human trafficking, and the shortcomings of the American child welfare system. We also discuss potential solutions—improving parenting, adoption practices, foster care, childcare, and education, increasing child sponsorship, providing more jobs and raising the wages of workers, reforming the child welfare system, and abolishing human trafficking. We present various ways to help children (and their families) in developing nations, including expanding microfinance, combating disease, supplying uncontaminated water, and reducing violence. We feature the stories of individuals who have overcome child poverty, organizations and programs that are alleviating poverty, and interviews with practitioners who are making a difference. We discuss what many congregations, parachurch and secular organizations, politicians, government programs, and businesses are doing to improve the quality of life for the world's impoverished children. We conclude chapters with what readers can do to aid poor children. Together we can make a difference.

52. Edsall, "What Makes People Poor?"; Shipler, *Working Poor*; Sawhill, "Intergenerational Mobility."

53. Stiglitz, "Inequality."

54. Kristof, "Canadian Dream."

55. Stiglitz, "Inequality."

2

Solving the World's Water and Food Crisis

Lord, to those who hunger, give bread. And to those who have bread,
give the hunger for justice.

LATIN AMERICAN PRAYER

Give a man a fish and you feed him for a day;
teach a man to fish and you feed him for a lifetime.

MOSES MAIMONIDES, JEWISH PHILOSOPHER

On September 9, 2006, Scott Harrison invited hundreds of his friends to a party in New York City to celebrate his thirty-first birthday. He charged them $20 to attend. Is he a megalomaniac who thought people would be honored simply to come to his party? Nine months later, on June 1, 2007, a team of twenty-one ordinary female and male athletes from thirteen different countries set out from New York City on a ninety-five-day journey. Running twenty-four hours per day, they collectively traversed 15,200 miles as they crossed eleven European nations, Mongolia, China, Japan, and Canada. Each athlete ran ten miles per day, and collectively they handed off a baton more than 1,500 times. Why did these twenty-one people spend more than three months of their lives jogging on three continents? Had they suddenly become fitness fanatics? Both Harrison and the runners undertook their respective activities for the same reason: to publicize and try to end what they deemed the preeminent crisis of the early twenty-first century—the world's lack of safe water. Reinforcing this contention, when sixteen development experts were recently asked which poverty interventions are most successful, they ranked providing clean water to rural villages as number one.[1]

After working for several years promoting prominent nightclubs and fashion events in New York City, Harrison felt desperately unhappy and spiritually bankrupt. In 2004 he volunteered with Mercy Ships, which recruits surgeons to operate on thousands of indigent people throughout the world who have no access to medical care. Harrison soon became the ship's photojournalist and spent months documenting human suffering in Africa. He was especially moved by his visits to many remote villages in Liberia where thousands had no electricity, running water, or sewage system.[2] His birthday celebration in 2006 raised $15,000 to construct three wells in a refugee camp in Northern Uganda. Since then, charity: water, the organization he soon founded, has financed more than 20,000 projects, primarily involving freshwater wells, rainwater catchments, and sand filters, and has brought potable water to more than six million poor people in Africa, Asia, and Central and South America.[3]

Similarly, the runners sought to motivate people to "alleviate the catastrophic burden placed on over a billion people who, every day, must drink unsafe local water, or travel long distances on foot to search for safe water for themselves and their families." They pointed out that about one in six people around the world does not have clean water for drinking, cooking, or bathing. To accomplish their aims, a book of photographs and analysis titled *Blue Planet Run: The Race to Provide Safe Drinking Water to the World* was published and the Blue Planet Run Foundation was created to supply safe drinking water to 200 million people by 2027. Today this global network includes more than 100 organizations that operate sustainable water and sanitation programs in twenty-seven countries.[4] Many other organiza-

1. Wydick, "Cost-Effective Compassion."
2. "Scott's Story," http://www.charitywater.org/about/scotts_story.php.
3. "charity: water," https://www.charitywater.org/projects/.
4. "Blue Planet Network," http://blueplanetnetwork.org/BPR/. See Smolan and

tions are also working to provide safe water for the 1.1 billion people who lack it.[5]

Think what your life would be like if you could not go to your faucet or refrigerator to get a glass of clean water any time you wanted one. Few people in the West consider this a luxury, but millions of others around the world would.[6] Millions of people in developing nations live in villages or rural areas where the only source of water is a polluted river, stream, or swamp. Imagine carrying eighty pounds of water in a can on your head or back for five miles once or twice a day, digging in the sand to obtain water, or waiting at a well for several hours for your turn to draw water.[7] While an average American household uses about one hundred gallons each day, families in the developing world use only five gallons a day.[8] Consequently, after carrying water home, the poor have to choose whether to use it for drinking, cooking, bathing, or washing dishes and clothes because they do not have enough water for all these purposes. Worldwide, the indigent spend billions of hours procuring water, time that children could instead use to attend school or play and adults to generate much needed income.

In the developing world, either the lack of water or contaminated water causes numerous health problems, including the death of almost two million children every year.[9] Impure drinking water, improper hand washing, and inadequate sanitation cause diarrhea, which alone leads to an estimated 842,000 deaths per year.[10] Filthy latrines, open sewage, and the lack of places to bathe make matters worse. Strikingly, more people today own a mobile phone than have a toilet in their home.[11] Every minute a child dies as a result of a water-related disease such as roundworm, whipworm, or hookworm. Throughout much of the world, "the toddlers of the poor waddle across minefields of microbial threat."[12] These diseases also stunt

Erwitt, *Blue Planet Run*.

5. *Human Development Report, 2006*.

6. See Roth, "Extra Hour Each Day."

7. "Our Mission," http://www.charitywater.org/about/mission.php.

8. Lenda, "Water Crisis."

9. *Human Development Report, 2006*, 6.

10. "Progress on Drinking Water and Sanitation." We could totally eliminate this problem through oral hydration therapy, which costs pennies per use, and is available for free in many areas of the developing world (Karlan and Appel, *More Than Good Intentions*, 42).

11. "Safe Water," water.org; "Why Water," http://www.water.cc/whywater.

12. Todd, *Hope Rising*, 51.

growth, produce debilitating anemia, diminish children's cognitive potential, and lead millions of them to miss many days of school. Among other benefits, access to clean water cuts infant mortality in rural villages in half at a cost of only $10 per child per year.[13]

Countless women and girls spend as many as twenty hours per week collecting water, which also limits their school attendance and often destroys their dreams of becoming physicians, teachers, lawyers, or nurses. Demographers predict that one billion women could enter the global workforce in the next ten years, but the time they will expend searching for safe water will impede their ability to do so.[14]

Thankfully, conditions are improving. Since 1990, two billion people, who previously used water that could sicken or kill them, have gained access to clean water.[15] Moreover, during the last century, the world's use of water increased more than twice as rapidly as did its population.

Nevertheless, the World Economic Forum contends that a water shortage is the greatest risk facing the world during the next decade.[16] The lack of safe water and healthy sanitation inhibits economic development, causes disease, and perpetuates the cycle of poverty.[17] The UN warns that the situation could become worse by 2025. As industrial development, population growth, and improving lifestyles create greater demands for water, experts estimate that unless we act quickly and vigorously almost one-quarter of the world's people will live in areas where water is scarce and two-thirds will live in regions where water resources are strained.[18] Affluent nations must help developing countries supply more uncontaminated water and increase their conservation and recycling of water to improve life for today's and tomorrow's children.

Fortunately, action is being taken. In 2014 the US Congress passed the Water for the World Act to increase people's access to safe water, sanitation, and hygiene in the nations with the greatest needs. The World Economic

13. This is the estimate of the World Health Organization.

14. "Third Billion," http://www.strategyand.pwc.com/global/home/what-we-think/third_billion.

15. "Progress on Drinking Water and Sanitation," http://www.unicef.org/media/files/JMPreport2012.pdf.

16. "Third Billion."

17. Damon and White, "Journey to Sundance."

18. "Freshwater Crisis," http://environment.nationalgeographic.com/environment/freshwater/freshwater-crisis/; Hjelmgaard, "Bringing Water to the Masses."

Forum's Global Agenda Council on Water is challenging business leaders around the world to provide equitable access to water in emerging markets.

Meanwhile, many non-governmental organizations are also working to provide clean water and better sanitation for the millions who lack it. In 2009, for example, civil engineer Gary White and actor Matt Damon created Water.org. Water.org partnered with Belgian beer manufacturer Stella Artois at the 2015 Sundance Film Festival to launch the "Buy a Lady a Drink" campaign to reduce the trips millions of women and children around the world take every day to collect water. Water.org also produced a film about Anita, an Indian woman, which aired at the festival. The installation of a water tap in her home transformed the life of Anita's family. Her children now go to school instead of waiting in line at a local water source. She works in a family business and grows her own food instead of frequently making a long journey to town to buy vegetables.[19] By working with local partners to provide innovative long-term solutions to water problems, Water.org has significantly changed the lives of thousands of other people in Africa, South Asia, and Central America.[20]

Numerous Christian organizations are also providing clean water to the world's poor. Since 1977, Lifewater has aided 2.5 million vulnerable children and their parents who live in remote regions in forty countries by eliminating life-threatening diseases through its community-focused hygiene and sanitation programs.[21] Living Water International, created in 1997, has trained thousands of volunteers and professionals in shallow well drilling, pump repair, and hygiene education who have completed more than 15,000 water projects in poor regions of Africa and Latin America.[22]

More than eighty organizations, Christian and secular, are working to provide clean water and improve sanitation around the world. They distribute hygiene kits and construct latrines and hand-washing stations. These organizations also make water filters from basic local materials and teach residents of poor communities to wash their hands, cook with clean utensils, and draw water from uncontaminated sources.[23]

The alternative birthday party through charity: water is an innovative approach. Every year parents spend millions of dollars on parties to

19. Damon and White, "Journey to Sundance."

20. "About Us," http://water.org/about/.

21. "Lifewater," http://lifewater.org/impact/.

22. "About Living Water," http://www.water.cc/aboutlivingwater.

23. "Water for the Ages."

celebrate children's birthdays by renting facilities, buying pizza, and supplying cake and children receive many presents and gift cards. Children could instead emulate the example of six-year-old Lory. He became upset when he learned that contaminated water harmed millions of children. Rather than bringing him presents, Lory asked family members and friends to donate $6 each to help furnish clean water for people in Africa. Through this and other means, he collected $2,386 that provided a clean water source for thirty-six Rwandans. While not as lucrative as Lory's, the average charity water birthday campaign raises about $770. If a mere one percent of Americans participated in this program each year for the next ten years, it would provide 100 million people with safe drinking water.[24]

More than a million residents of Kibera, a Nairobi slum, live in an area smaller than New York City's Central Park. Kibera has no running water, its roads function as open sewers, and one-fifth of its children die before the age of six. Some residents use makeshift hoses to hack into the municipal waterline, which contaminates the water they withdraw. Thousands of families purchase this dirty water at exorbitant prices. Pentair, a global water services company, recently drilled a well and put kiosks in Kibera, enabling residents to buy pure water for a small fee.[25]

Convenient access to clean water changes people's lives dramatically. The drilling of wells in hundreds of villages and rural areas has enabled more young girls to go to school, women to become economically productive, and children to live beyond their fifth birthday.[26] Consider the example of Murinja, Rwanda. Four times each day, fifteen-year-old Jean Bosco, like many other village children, walked a long distance to fill five-gallon cans with water from a muddy, stagnant, foul-smelling pond. Living Water International drilled a well in his village giving Jean and dozens of other children more time to attend school, do other chores, and play with friends. They no longer have to boil water to prevent the diseases that using unclean water causes. Now a nearby clinic uses wholesome water to treat the sick.[27]

As noted, improving water and sanitation especially benefits women. When communities have a clean, easily-accessed water supply, women spend less time caring for sick family members and can earn more income. Because women and girls are often assaulted or raped on their trips to

24. "Birthday Parties," https://www.charitywater.org/birthdays/history.php.

25. Sohn, "Coke."

26. Hjelmgaard, "Bringing Water to the Masses."

27. Havens and Walling, "Jean Bosco."

procure water, their lives become safer. Meanwhile, improved sanitation systems allow girls to stay in school after they reach puberty because they can handle menstruation more effectively.[28] Moreover, numerous organizations that provide clean water, better latrines, and improved hygiene partner with women, which helps elevate their status. Women typically take the lead in helping their communities practice better hygiene, including regular hand washing.[29]

While providing pure water through wells and rainfall collection systems is crucial, so is ensuring that farming practices do not contaminate clean water sources. Consequentially, many organizations that focus on alleviating other aspects of poverty also address water issues. Arguing that "clean water is the foundation of health and prosperity," Heifer International, for example, teaches families and communities how to manage their water resources.[30] All of these improvements to the water supply of developing nations help their residents have a better life.

The Challenge of World Hunger

Hunger problems are closely connected with the world's water crisis. Since 1980 the percentage of the planet's people who live in extreme poverty and, therefore, do not have enough to eat has been substantially reduced, but the total number, 850 million, has remained about the same because of the increase in the world's population. Every night one out of eight people in the world goes to bed hungry. One out of five people is undernourished. Many of us chastise our nineteenth-century forebears for not abolishing slavery, but when future generations look back on our day, they can justifiably censure us for not ending the tragedy of human hunger. Although two-thirds of the world's 850 million malnourished people live in Asia, sub-Saharan Africa has the highest percentage (25) of persistently hungry individuals. A significant number of the hungry are children. Globally, the mental and physical development of one in four children under age five is stunted because of malnourishment (including 40 percent of all African children). Moreover, one in six children—about 100 million—in the world's poorest countries is underweight because of acute or chronic hunger.[31] Worldwide

28. "Clean Water," http://www.care.org/work/health/clean-water.

29. Ibid.

30. "Heifer International," http://www.heifer.org/ending-hunger/index.html.

31. Green, "Ending World Hunger"; "Hunger Statistics," http://www.wfp.org/hunger/

300 million children go to bed every night with an empty stomach.[32] Many poorly-nourished children are frequently ill. Malnutrition exacerbates the effects of every childhood disease, including malaria and measles.[33] In addition to the 850 million people who are persistently hungry, the United Nations Food and Agriculture Organization (FAO) calculates that more than another billion suffer from micronutrient deficiencies.[34]

The FAO estimates that half of the world's hungry people are smallholder farmers and their families who eke out an existence on land with poor soil that is prone to drought or floods. About 20 percent are families who own no land and earn money by working for farmers. Another 10 percent of the hungry survive by raising animals, fishing, or using forest resources. The final 20 percent live in shanty towns on the edge of large cities in developing nations where they do various odd jobs or scavenge to avoid starvation.[35]

Many assume that the reason millions are hungry is that the world does not produce enough food. This supposition, however, is false. Food production per person is currently the highest it has ever been. For several decades, the world has produced enough calories, about 2,700 per day per person, not only to feed the planet's 7.3 billion people, but to adequately feed the United Nations' projected 2050 population of nine billion. Although the world's population has increased 70 percent since 1985, its farmers, who have achieved increased yields per acre by using better seeds and strains, and more irrigation, fertilizer, and mechanization, produce 17 percent more calories per person. In addition, the world's cultivated land has doubled as peasants, displaced by agribusinesses, grow crops on hillsides and in tropical forests. Unfortunately, these developments, especially as pesticide use rises, groundwater levels drop, and erosion intensifies, often harm the environment.

The problem, therefore, is not that the world's food supply is inadequate. Rather, the problem is that many calories the world produces do not go to feed humans and that millions of indigent individuals do not have enough land to grow food, the energy to produce it, or sufficient income to buy it. Being extremely poor (earning less than $1.25 per day) makes

stats; "State of the World's Children," http://www.unicef.org/sowc09/.

32. Thurow and Kilman, *Enough*, xiv.

33. "Hunger Notes."

34. Bittman, "Feed the World."

35. "Who Are the Hungry?" http://www.wfp.org/hunger/who-are.

people physically weaker and less able to earn the income they need to avoid hunger.[36] Discrimination, inadequate distribution systems, unjust or inept governments, conflict, war, drought, and flooding also contribute to one billion of the world's people consuming less than 1,900 calories each day. In addition, a third of the world's food is consumed by animals, at least a third is wasted, and about five percent goes to produce biofuels.[37] Some experts estimate that half of all the world's food is wasted after it is harvested because of poor storage facilities, inadequate transportation (made worse by the lack of roads and bridges), and misuse in kitchens and restaurants.[38] A variety of factors force peasants off their land or cause famine: cruel dictatorships (such as North Korea), war and ethnic persecution (including South Sudan, the Democratic Republic of the Congo, and Syria), drought, or other calamities. So do land speculation and the seizure of farms and water sources by wealthier citizens, sometimes facilitated by government officials who view poor farmers as inefficient. As a result, millions of peasants flee to cities where they work (often sporadically) at low-paid jobs, occupy miserable housing, and often eat worse than before.[39]

The world's current food system is environmentally harmful, economically unsustainable, and unjust. While the more affluent half of the world's people eat well, the other half struggle to feed themselves.[40] Increasing prosperity and the effort to create alternative sources of fuel are making the world's hunger problems worse. As hundreds of millions of people in China and India move toward middle-class standing, the demand for dairy products and grain-fed meat escalates. As a result, global grain reserves have plummeted and many regions are more vulnerable to natural disasters. Moreover, these developments have increased the price of food. The pressures of a larger population, greater demand, and ecological changes (expanding deserts, sinking water tables, lakes that are drying up, and climate changes) are making it more difficult to grow staple crops, especially in tropical regions.[41] Unless we act now, rising demand for food, increases in global food prices, and environmental devastation are likely to increase hunger, cause civil unrest in many countries, and topple governments.

36. Patel, Holt-Gimenez, and Shattuck, "Ending Africa's Hunger."
37. Bittman, "Feed the World"; "Hunger Notes."
38. Green, "Ending World Hunger."
39. Bittman, "Feed the World."
40. Ibid.
41. Thurow and Kilman, *Enough*, xv–xvi.

Leading Organizations Combatting World Hunger

Thankfully, numerous organizations are working energetically and effectively to alleviate hunger. The efforts of UNICEF, the United Nations' World Food Programme, Heifer International, CARE, Oxfam, and Farming First are especially notable. Established in 1946 to help children in countries devastated by World War II, UNICEF today works in 190 countries and has saved more children's lives than any other humanitarian organization. It provides emergency food during natural disasters and famines and community clinics that furnish nutrition education and support for young mothers. UNICEF also supplies vaccines, antibiotics, micronutrient supplements, and insecticide-treated bed nets and teaches women how to breastfeed and families how to practice safe hygiene.[42] The World Food Programme, the United Nations' other key agency in combatting hunger, aids eighty million people in the world's seventy-five poorest countries by quickly furnishing food during emergencies and empowering indigent farmers to help themselves.[43]

Heifer International, which began in 1944, gives cows, chickens, pigs, and other animals to poor farmers in more than thirty countries. These animals supply milk, cheese, eggs, honey, and other essential products. They plow fields, help increase crop yields, and transport goods to market. Every family that receives an animal is required to give one of its offspring to another needy family. On average, progeny are passed on for nine generations. Heifer International has helped more than twenty-two million families increase their income and has enabled many children to receive more education.[44]

Since its founding in 1945, CARE has played a leading role in fighting global poverty. Originally known for giving "care" packages to the indigent, the organization today focuses on equipping poor women to help their families and communities escape destitution. CARE works with local community leaders to improve education, stop the spread of HIV, provide clean water and better sanitation, increase economic opportunities, and preserve natural resources.[45]

42. "UNICEF," http://www.unicef.org/; "7 Top Hunger Organizations," http://www.foodandnutrition.org/September-October-2013/7-Top-Hunger-Organizations/.

43. "Our Work," http://www.wfp.org/our-work.

44. "Heifer International," http://www.heifer.org/ending-hunger/index.html.

45. "History of Care," http://www.care.org/impact/our-stories/care-history.

Founded in 1995, Oxfam is an international confederation of seventeen independent non-governmental organizations that each represent a different country. Oxfam supplies clean water, food, and hygienic materials to victims of war and natural disasters. Working in ninety countries, its staff also strive to devise fairer land policies, improve the operation of the international food system, and provide basic health, educational, and financial services to the indigent.[46]

Established in 2009, Farming First is a global coalition of 154 organizations representing farmers, scientists, engineers, industrial leaders, and agricultural development NGOs. It highlights how better agricultural practices can increase food security, inhibit climate change, expand biodiversity, and increase farmers' income. Farming First strives to safeguard natural resources, increase harvests, expand access to markets, and foster research about sustainable development.[47]

Hunger in the United States

Although hunger problems are more severe in developing nations, they also exist in the United States. Currently about 49 million people (roughly 15 percent of the American population), including almost 16 million children, live in food insecure households. Numerous organizations strive to alleviate hunger in the United States. Especially impressive is the work of Feeding America. Established in 1979, it sponsors 200 food banks and 60,000 food pantries and meal programs throughout the country. Each year it supplies about 3.3 billion meals to needy individuals and families. While the National School Lunch Program, operated by the federal government, provides free or reduced-priced meals to more than 21 million children during the school year, Feeding America provides nutritious meals and snacks to hundreds of thousands low-income children on the weekends and during the summer.[48]

The federal government's Supplemental Nutrition Program (SNAP) "offers nutrition assistance to millions of eligible, low-income individuals and families" and benefits communities economically. SNAP is by far the nation's largest hunger program. Its staff work with state agencies,

46. "Oxfam International," http://www.oxfam.org/.

47. "Farming First," http://www.farmingfirst.org/about-us/.

48. "Hunger in America," http://www.worldhunger.org/articles/Learn/us_hunger_facts.htm; "Feeding America," http://www.feedingamerica.org/hunger-in-america/.

neighborhood and faith-based organizations, and nutrition educators to ensure that those eligible for assistance know about the program and can apply to receive its benefits.[49] Many Americans incorrectly believe that the SNAP program is plagued by fraud, inhibits recipients from working, subsidizes able-bodied loafers, makes people dependent, and provides only a minor portion of people's food needs. In reality, studies show that the rate of fraud and waste in the SNAP program is less than one percent. The average household receives $281 per month, and the typical individual receives $133. Who would refuse to work in order to try to live on this paltry amount? In our work with the Christian Assistance Network, my wife and I have been often amazed, given how little income many of our clients have, that their SNAP benefits are so low. In 2011, 87 percent of households receiving food stamps included a child, an elderly person, or a disabled individual. In 2013, 44 percent of SNAP participants were under age eighteen. Half of all Americans will use food stamps as children and so will half of all Americans sometime between ages eighteen and sixty-five. Because the typical SNAP amount is so small and using food stamps involves social stigma, few people want to be dependent on them. More than 50 percent of SNAP recipients work, and 80 percent of the others who are able-bodied take a job within a year after their benefits begin. The SNAP program costs about $2 billion a year, which is only 2 percent of the federal budget.[50]

Ending World Hunger

In addition to increasing funding for humanitarian efforts, numerous other actions can alleviate world hunger. Especially crucial are removing impediments (governmental, societal, material, and psychological) that make life more difficult for the poor and helping them gain the knowledge, skills, and resources they need to provide for themselves. We must move from furnishing aid to promoting development. Foreign aid can be helpful under certain conditions and is essential during emergencies caused by drought, typhoons, and wars. However, aid can also produce sizeable national debt, foster political corruption, depress local markets (which reduces the income of local farmers and business people), and lead to dependence. In

49. "Supplemental Nutrition Assistance Program," http://www.fns.usda.gov/characteristics-supplemental-nutrition-assistance-program-households-fiscal-year-2013.

50. Johnson, "Six Myths"; "Characteristics of SNAP Households"; Sherter, "Food Stamps."

the 1960s Africa exported 1.3 million tons of food each year, while today it imports almost 25 percent of its food. The cost of paying off international development loans and misguided national policies have both substantially contributed to this outcome.[51] To be politically and economically secure, countries must develop their own stable food supply.

Three critical steps in reducing world hunger are discussed in other chapters: improving schools to empower poor children to escape the trap of poverty, sponsoring children, and helping the destitute save money and obtain loans. A fourth is to increase indigent adults' knowledge about family planning and birth control to enable them to limit the size of their families if they choose. Governments, organizations, and individuals can engage in many other actions to alleviate poverty and provide a better life for children. For example, Brazil and Ghana have demonstrated that giving cash transfers to the destitute, increasing the minimum wage, and assisting individuals, especially women, who farm small plots can substantially decrease hunger.[52]

High transportation costs, food spoilage, and unreliable and inadequate water supplies hamper food production in many developing nations today. Therefore, their governments, aided by grants and experts from affluent countries, foundations, and charitable organizations, must help communities and farmers manage land more effectively, conserve soil and water, control flooding, and stockpile water for future use. Governments need to construct more roads and bridges, erect warehouses, granaries, and farmers' markets, build more irrigation systems, clear land, plant trees, and build or renovate schools. Teaching poor citizens how to better manage natural resources, handle their finances, and generate more income is also essential.[53]

The governments of developing nations and humanitarian organizations must also work together to create more stable markets, improve the status and opportunities of women, help the indigent establish legal title to their land (which is discussed in the next chapter), encourage farmers to utilize more ecologically-sound practices, reduce conflict and war, and change the attitudes of the destitute. Poor farmers must often sell their

51. Patel, Holt-Gimenez, and Shattuck, "Ending Africa's Hunger." See also Perkins, *Geopolitics*; Gruden and Asmus, *Poverty of Nations*, 65–74; Easterly, *White Man's Burden*; Moyo, *Dead Aid*.

52. Green, "Ending World Hunger."

53. "Food Assistance for Assets," http://www.wfp.org/food-assets; "What Causes Hunger," http://www.wfp.org/hunger/causes.

products when prices are low, which decreases their income. Helping poor farmers combine their resources and sell their crops at higher prices, which, in turn, enables them to produce more, can alleviate this problem. The World Food Programme (WFP) provides technical expertise to enable farmers to boost their production of staple food commodities and increase their sales to WFP and other buyers at fair prices, thereby augmenting their earnings. This has greatly improved the lives of hundreds of thousands of small farmers, especially women, in many developing countries.[54] However, when food prices rise, indigent urban workers are forced to purchase cheaper, less nutritious foods, which increases malnutrition, especially among children.[55] Therefore, helping the urban poor increase their income and reduce their housing costs is also important.

To enhance the lives of children, we must improve conditions for their mothers. Women are generally paid less than men for their agricultural work, do the lion's share of household work, and are usually excluded from making decisions about agricultural practices.[56] In numerous African nations, women produce most of the food, but men control family finances, and many of them squander money on alcohol, sex, and drugs. Women are much more likely than men to save money, use loans to establish viable businesses, and upgrade their farms, and they repay loans at much higher rates than men do.[57]

Picture two women farmers in Kenya. Both raise maize on small plots of land. One produces two tons of maize per acre, while the other produces only one-fourth that amount, leading to tremendous differences between their families. The first family has enough to eat, decent housing and clothing, and healthy children. The second family struggles to survive. What accounts for this difference in production? Like many other farmers since the Green Revolution began in the 1960s, the first woman is using improved hybrid crop varieties, fertilizer, and planting techniques that boost yield per acre.[58]

In 2006 Andrew Youn co-founded One Acre Fund to help African farmers implement these Green Revolution techniques that doubled the

54. "Purchase for Progress," http://www.wfp.org/purchase-progress.

55. "What Causes Hunger?" See also Conway, *One Billion Hungry,* and Timmer, *Food Security and Scarcity.*

56. "Agriculture," http://www.care.org/work/world-hunger/agriculture.

57. Kristof and WuDunn, "Women's Crusade."

58. Bornstein, "Green Revolution."

world's food production between 1960 and 1990. Today his organization employs 2,500 staff who provide training and market assistance to 280,000 smallholder farmers in Kenya, Burundi, Rwanda, and Tanzania, and it hopes to serve a million families by 2020. Meanwhile, many companies have been created to improve seed varieties, and African governments are partnering with fertilizer manufacturers to reduce costs.[59]

In conclusion, to lessen world hunger, the world's wealthy nations must provide more carefully targeted and monitored development aid, assist poor farmers in developing nations to grow more food, and help improve the infrastructure of these countries. Affluent nations must also prod African countries to invest more money in agriculture, protect the property of farmers, and prevent armed conflict between and within nations.[60] Motivating the poor to adopt a more positive mindset is also crucial to ending hunger.[61]

What We Can Do to Solve the World's Water and Hunger Problems

Norman Borlaug, the architect of the Green Revolution, declared in 1970: "we will be guilty of criminal negligence . . . if we permit future famines."[62] For more than forty-five years, we have known how to avert famine and end world hunger. A world that put astronauts on the moon, invented the Internet, and almost conquered AIDS should be able to eradicate humanity's oldest scourge. Nevertheless, every day 21,000 people living in the developing world die as a result of malnutrition and related diseases.[63]

We cannot prevent natural disasters or stop all the malevolent actions of dictators that produce food and water problems in numerous nations. The world's chronic hunger and water shortages, however, are largely caused by human ignorance, selfishness, and lethargy, on the one hand, and well-intended, but misdirected, actions of individuals, organizational leaders, and government officials, on the other. We have the ability to end

59. Ibid. See also Tina Rosenberg, "Green Revolution"; Sanchez, "Plentiful Food Production."

60. Thurow and Kilman, *Enough*, 265–73.

61. Ferrari, "World Hunger."

62. Borlaug, "Green Revolution."

63. Thurow and Kilman, *Enough*, xiii–xiv; "Hunger and World Poverty," http://www.poverty.com/.

this calamity. We have enough resources to provide everyone with adequate food to eat and clean water to drink.[64] For $30 billion a year, the FAO estimates, we could abolish world hunger.[65] This amount is less than 2 percent of what the world's nations collectively spend each year on their military budgets. Providing the additional calories the 13 percent of the world's chronically hungry people need would require a mere 1 percent of the food we currently produce. Several studies indicate that we could provide clean water to every person in the world for about $20 billion.[66]

Christians can take several steps to help provide clean water for everyone and end world hunger. We can limit our consumption of water and food. We can reduce our personal waste. Christians can give generously to organizations that furnish pure water, alleviate hunger, and work to help people supply their own needs in the future. We can prod the governments of developing nations to take steps to solve their water problems and reduce the hunger of their citizens. Christians can support organizations like Bread for the World that lobby members of Congress to fund the food programs at home and abroad that most help beneficiaries and hold both recipient nations and individuals accountable.

Many of us can also change what we eat. The diet of most Westerners includes large amounts of meat, fruit, and other foods that require much greater resources to produce than the more plant-based diet of people in other parts of the world.[67]

Decreasing food and water waste is crucial too. Experts calculate that 30 percent of all food produced is squandered rather than consumed.[68] In wealthy nations most waste takes place in restaurants, cafeterias, and homes. It happens because of consumer preferences (expectation of unblemished fruit and vegetables) and supermarket strategies such as "buy one, get one free." Raising awareness about world hunger, educating consumers to make better choices, increasing prices for food, enacting government regulations, and developing campaigns (like the United Kingdom's "love food, hate waste") can all help reduce waste.[69]

---

64. Thurow and Kilman, *Enough*, xvi–xvii. See also Leathers and Foster, *World Food Problem*; Butterly and Shepherd, *Hunger* and Patel, *Stuffed and Starved*.

65. "Scourge of Hunger."

66. Todd, *Hope Rising*, 52.

67. Godfray, "9–10 Billion People," 113–14.

68. E.g., WRAP, *Food We Waste*.

69. Cheng-Tozun, "The Food Supplier"; Godfray, "9–10 Billion People," 115–16. See

Failing to end world hunger will have disastrous consequences. We are biblically and morally obligated to ensure that all the world's people have clean water and enough food to eat. God has blessed us with the resources to accomplish this. As stewards of the planet God has created and disciples of Christ, we must act quickly, compassionately, and wisely to end the scourges of contaminated water and world hunger.

---

also Sachs, *Fork*.

3

Reducing Global Violence and Protecting Property Rights

No longer will violence be heard in your land,
nor ruin or destruction within your borders.

Isaiah 60:18

Where justice is denied, where poverty is enforced, where ignorance prevails and where any one class is made to feel that society is in an organized conspiracy to oppress, rob and degrade them, neither persons nor property will be safe.

Frederick Douglass, 1886

Evans, a forty-five-year-old Kenyan father of six children, worked as a security guard for a company that sold building materials. One night armed thieves stole $35,000 worth of goods, after tying up Evans and his fellow guards and locking them in a room. When the police arrived the next morning, they charged Evans and his coworkers with failing to prevent a felony. The stunned and distraught Evans suffered a stroke immediately after his arrest that impaired his speech and prevented him from defending himself to the police or in court. Although Evans had not committed a crime, he was placed in prison. After a month in jail, he was released because his family raised bail money by selling their cow and using their land as a form of security. Evans lost his job, and his family had to rely on handouts from relatives. Four of their children had to move to their grandmother's house several hours away. Evans was free, but he had no income to cover either the physical therapy or prescribed medications he needed to speed his recovery.

Moreover, the prospect of enduring a lengthy court case to clear his name loomed. After learning about his case, attorneys from International Justice Mission (IJM), a global organization that strives to protect the poor from violence in the developing world, began fighting in court to refute the bogus charges. Meanwhile, IJM social workers helped Evans's wife establish a small grocery business to support their family. Despite his innocence and the lack of evidence against him, it took almost eighteen months of relentless action by IJM lawyers to get Evans (and the other security guards) acquitted. During this process and following his exoneration, IJM Kenya's aftercare team helped pay for Evans's medical treatment and school fees for his children. Without IJM's legal and financial assistance, it is unlikely Evans could have won his legal battle, recovered from the psychological trauma of his false arrest and imprisonment, or rebuilt his life.[1]

Corrupt judicial systems, coupled with the threat and use of violence, contribute immensely to the impoverishment of children and their families in today's world. The United Nations estimates that more than 60 percent of the world's 7.3 billion people have little legal protection. The public justice systems of the countries in which they live are too dysfunctional and crooked to safeguard the destitute from attacks on their person or property. Throughout the developing world, most "poor people regard the police as agents of oppression, not protection." They lament that justice and police protection are provided only for prosperous businesses, the wealthy, and individuals with connections.[2] The police's lack of training and abuse of power and the failure of the courts to uphold justice produce devastating consequences. Corrupt police extort bribes and brutalize millions of innocent indigent citizens or hold them in harsh pre-trial detention.[3] Long delays in prosecution and inadequate numbers of police, judges, and attorneys thwart justice and enable the powerful, greedy, and ruthless to exploit

1. "Evans Is Now Free."
2. Narayan and Petesch, *Voices of the Poor*, 471.
3. "Police Abuse of Power," https://www.ijm.org/casework/police-abuse-of-power.

the vulnerable and voiceless without fear of being apprehended or prosecuted. As a result, for billions in the world's developing nations, "violence is an everyday threat, as much a part of what it means to be poor as being hungry, sick, homeless or jobless."[4]

On a global level, the violence committed by soldiers, terrorists, criminals, and gang members also exacts a huge personal, social, and financial toll and significantly harms children. Every year half of the world's two billion children endure some sort of violence. These children also have a greater risk of suffering from chronic diseases, drug abuse, and serious mental health problems.[5] Youth violence, which includes physical fighting, sexual and physical assault, and homicide, is a worldwide social ill. Each year 200,000—or nearly half of the world's homicide victims—are between ten and twenty-nine. For each young person whose life is taken, thirty young people sustain injuries in fights that require treatment in a hospital or clinic.

Meanwhile, youth crime is increasing in much of the world, fueled by larger numbers of people under the age of twenty, many of whom live in abject poverty in conflict-ridden developing nations. Youth who are marginalized as immigrants, cannot find jobs, or are objects of fear and suspicion often join criminal gangs not only to sustain themselves, but to gain companionship, support, respect, and protection. Destitute, desperate, and despondent, they are easily enticed into committing criminal acts. Violence perpetrated by and against youth detrimentally affects their psychological health and social functioning, leading to fear, lowered expectations, infrequent school attendance, and callous behavior. It reduces people's productivity, substantially increases the cost of nations' criminal justice, medical, and welfare services, and undermines social stability.[6]

In addition to stranger violence, hundreds of millions of children around the globe are physically, emotionally, and sexually abused by those they trust—family members, caregivers, clergy, coaches, and teachers. In many countries one quarter to one half of all children report that they have experienced severe physical abuse, including being kicked, beaten, or tied up by their parents. Much of this maltreatment is inflicted as punishment for misbehaving, which parents, prevailing social customs, and often laws

4. Haugen, "Equal Protection."

5. "Toward a Violence-Free Generation," http://www.cdc.gov/violenceprevention/vacs/index.html.

6. "Youth Violence," http://www.who.int/mediacentre/factsheets/fs356/en/.

defend as proper means of discipline. Global studies report that about 20 percent of women and 5–10 percent of men are sexually abused as children. Countless other children suffer from emotional abuse and neglect. These various forms of maltreatment contribute to a wide range of adverse physical and mental problems in adolescence and adulthood, including suffering depression, being victims or perpetrators of violence, and engaging in such high risk social behaviors as heavy drinking, drug abuse, and unprotected sex. Abuse of children also has an immense economic impact. It increases the cost of medical, psychological, welfare, and special education services and foster care. Later, as adults, victims often commit crimes, are incarcerated, earn less money, and pay fewer taxes.[7]

"By any measure," writes one scholar, including media stories, published research, the number of organizations and individuals working to help children, and the actions of governments, the mistreatment of children has attained an unprecedented "level of global attention."[8] Unfortunately, however, most nations are focusing on intervening after abuse occurs rather than working proactively to prevent it. The World Health Organization (WHO) argues that significantly reducing child abuse requires a coordinated effort among family planning and reproductive health services, housing authorities, child care providers, community nursing programs, religious institutions, and the media. Together these entities can mitigate the underlying causes of and lessen the risk factors connected with child maltreatment and strengthen practices and policies that protect children.[9]

Rape, dating violence, bullying, and trafficking of children are also major global problems. Each year an estimated 150 million girls under the age of eighteen around the world suffer some form of sexual violence. About 45 percent of girls whose first sexual experience occurred before age fifteen report that it was forced upon them.[10] A WHO study of forty developing countries found that substantial numbers of both boys and girls are victims of bullying.[11] Millions of children are forced into prostitution, pornography, military service, and slave labor.

7. *Preventing Child Maltreatment*, 11, 13.

8. Conte, "Introduction," 1.

9. *Preventing Child Maltreatment*, 33–34. See also Conte, *Child Abuse and Neglect.*

10. "Statistics on Violence," http://www.endvawnow.org/en/articles/299-fast-facts-statistics-on-violence-against-women-and-girls-.html.

11. "Youth Violence."

Criminal Justice, Protection, and the Poor

Their lack of legal protection deeply harms the impoverished in many parts of the world. "The locusts of lawless violence," Gary Haugen, the founder of IJM, and attorney Victor Boutros lament, "swarm unabated in the developing world" and destroy the prospects and hope of the destitute. The world's poorest billions live in constant fear of being imprisoned, raped, robbed, losing their property, or even being enslaved. Because recurrent violence produces health problems, inhibits children's education, and reduces people's opportunities, the poor can improve their lives only if basic law enforcement is provided. As Haugen and Boutros contend, "if you are *not safe*, nothing else matters." Residents of urban slums in the developing world classify violence as their "main problem." Most of them, especially girls and women, declare that they do not feel safe anywhere, not in factories, the marketplace, or streets, at the bus station, or on the way to school, and, tragically, not even at home.[12]

While governments of wealthy nations, aid organizations, and concerned individuals have spent trillions to help the developing world, they have done almost nothing to ensure that their criminal justice systems safeguard the basic rights of their poorest citizens. Donors and development agencies have made little effort to help the world's poorest nations develop professional and accountable police and effectively functioning courts and child welfare agencies that are indispensable to curbing violence and protecting people and property. This occurs in part because disease, squalor, shanties, homelessness, contaminated water, trash, and joblessness are easy to see, while the horrific aspects of the criminal justice system—the frequent beatings and rapes of those arrested, illegal detentions, appalling prison conditions, and police corruption—are much less visible.

Moreover, inept police and overburdened courts fail to deter crime. As Haugen and Boutros argue, "very high rates of common criminal violence" are often as detrimental to a nation's social and "economic development as a civil war, economic shocks, or the worst natural disaster." Vicious acts or the fear of violence thwarts the development of the knowledge and skills the poor need to escape destitution, undermines the social fabric, and harms community and family relationships. They also contribute to depression, alcohol and substance abuse, post-traumatic stress disorder, and suicide.[13]

12. *Challenge of the Slums*; Haugen and Boutros, *Locust Effect*, 75.

13. Haugen and Boutros, *Locust Effect*, 16, 109 (first quotation), 101 (second quotation), 103, 105.

Their frustration with incompetent and corrupt police, congested courts, and overwhelmed prosecutors and judges lead many affluent individuals in developing nations to buy their own protection. In India, for example, four times as many people work for the private security industry as serve in the country's police force. Destitute people, especially women and children, however, are forced to rely on "underpaid, under-trained, undisciplined and frequently corrupt police forces for protection and all-but-paralyzed courts for justice." Consequently, those who can pay for safety obtain it, while those who cannot, live in fear and are often victims of violence and injustice. When wealthy elites have little incentive to help maintain a reliable system of public security, it becomes worse.[14]

Gender Violence and Land Grabbing

Gender violence (domestic abuse and coerced sex) affects every facet of the developing world—schools, alleys, homes, workplaces, places of worship, and orphanages as well as commercial transactions. Females between fifteen and forty-four, especially poor ones, are more likely to suffer death or disability as a result of gender-based violence than of war, traffic accidents, malaria, and cancer combined. In many African countries, more than 25 percent of girls are forced at least once to have sex.[15] Most poor females do not report rape because they know that the police will probably do nothing to try to apprehend their assailants and they will wait months before their case is heard. About one in seven girls in the developing world is forced to marry before reaching the age of fifteen (and their relationships typically involve force, pain, and fear), and every year more than two million girls endure genital mutilation.[16] Appallingly, sexual violence is rampant in schools.

Land grabbing is a huge problem in developing nations. As a Bangladeshi economist and UN official argues, "with limited and insecure land rights, it is difficult, if not impossible, for the poor to overcome poverty."[17]

14. Ibid., 51 (quotation), 188–96; Haugen, "Equal Protection"; "Violence against Women," http://www.unifem.org/campaigns/sayno/docs/SayNOunite_FactSheet_VAW-worldwide.pdf.

15. "Violence and Health"; *Human Rights Reports: Ethiopia*, http://www.state.gov/j/drl/rls/hrrpt/2009/af/135953.htm.

16. Jejeebhoy and Bott, *Non-consensual Sexual Experiences*.

17. Rashid, "Land Rights."

About 1.5 billion of the world's poor live in urban settlements and slums and have no secure claim to their homes. In addition, millions of destitute farmers can be easily forced off their land because no reliable records demonstrate that they own it. In sub-Saharan Africa, 90 percent of all rural residents have no proof that they own their land and houses. Consequently, they fear losing the plots they farm to ruthless relatives, more affluent neighbors, or domestic or foreign agribusinesses.[18] Moreover, when the economic potential of land increases because new roads connect rural areas with markets or irrigation is introduced, small farmers often lose out to more powerful interests. People are understandably reluctant to improve property by adding new buildings or adopting new innovations and technologies that may be taken from them. Land insecurity also affects which crops people grow and whether they produce only for themselves or for commercial purposes. Proof of ownership encourages people to diversify their sources of income by using their land as collateral or renting it. The lack of legal ownership, therefore, fuels social instability and conflict around the world and increases poverty.

Even when poor people do have proof of ownership, the police are often neither willing nor able to protect their property. The police often fail to help victims because of their limited resources, indifference, or categorizing efforts to pilfer their property as "family matters." In the absence of documented property rights and police protection, brute force and cultural norms typically determine who controls what. This is particularly a problem for women in developing nations. When their husbands or parents die, heartless relatives or neighbors often steal the land and homes of widows and orphans, sometimes using lies, threats, or violence to accomplish their ends, with little fear of repercussions. A widow's relatives are the most likely candidates to purloin "everything from cows to cooking utensils, bank savings to farming equipment, homes to clothing, leaving her and her children destitute and vulnerable to exploitation, abuse, and violence."[19] In sub-Saharan Africa, for example, women produce 80 percent of the food while owning only about 1 percent of arable land. When their husbands die or abandon them, women, who are viewed as less valuable and subordinate in many African cultures, often lose their land and source of livelihood. Currently half a billion children living in low-income countries depend on the care and financial support of more than 115 million desperately poor

18. "Property Grabbing," http://www.ijm.ca/property-grabbing.

19. Ibid.; Haugen and Boutros, *Locust Effect*, 81 (quotation).

widows. Mothers who lose their homes, land, and belongings can rarely provide sufficient food or basic medical care for their children.[20]

Numerous organizations, including the International Fund for Agricultural Development, work to map land, record natural resource rights, verify the rights of groups to use areas for grazing and fishing, document the land ownership of poor farmers and their right to participate in irrigation projects, and strengthen women's land tenure. Others, most notably IJM, help poor people regain land stolen from them. When people obtain legal title to property, agricultural production increases significantly. For example, the registration of land in Ghana helped generate eleven times more land-based revenue in 2010 than in 2003.[21]

The story of Irene, a Zambian woman, illustrates the problems insecure property rights cause. After the death of Irene's father in 1987, her uncle stole his property, leading her mother to struggle to pay their family's basic expenses. Learning years later what had happened, Irene, at age twenty-three, was determined to regain her family's property and to lift them out of poverty. After an eight-year legal battle with help from IJM attorneys, in 2013 a judge ordered her uncle to return the property he had stolen. Throughout this process, IJM helped Irene pay for her courses at a local university as she pursued a degree in social work, and she volunteered with an IJM Aftercare team to aid others.[22] IJM staff also train African community leaders and police how to effectively enforce laws against property grabbing.[23]

Police Corruption and Dysfunctional Courts

As noted, police corruption and brutality cause immense problems for the poor in much of the developing world. The police often hold suspects in jail despite a lack of evidence. They frequently frame indigent, uneducated people to solve criminal cases quickly. The police also often torture suspects to extract confessions and gain information. Many destitute individuals are imprisoned simply because they were present at a crime scene or did

20. Haugen and Boutros, *Locust Effect*, 79–81; "Africa's Homeless Widows." See also De Soto, *Mystery of Capital*.

21. "Land Tenure Security," https://www.ifad.org/topic/overview/tags/land; "Africa's Land Reform Policies."

22. "IJM: Zambia."

23. See "IJM Findings," https://www.ijm.org/studies.

not have the money to bribe a crooked officer. Consequently, the police in many low-income nations are viewed as enemies, not allies; poor parents often instruct their children to run away from the police if they encounter trouble instead of going to them for help. Most police are not trained in professional methods of investigating crime and are not accountable to the public. Many officers assault citizens physically and sexually. People interviewed in the World Bank's *Voices of the Poor* repeatedly stressed that rather than "upholding justice, peace and fairness," the police and criminal justice system persecutes the impoverished and makes them "more insecure, fearful, and poorer."[24] The indigent in many developing nations view the police as simply "another armed, predatory gang" "that steals, rapes, extorts from, and assaults them."[25] Even worse, the police sometimes engage in drug smuggling, human trafficking, illegal mining, and other criminal activities. These various corrupt practices greatly harm the world's poorest people.

In many developing countries the court system is also very dysfunctional. It is understaffed, works incredibly slowly, and often reaches faulty verdicts. Because lawyers are scarce and costly, few accused poor people can employ one. Moreover, many lawyers and judges in developing nations have neither attended law school nor received any formal legal training. The dearth of attorneys and judges, coupled with their incompetence, creates massive backlogs in cases and long delays.[26] To avoid wasting years of their lives in prison, the poor need effective advocates; some Kenyans, for example, have been detained as long as seventeen years before being tried. Courts typically use the official languages of their nations, which many defendants do not understand. For an accused Ugandan sitting in a courtroom listening to a trial that has potentially profound consequences for his life, conducted in English, a language he does not comprehend, is bewildering, frightening, and frustrating. In addition, indigent citizens who are falsely arrested lose their jobs and usually their homes and often leave prison sick and demoralized. When an innocent breadwinner is incarcerated, poor families struggle mightily to feed, house, clothe, and educate their children.[27]

24. Narayan et al., *Voices of the Poor*, 163.

25. Haugen and Boutros, *Locust Effect*, 87 (quotation), 135.

26. Ibid., 146–47, 149–51.

27. "Police Abuse of Power"; Haugen and Boutros, *Locust Effect*, 92.

Reforming Criminal Justice Systems

Improving criminal justice systems and giving the poor legal protection involves convincing international aid organizations to make this a higher priority and overcoming resistance from government officials who are reluctant to allow outsiders to intervene in the operation of their legal systems. Haugen and Boutros implore nations and aid organizations to make people's right to justice and safety an essential development goal. Until they do, most destitute residents of low-income nations will not be able to improve their lives.[28] The United States Agency for International Development and the World Bank have devoted only 1 percent of their aid to reforming the justice systems of the developing world. The funds international agencies and donors have donated to promote the rule of law or enhance law enforcement have instead been used primarily to rebuild a few embattled nations such as Iraq and Afghanistan, combat transnational crimes of drugs and terrorism, and create attractive conditions for capital investment and commercial activity. Haugen and Boutros urge nations and organizations to give "economic assistance, favorable trade status, and diplomatic partnership" principally to developing nations that "make concrete commitments" to construct criminal justice systems that provide effective law enforcement for the indigent.[29]

Recognizing that the "forces of predatory violence" will not simply disappear, IJM works in developing nations to improve judicial systems, train police, prosecute criminals, "end the culture of impunity, and deter acts of violence against the poor." It helps widows, victims of human trafficking and property theft, and their families regain their houses and land, generate income, receive medical care and counseling, and ensure that their children can attend school.[30] Although the attempt to create "effective public justice systems in the developing world is costly, difficult, [and] dangerous," IJM seeks to convince world leaders that reforming these systems is indispensable to stopping violence and upgrading the lives of the destitute. Improving the functioning of the judicial system also requires changing other factors that contribute to violence—"cultural norms, gender bias, economic desperation and inequality, lack of education, [and] marginalization of vulnerable groups." To accomplish this, the police must be trained in

28. Haugen and Boutros, *Locust Effect*, 203, xiv; Haugen, "Equal Protection."

29. Haugen and Boutros, *Locust Effect*, 202–3, 257.

30. Ibid., 110, 117 (quotations in that order); "Property Grabbing."

professional methods of gathering information, investigating crimes, and conducting surveillance. They must be paid better to attract more qualified candidates, and more police must be assigned to the vastly underserved areas where the poor live.[31]

Haugen and Boutros point out that during the nineteenth and early twentieth centuries many of today's most economically advanced nations fought fierce battles to rescue their dysfunctional, corrupt public justice systems "from abuse for private gain," misuse by the politically powerful, and "outdated, unprofessional, and ineffectual practices." Therefore, while creating just, effective criminal justice systems in developing nations is admittedly expensive and very challenging, the historical record indicates that it is possible. Transforming these poorly performing systems in wealthy countries required committed community leaders, reform-minded elites, improving the pay and working conditions of criminal justice system employees, and building public trust. Because reforming the criminal justice systems of developing nations is such a mammoth and complex task, IJM leaders suggest pursuing "targeted, experimental projects" in selected countries. Successful endeavors in the Philippines, Brazil, Georgia, Sierra Leone, and Peru, they argue, indicate that deeply dysfunctional systems can be reorganized, endemic police corruption can be ended, forced labor can be prevented, and powerful predators can be held accountable.[32]

Haugen and Boutros also challenge the widespread assumption that all public officials in developing nations are "hopelessly corrupt, apathetic, and brutish." They estimate that while 15 percent of criminal justice personnel seek to use their authority "for purely predatory purposes," another 15 percent desire "to do good and serve the public." The other 70 percent wait to see which group will control the criminal justice system's culture and rewards—job retention, promotions, desirable assignments, and other benefits. If the virtuous 15 percent seem likely to prevail, the middle 70 percent will quickly "clean up their acts to stay out of trouble."[33]

John Richmond is a US Justice Department prosecutor who specializes in human trafficking. From 2002 to 2006, he worked for IJM in Chennai, India, to rescue people from forced labor. His team of social workers, advocates, investigators, and attorneys gathered evidence and aggressively pushed the police and judges to release hundreds of Indian individuals and

31. Ibid., 118 (first quotation), 122 (second quotation), 131, 138–39.

32. Ibid., 224 (first quotation), 225, 229–36, 241–75, 241 (second quotation).

33. Ibid., 254–55 (first two quotations from 254, third from 255).

sometimes whole families from bonded labor in brick kilns, rock quarries, rice fields, and other locales. As part of his current position, Richmond conducts seminars around the world to train law enforcement personnel how to improve their criminal justice systems. The key to upgrading the legal systems of developing nations, Richmond argues, is investing in human capital. Spending money to better train police, judges, and attorneys in crime detection, investigation, and prosecution, he maintains, can within a decade produce a critical mass of law enforcement personnel who can make their criminal justice systems more swift, just, and effective.[34]

The ultimate goal, however, must be not simply to construct legal institutions that are powerful enough to effectively restrain violence, but to create a political culture where less of that restraint is needed because citizens internalize moral norms. This is best achieved through improving parenting and schools, increasing religious involvement, and elevating moral standards.[35]

Gangs in Global Context

The large membership and extensive criminal activities of gangs also negatively affect millions of children around the world. Gangs are deeply entrenched, powerful groups that extort money, sell drugs, and commit numerous violent acts. Gangs are flourishing today in many parts of the developing world. Gangs especially impact the lives of many of the billion people who live in urban slums. Although the composition and activities of gangs around the world vary significantly, their members are very similar: they are primarily poor, urban, minority group males between ages fourteen and nineteen who come from disorganized, abusive, and drug-using families.[36] Many youth in other nations adopt the cultural aspects of American gangs that they encounter in music, online, or through movies and television.[37]

As discussed in more detail in the next chapter, to prevent gang involvement and reduce juvenile delinquency, we need to prod countries to

34. Interview at Grove City College on February 24, 2015.

35. Joustra, "Gary Haugen." See also the work of The Institute for Global Engagement (https://globalengage.org/) and Religious Freedom and Business Foundation (http://religiousfreedomandbusiness.org/).

36. Hartjen, *Youth, Crime, and Justice*, 69; Zissis, "Gang Truce."

37. Hazen and Rodger, *Global Gangs*; "Reducing Gun Violence," https://www.publicsafety.gc.ca/cnt/rsrcs/pblctns/rdcng-gn-vlnc/index-eng.aspx.

use preventative strategies, handle youthful offenders less punitively, and strive to redirect them. Almost all the world's nations have promised to honor standards for treating youthful offenders established by the United Nations and Amnesty International. Unfortunately, however, numerous countries employ a deterrent, punitive, "crime-control" approach to ensure public safety instead of adopting a "best interest of the child" approach that emphasizes treatment and care of juveniles. The standards nations have pledged to follow can be used to pressure transgressing ones to focus on reforming rather than penalizing youthful offenders.[38]

Some individuals are taking innovative steps to lessen the devastating effects of youth violence. For example, Laddawan Chaininpun, a resident of Chiang Mai, Thailand, was appalled when her grandson joined its largest and most disreputable gang—Na Dara (NDR). She concluded that gang membership thrived largely because the city's youth had few constructive alternatives. By demonizing gang members as violent criminals, Laddawan argued, the police and media ostracized youth and pushed them to join gangs for protection. Consequently, she decided to work with her grandson's gang instead of against it. She counseled members on personal and family matters and helped mediate their disputes with the police. Recognizing that the gang structure provided friendship and encouragement during a critical development period for youth, she reasoned that NDR could accomplish more positive ends. She helped convince her grandson's gang to ban drug usage. The successful transformation of NDR led Laddawan to found the Chiang Mai Youth Community that works to convert gangs into organizations that help youth become responsible adults while eschewing drug use, violence, and other destructive behaviors.[39]

Eleven thousand miles way, Favio Chávez devised a creative alternative to the gangs that plague Cateura, a small community built on a garbage dump on the outskirts of Paraguay's capital of Asunción. Alarmed by Cateura's widespread illiteracy, dire poverty, drugs, and gangs, the ecological technician concluded that the children of the 2,500 families who recycled trash needed something positive to do to encourage them to avoid their community's gang culture and to aspire to have better lives. Chávez, who had previously been a music teacher and the choir director of his church, decided to teach a handful of students using his own instruments. When many more children were eager to learn, he enlisted the help of a trash

38. Hartjen, *Youth, Crime, and Justice*, 69.

39. "Peace and Conflict," http://www.tigweb.org/global-issues/.

picker to make instruments out of scraps of wood, forks, jars, oilcans, and other junk in the landfill. Today hundreds of Cateura's children play violins, cellos, flutes, drums, and other instruments made from trash. Older children tutor younger ones, and the "Recycled Orchestra" performs works by Bach, Mozart, and Beethoven. Thanks to a 2013 CBS *60 Minutes* episode and the 2015 documentary *landfillharmonic*, scores of instruments have been donated to the community, the orchestra is being invited to perform around the world, and Paraguay's most famous musician, Berta Rojas, frequently flies from her home in Maryland to teach lessons to children. The money the orchestra has earned by its performances has financed the building of a facility that houses a music school for 200 children and provides free craft classes for Cateuras's residents. Moreover, the orchestra's income is supplying college scholarships for the community's youth. Chávez, the "pied piper of Paraguay," is helping Cateura's children stay out of gangs, giving them hope, and calling global attention to extreme poverty.[40]

What We Can Do to Reduce Global Violence and Protect Property Rights

Christians can support IJM and other organizations that strive to improve criminal justice systems around the world in order to curb violence, ensure that the indigent receive fair trials, and protect the property of the poor. We can urge developing nations to give higher priority to reforming their criminal justice systems, preventing child abuse, and reducing the factors that make gangs attractive. We can implore aid organizations to devote more of their funds, resources, and staff to further policies and activities that increase the safety and security of the poor in these countries. Christians can help people settle disputes peacefully and work to lessen the tension and friction that contribute to violence. These steps can greatly aid the indigent in their quest to improve their economic circumstances and social interactions and to provide a better life for their children.

40. "Favio Chavez," https://gocampaign.org/heroes/favio-chavez/; "Recycled Orchestra"; "landfillharmonic," http://www.landfillharmonicmovie.com/.

4

Curbing Gang Membership and Youth Violence in the United States

Rescue me, Lord, from evildoers; protect me from the violent.

PSALM 140:1

During the last fifty years, the United States has experienced an epidemic of youth violence. Gang activities negatively affect many children's lives and impose huge economic costs on communities by reducing property values and business and tax revenues. Thousands of families flee neighborhoods where gangs operate.[1] Crime and violence impair the emotional, physical, and economic well-being of children and make it more difficult for them to be educated and reach their full potential. In 2012, an estimated 850,000 Americans belonged to 30,700 gangs in 3,100 communities and gang members killed 2,363 people. That year, about 630,000 American youth were treated in emergency rooms because of injuries resulting from violence.[2] Homicide is the principal cause of death among

1. Ritter, Simon, and Mahendra, *Preventing Gang Membership.*

2. "National Gang Center," https://www.nationalgangcenter.gov/; "Youth Violence Datasheet," http://www.cdc.gov/ViolencePrevention/pdf/yv-factsheet-a.pdf.

African-American teenagers and the second leading cause of death for Latino teenagers.[3] Teenagers commit 16 percent of all violent crimes and 26 percent of all property crimes in the United States. Arresting, prosecuting, incarcerating, and trying to rehabilitate juvenile offenders requires a substantial amount of the time and resources of the police and courts and strains state budgets. These activities and the related medical expenses and lost productivity of their victims cost our nation billions each year.[4]

The physical, emotional, and sexual abuse of children also plagues America. Each year state and local agencies receive more than three million referrals (involving about six million children) of child maltreatment, and many cases are not reported. In the vast majority of cases, the abuser is a parent, usually a low-income one. About one third of abused children grow up to become abusers, thus perpetuating this tragedy. Every year child abuse costs the US about $125 billion as a result of providing child welfare and protection, health care, law enforcement and court fees, special education expenses, and unemployment benefits.[5] While various types of violence and crime negatively affect children, space permits focusing only on the detrimental impact of gangs and juvenile delinquency.

Although the number of American youth who belonged to gangs and their detrimental effects on our society peaked in the late 1990s, gangs continue to thrive and harm both their members and numerous communities. Nearly half of high school students and 35 percent of middle school students claim that gangs operate in their schools. Almost one in twelve youth report that at some point in their teenage years they belonged to a gang.[6] Most members of gangs in the United States are African-American or Latino youth (principally of Mexican or El Salvadoran ancestry). Gang

3. "Violence and Injury Prevention," http://www.who.int/violence_injury_prevention/publications/violence/youth_guidelines/en/.

4. "Violence-Free, Healthy, and Prospering Communities," http://youth.gov/feature-article/creating-violence-free-healthy-and-prospering-communities-requires-your-voice.

5. Child abuse and neglect are twenty-six times higher in low-income families than in middle and upper-class ones. See Sedlak and Broadhurst, *Child Abuse and Neglect*; "Child Abuse Facts," http://www.safehorizon.org/page/child-abuse-facts-56.html; "Child Abuse Statistics," https://www.childhelp.org/child-abuse-statistics/.

6. Egley Jr. and Howell, *2010 National Youth Gang Survey*; *American Attitudes on Substance Abuse*; Snyder and Sickmund, *Juvenile Offenders*.

members in the United States commit many more violent acts, especially lethal ones, than do their counterparts in most other nations.[7]

Many young teens join gangs because their race, ethnicity, socio-economic status, or limited education leads them to feel alienated and marginalized. They belong to gain protection, social and psychological support, a sense of respect, and money; increase their status; have fun; defy authority; and spend time with friends.[8] "What lured me" into a gang as a teenager, explains Yusuf Shakur, the director of Detroit's Urban Youth Leadership Group, was that its members "made me feel like I was something special."[9] The teenagers most likely to join gangs are aggressive, poorly-performing students who grow up in dysfunctional homes and have friends and siblings who belong to gangs.[10] Drug usage and dependency also play a major role. Gangs make large amounts of money by selling drugs; members have easy access to illegal drugs and often commit crimes to fund their habits.[11] As a Cincinnati gang member who began selling drugs and stealing at fifteen explains: "When your mom's a crackhead, your dad's in the joint, your brother sells drugs, and your best buddy got a Cadillac and Jordans—what else you going to do? You got no other role models."[12] Contrary to stereotypes, large numbers of girls join gangs. Girls who have been physically and sexually abused at home often join gangs because they believe that doing so will protect them from further mistreatment.[13]

Reducing the Membership and Influence of Gangs

To reduce the allure and detrimental impact of gangs, involvement in them must be made less appealing. Youth need alternative sources of camaraderie, affection, meaning, and income to avoid gangs. Eliminating risk

7. Hazen and Rodger, *Global Gangs*; "Reducing Gun Violence."

8. Duffy, "Introduction," 4; "Prevent Gang Membership," http://www.cdc.gov/violenceprevention/youthviolence/preventgangmembership/.

9. Quoted in Ritter, Simon, and Mahendra, *Preventing Gang Membership*, 5.

10. "Gang Violence Reduction Program," https://www.nationalgangcenter.gov/spt/programs/71; Hill et al., "Childhood Risk Factors," 300–22; Hawkins et al., "Predictors of Youth Violence," 1–11.

11. "Gang Prevention"; "Gang Violence Reduction Program"; "Youth Violence"; Hill et al., "Childhood Risk Factors," 300–22; Hawkins et al., "Predictors of Youth Violence," 1–11.

12. Seabrook, "Don't Shoot."

13. Miller, "Girls in the Gang," 183; Zahn, *Delinquent Girl*.

factors, decreasing gang influence, and elevating the costs of participation is also imperative. Success depends on devising and implementing better prevention, intervention, and suppression strategies. Strengthening families, training parents how to deal with disruptive and delinquent children, and providing adult supervision and recreational and social opportunities for youth after school and on weekends is critical. So is training teachers how to better manage troublemaking students, equipping teachers and administrators to better resolve student conflicts, creating youth violence prevention programs, increasing tutoring for academically struggling students, and providing more counseling and mental health services. Implementing programs to help adolescents handle anger, resolve conflicts, and develop skills that help resolve interpersonal problems is crucial. Also important is ensuring that families have adequate income, food, shelter, and prenatal care, providing affordable childcare and preschool programs that foster both academic and social skills, and furnishing safe and loving care for children who cannot live with their parents.[14]

Three programs have been particularly effective in reducing gang membership and violence in the United States: Boston's Operation Ceasefire, Project Safe Neighborhood, and the federal Weed and Seed program. Since the mid-1990s, Operation Ceasefire has enabled criminal justice personnel, social workers, and religious leaders to work together to decrease the violence of a small group of chronic youth offenders who are promised both support from social service agencies and community organizations and that they will be punished if they fail to comply. Since its initial success in Boston, this strategy has been employed in sixty other cities. Established in 2001, Project Safe Neighborhood seeks to reduce gang violence through collaboration among local, state, and federal resources. This program fosters coordination between law enforcement, community organizations, and houses of worship and is sensitive to the problems and needs of particular communities. Weed and Seed, a federal initiative that started in 1991, also focuses on neighborhoods rather than cities. Its goals are to "weed" out gang activity, drug abuse, and violent crime and to "seed" troubled areas through prevention and intervention programs while rebuilding homes and the infrastructure in these neighborhoods.[15]

14. "Gang Prevention"; Roling and Pritchard, "Social Enterprise"; "Best Practices," http://www.health.state.mn.us/injury/best/best.cfm?gcBest=youth; "Youth Violence."

15. Gebo and Bond, "Gang Reduction Responses," 6–9.

Operation Ceasefire, developed by David Kennedy, a professor at John Jay College of Criminal Justice in New York City, is widely hailed as the most successful program. He explains that most serious violent crimes are committed by chronic offenders who belong to gangs or drug-dealing enterprises. These individuals commit 50 to 75 percent of all murders in the United States. Traditional law enforcement practices in poor, often black, neighborhoods, Kennedy asserts, have been intrusive and ineffective. Stopping suspects on the street and arresting individuals for drug usage, "trespassing," and other misdemeanors has angered many residents of distressed neighborhoods and led them to distrust authorities.

Cities that have long had high rates of homicide, including Philadelphia and Oakland, have recently reduced its incidence by using community-based interventions rather than arresting and incarcerating youthful offenders. In this approach, law enforcement, social service, and community leaders identify gang members with extensive criminal histories and require them to attend "call-ins." At these meetings, authorities demand that gang members stop their violence, detail the legal consequences of not doing so, and offer to help them change their lifestyle. "If they do not stop," gang members are warned, "the consequences will be swift, and certain, and severe, and punishment will be handed out not just to the individual involved in the shooting but to everyone in that individual's gang." This strategy, Kennedy argues is transforming the previously hostile, adversarial relationship between police and "troubled, oppressed, and deeply angry minority communities." Focusing on intervention rather than on arrest and imprisonment enables law enforcement personnel to gain the trust of residents of impoverished communities and convinces many of them to cooperate with the police to reduce gang activity and youth crime. These relationships also give police greater legitimacy; instead of being seen as antagonists, they are viewed as partners acting in the community's best interest.[16]

Success Stories

Operation Ceasefire has recently worked effectively in Los Angeles where the Watts Gang Task Force established a working partnership between the city's police force, community leaders, former gang members, and mothers and grandmothers of gang leaders to collect intelligence and intervene to prevent trouble before youth are either injured or arrested. In two years,

16. Kennedy, "Falling Body Count"; Seabrook, "Don't Shoot."

violent crime in the Watts area decreased by more than 60 percent and drive-by shootings almost completely stopped.[17]

Cincinnati is another success story. Tired of dealing with the tragic aftermath of gang conflicts to settle scores, carry out vendettas, and control turf, city leaders invited Kennedy to help them implement Operation Ceasefire. Law enforcement personnel gathered information about gang's structure, leaders, size, places of operation, alliances, criminal activities, and levels of violence. They identified sixty-nine gangs with about 1,000 members. During the next several months, the police named 800 of them and charted the connections and conflicts among them. Cincinnati formed a Ceasefire team that included attorneys, cops, probation and parole officers, social service providers, and "outreach" workers, some of whom were former convicts, who acted as liaisons with gang members.[18]

At the first meeting of the Ceasefire team with gang members, the city's chief of police told them: "We know who you are" and "what you're doing. If your boys don't stop shooting people right now, we're coming after everyone in your group." (To reinforce this message, at a later meeting, gang members were shown surveillance footage in which some of them were selling drugs.) A physician who had treated many injured and dying gang members as well as innocent children caught in their crossfire told gang members that they "were better than their violent actions implied." Mothers of two sons murdered by gang members shared their feelings of grief and loss. Authorities promised to provide life coaching and personal and vocational counseling to youth who wanted to escape gang life. Social workers were introduced who could help gang members get jobs or more education. Clergy, victims and their families, and ex-gang members all informed offenders: "What you are doing is wrong, and we know you can do better." This approach worked, as homicides declined in Cincinnati by 50 percent over a two-year period.[19]

17. Kudler, "LAPD's Radical Solution"; Buntin, "What Does It Take?"

18. Seabrook, "Don't Shoot."

19. Ibid. See also Kennedy, *Deterrence*; Kennedy, *Don't Shoot*; and "Interrupting Violence." Gary Slutkin developed a similar approach called CeaseFire that uses community members to mediate with gangs while working to change behaviors in high-risk individuals and their communities. See Kristof, and WuDunn, *Path*, 7–8, 142–49.

An Ounce of Prevention is Worth a Pound of Cure

While various forms of intervention are valuable, prevention is even more important. During the course of his life, a chronic criminal offender costs society an estimated $4.2 to $7.2 million; by contrast, scholars argue that spending a mere $3,000 on such an offender by age ten would very likely have prevented his future criminal actions.[20] Another study concludes that every dollar invested in prevention saves taxpayers seven to ten dollars, primarily by reducing spending on prisons.[21] Unfortunately, federal, state, and local governments unwisely focus much more on intervention into and suppression of gangs than on trying to stop youth from joining them. Police, public health professionals, educators, business and community leaders, and social workers need to work collaboratively to devise a comprehensive strategy to prevent children from participating in gangs. Communities must provide tutoring, mentoring, life-skills training, and supervised recreational activities and promote effective parenting. Parents can help by establishing warm affective bonds with their children, providing consistent discipline, carefully monitoring their children's behavior, and keeping them from negative peer influences.

Innovative Strategies: Boxing and Chess

Meanwhile, some courageous individuals have developed creative approaches to diminishing gang involvement and youth violence. While volunteering with Chicago's Department of Children and Family Services, Sally Hazelgrove asked many youth who lived in a public housing project on the South Side why they belonged to gangs even though it was likely to lead to their imprisonment or death. They did so, they reported, to gain love, respect, and a purpose for living. Gang members explained that they had grown up in impoverished homes where their emotional needs were not satisfied. Consequently, gangs that provided camaraderie, meaning, and opportunities to make money were greatly appealing. To help these youth and decrease the violence the city's 150,000 gang members perpetrated, Hazelgrove decided to replicate the positive aspects of gangs. After gang members said that boxing would provide an attractive alternative to gang involvement, she opened the

20. Cohen, Piquero, and Jennings, "At-Risk Youth," 391–434; Cohen and Piquero, "High Risk Youth," 25–49; Heckman, "Disadvantaged Children," 1900–02.

21. "Violence-Free, Healthy, and Prospering Communities."

Crushers Club in 2009 in Englewood near where many of them lived. The tough but tender Hazelgrove recruits boys ages nine to eighteen who have either joined gangs or are at risk to do so and provides training in boxing, mentoring, spiritual nurture, and a "second family."[22] At the gym, older youth mentor younger ones. Funding from foundations, businesses, and colleges enables the club to operate and pay twenty-one "leaders" about $5,000 a year, a tiny fraction of the $85,000 it costs Illinois to incarcerate a juvenile for a year. To be hired and work as a "leader," youth must repudiate gang membership, obey the law, and be positive role models.

By promoting "respect, discipline, ownership, and love," the Crushers Club strives to give its members a "fighting chance" to create a better life. Club members train four days a week and eventually box in amateur matches. They also showcase their talents at Friday Night Fights to which the whole community is invited. Crushers recently added a music studio with professional quality equipment. Hazelgrove's approach is working: 90 percent of club members have improved their school attendance and academic performance; according to their parents, they are less defiant at home; and while 85 percent of juveniles who are arrested commit another crime within three years, only 10 percent of the club's members do.[23]

In the nation's capital, Eugene Brown is also helping at-risk youth make good decisions, observe the law, and find meaning in life. Brown grew up as a troubled teenager in a rough section of Washington, DC. Disillusioned after Martin Luther King Jr.'s assassination in 1968, Brown became addicted to heroin. To support his habit, he turned to armed robbery, was arrested, and spent eighteen years in prison. While there, he became a stellar chess player. After being released, he returned to Washington, a city infamous in the 1980s for its many gangs, youth murders, and failing inner-city schools. Brown drove his old station wagon through the city's toughest neighborhoods to recruit disadvantaged children to play chess. He purchased a run-down house in northeast Washington where he has taught the game to thousands of low-income boys and girls.[24] Brown teaches many of these adolescents to play chess proficiently, and some of them have received college scholarships to play. His larger goal, however, "is get them to think before they move." His Big Chair Chess Club, Inc. seeks to help inner-city

22. "Your Chicago: Crushers Club."

23. "Crushers Club," http://crushersclub.org/; Hazelgrove, "Street Gangs"; Alvarez, "Crushers Club"; Subramanian, "This Woman Fought."

24. Graham, "Saving Power of Chess."

children and adults develop life skills and to improve their concentration, patience, and self-discipline. Brown wants to keep youth from doing what he did: making "impulsive decisions that end up costing them the rest of their life."[25] For more than three decades, Brown has had "an astounding impact" on the lives of hundreds of Washington's underprivileged youth who have learned how the tactics that win chess matches help them develop a "positive strategy for life." Brown's life is a testimony to his philosophy that even though the game of life may "take treacherous turns," it "is never over until the last move has been made."[26]

Members of the Big Chair Chess Club team have won trophies at National Scholastic Tournaments in Charlotte and Nashville as well as at the Super National Tournament in Kansas City. The club has taught chess to thousands of students at numerous Washington DC schools, including pupils at Kimball Elementary School who have won seven city championships. All the club's funding comes from community members and business sponsors. Brown's organization also helps youth gain life skills and job training and placement and provides apprenticeship programs, computer literacy skills, and after-school tutoring. In addition, he has developed programs to aid youth and adults in their readjustment to society after their incarceration ends. Brown has been profiled on ABC's *20/20* and has produced a documentary on Washington's black chess scene. The inspirational 2013 movie, *The Life of the King*, starring Cuba Gooding Jr., portrays his life story.[27]

The Pact

Sampson Davis, Rameck Hunt, and George Jenkins grew up in an impoverished neighborhood in Newark, New Jersey, beset by gang violence, drug abuse, and crime. "The sounds of gunshots and screeching tires late at night," they report, "were as familiar to us as the chirping of insects" are to those who live in rural areas. All three were raised by single mothers and had no male role models to help them deal with the tough street life. At age thirteen, Davis started working with crack dealers. He was soon arrested for armed robbery and placed in a juvenile detention center. Deciding to view the two-year suspended sentence he received as an opportunity to have a

25. Graham, "Saving Power of Chess."

26. "Take Care of the King."

27. "Eugene Brown," http://www.chessmaneugenebrown.com/#!about2/c18b. See also Thomas-Lester, "Kings of a Different Game"; "Eugene Brown Teaches."

different life, Davis befriended Hunt and Jenkins, two of his classmates at a Newark magnet school. Convinced that education was the path to a better future, in 1989, at age sixteen, these three bright African Americans made a pact to become physicians. They supported each other academically and socially, pushing each other to work hard and stay out of trouble. All three graduated from Seton Hall University and then from either medical or dental school at Rutgers University.[28]

Today they all practice in the Newark area and work to improve their community. They have collaborated on three books that chronicle their experiences: *The Pact: Three Young Men Make a Promise and Fulfill a Dream* (2003), *We Beat the Street: How a Friendship Pact Led to Success* (2006), and *The Bond* (2008), which chronicles the problems of growing up without a father and discusses ways to increase the role of fathers in low-income communities. All three have received numerous accolades and awards, including the Essence Lifetime Achievement Award. In addition to their friendship, they attribute their success to their mothers, mentors, and intrinsic motivation. They overcame the obstacles of their background by focusing on three D's—dedication, discipline, and determination. The three doctors exhort youth growing up in impoverished, crime-ridden communities to surround themselves with positive peers and find adult mentors who can help them accomplish their goals.[29]

Davis co-founded the Violence Prevention Institute of New Jersey to provide educational and intervention programs to deter gang membership and violence. Participants are taught how to improve their school performance, develop better family relationships, deal more effectively with peers, stop detrimental social behaviors, and avoid gang involvement. The Institute also conducts research to help cities, states, law enforcement agencies, and school boards design strategies to reduce the criminal acts, violent behavior, and drug and alcohol abuse of youth and young adults.[30]

A Crusading District Attorney

The work of Ben David, the district attorney for New Hanover and Pender counties in southeastern North Carolina, is an impressive example of a

28. "The Pact" (quotation); Jones, "The Pact."

29. "Dr. Sampson Davis," http://www.drsampsondavis.com/about-dr-davis/; http://www.thehistorymakers.com/biography/dr-sampson-davis-39.

30. "Violence Prevention Institute," http://www.violencepreventioninstitute.com/.

holistic approach to reducing youth violence and crime. My wife and I heard him speak to an adult Sunday school class about the role his faith plays in his vocation at First Presbyterian Church in Wilmington where he serves as an elder. David's enthusiasm, boundless energy, charisma, and passion for justice are readily apparent. Building on the work of David Kennedy (his book *Don't Shoot* is required reading for all David's staff), other pioneers in the criminal justice field, and the Harlem Children's Zone, the district attorney has established three innovative, interrelated programs—Teen Court, the Blue Ribbon Commission on the Prevention of Youth Violence (BRC), and Phoenix Hometown Hires—that are helping improve social conditions for the 275,000 residents of the two counties.

As an assistant district attorney for New Hanover and Pender counties, David created a Teen Court in 1999 based on one he had observed in the Winston-Salem area while working there after his graduation from Wake Forest Law School. David began this job on April 20, 1999, the day after the tragic shootings at Columbine High School in Colorado. That same day two sixteen-year-old boys foolishly posted a message at a Wilmington high school warning that "the end is near." Fear that a bomb had been planted in their school, almost 500 students went home. In the aftermath of Columbine, schools across the nation adopted a zero tolerance policy toward such pranks, and the boys were tried as adults. David concluded that a different approach was needed to help delinquent youth.[31]

To keep younger teenagers out of the adult correctional system, reduce recidivism, and promote rehabilitation, Teen Court gives first-time, nonviolent offenders between the ages of twelve and seventeen the opportunity to admit their guilt and receive a punishment assigned by a jury of their peers—other youth who are primarily volunteers from National Honor Society chapters, Key Clubs, or Boy Scout troops. Youth also serve as the bailiffs, clerks, and attorneys for the proceedings. The job of these juries is to determine sentences for the offenders. All defendants are required to do community service and to be jury members in subsequent Teen Court proceedings. Juries can also mandate that defendants write a letter of apology or an essay about their transgression, pay restitution, attend a seminar, or take an online class such as "Shoplifting 101." Teen Court forces youth to confess publicly that they made a mistake and accept responsibility for their actions. This approach has been very successful. For the last ten years

31. Interview with Benjamin David at the New Hanover County Courthouse on February 17, 2015.

more than 70 percent of those tried in the New Hanover or Pender Teen Courts committed no further offenses during the next twelve months, while 84 percent of the seventy-four defendants sentenced during the 2013–14 school year did not recidivate.[32]

David was elected district attorney in 2004, and four years later, he expanded his office's outreach by bringing local business people, politicians, faith leaders, school officials, and heads of nonprofits together to create the Blue Ribbon Commission for the Prevention of Youth Violence (BRC). The BRC identified a fifteen-block area on Wilmington's north side as the community most needing assistance. It marshalled the resources of businesses, churches, and nonprofits to revitalize the community, redesigned its local school, hired an advocate to help neighborhood residents utilize social services, and created a Youth Enrichment Zone (YEZ) Teen Council to enable middle school students to develop leadership skills and serve as role models and mentors for their peers. Council members meet weekly to plan Friday night movies, games, and speakers at the local teen center and arrange community service projects.[33]

Arguing that few people can escape a life of poverty, crime, and drug usage without a job that pays a livable wage and that destitute men and women with a criminal record have great difficulty obtaining such employment, David created Phoenix Hometown Hires in 2014. To break the cycle of intergenerational poverty, give people greater dignity and purpose, reduce recidivism, and furnish talented employees, the program prods Wilmington area business leaders to hire individuals who are either impoverished or non-violent felons. A "Scarlett Letter" prevents the latter group from finding a job. Numerous businesses are providing financial literacy training, funding the project, or hiring individuals. Program participants receive training through Cape Fear Community College and work with mentors who strive to help them succeed in their various workplaces. In 2016, ninety-eight companies hired 157 individuals.[34]

32. Interview with David; David, "Benefits of Teen Court," 30, 63; telephone interview with Shelia Evans, the Teen Court Coordinator, February 26, 2015; "Teen Court," http://www.theadrcenter.org/our-services/teen-court/.

33. Telephone interview with BRC director Jana Jones Halls, March 11, 2015. See also "Blue Ribbon Commission," http://www.brcyez.org/.

34. "Phoenix Hometown Hires." About 50 percent of those who have been hired have a criminal record; Telephone interview with Tommy Taylor, Cape Fear United Way, March 19, 2015.

To promote his goals, David also speaks annually to about 10,000 students at the thirty middle schools and high schools and encourages his forty-five staff to volunteer by giving them time off in exchange for their weekly community involvement. In his speeches, David accentuates personal responsibility, the dangers of drugs, and the destructive effects of bullying. David also tries to meet "at-risk youth where they live" and discusses "choices and consequences" with them "before they get into trouble." Because he speaks frequently at schools and participates in many public events, David argues, many area residents trust him. This prompts some of them to report crimes they have witnessed to him or tell him about abuse they have suffered. His staff coach community sports teams and volunteer at schools, homeless shelters, and domestic violence facilities. David personally serves through the National Center for Fathering's Watch D.O.G.S. program at the public school his children attend by working with the chess club.[35]

Inspired by his faith, especially the biblical injunctions to lift up the poor and oppressed, David is bringing together various groups in the two counties—business people, clergy, school administrators, political officials, leaders of nonprofits, and the poor—to create a more just and prosperous community. He works to promote racial reconciliation and prod citizens to care about justice. Many are inspired, he contends, by seeing others doing the right thing.

David maintains that law enforcement personnel should work to build trust with community residents, "use power graciously," speak truthfully, and focus on the long term rather than on immediate results. Central to this approach is recognizing people's dignity and treating them kindly and justly. Only love and respect, he contends, work in the long run. Implementing Kennedy's Ceasefire model, his office holds discussions among police officers, social workers, and gang leaders to decrease crime and drug usage in Wilmington's poorest neighborhoods. David applauds the "paradigm shift" advocated by Ronal Serpas, the police chief of Nashville, who argues that to "build stronger relationships and trust between police and the people they serve," police officers must be trained differently. The police must substitute a guardian approach for their current "warrior mentality," which leads them to view communities with high rates of crime and violence as "combat zones" and produces an adversarial relationship between the police and residents. Serpas calls for educating law enforcement personnel in

35. Interview with David; David, "Community-Based Prosecution," 390–92 (quotation from 390).

a health perspective that recognizes that people learn violent behavior from those around them. The police can prevent violence by better understanding what produces it and addressing its underlying causes. They need to be taught how to de-escalate violence and more effectively treat high-risk individuals. This can improve the relationship between the police and residents of high-crime neighborhoods and enable them to work together to change norms and behaviors that contribute to violence.[36] While numerous factors have helped reduce Wilmington's crime rate to historic low levels, including gentrification and the decline of crack cocaine usage, David's approach has played a significant role.[37]

What We Can Do to Curb Gang Membership and Youth Violence

Christians should actively work to change the factors that prompt youth to join gangs and provide constructive alternatives to gangs. We can serve as foster parents, tutor academically struggling students, mentor troubled youth, or lead a Bible study or discussion group at a facility for juvenile delinquents. Christians can encourage religious, social, or community organizations to labor to stop crime, decrease gang membership and activity, and reduce child abuse and bullying. We can provide comfort and support for children who live in dysfunctional families and crime-riddled neighborhoods or need assistance to avoid violence.[38] Christians can take free, online violence prevention training, available on the Centers for Disease Control's VetoViolence website (http://vetoviolence.cdc.gov/), to better understand the circumstances that contribute to violence and how to change them. We can also report any suspected cases of child abuse to community authorities. Churches and communities can create programs to give youth more opportunities for recreation, social interaction, and volunteering that fill the needs gangs often supply. Through these various activities, Christians can help redirect many at-risk children and enable them to have more fulfilling lives.

36. Serpas, "Dangerous Contagion"; phone conversation with David, April 8, 2015. See also "Contagion of Violence," http://www.ncbi.nlm.nih.gov/books/NBK190337/?report=reader.

37. Interview with David. See also David, "Community-Based Prosecution," 411; Evans, "A Closer Look."

38. "How to Minimize Gang Violence," http://www.ncgangcops.org/minimizeactivity.html.

5

Improving Education for Impoverished Children in Developing Nations

Education is the great equalizer of men.

HORACE MANN, 1847

Education has a crucial role to play in reducing child poverty. Well-educated individuals generally obtain better paying jobs, have superior health, and experience more gender equality. Strengthening children's cognitive, physical, social, moral, and emotional development by improving their health and educational opportunities, especially during the first five years of their lives, is imperative. Critical intellectual and physical growth occurs during these years that cannot be replicated later. We have limited power to change parenting practices, and many children have little or no involvement in religious or community activities. Schools are the only institutions in which most low-income children in many nations are required to participate. Therefore, increasing the number of them who attend and upgrading the quality of primary and secondary schools is essential. In developing countries, preparing impoverished students for college or technical schools and ensuring that they have the personal traits and funding to graduate from these institutions is also becoming essential.

The United Nations Declaration of Human Rights, adopted in 1948, asserts that "everyone has the right to education." The 1990 UN Convention on the Rights of the Child obligates member states to make universal primary education compulsory and secondary education accessible to all children. The world is making significant progress in increasing both the number of students who attend primary and secondary schools and enriching the education they receive. In 2005 the United Nations set a Millennium Development Goal "that all children should receive a primary education by 2015." Although this goal was not achieved, about 90 percent of all primary school-aged children in developing nations currently attend. Meanwhile, the number of children around the world attending secondary schools increased dramatically during the twentieth century and today stands at 58 percent.[1] Consequently, 77 percent of the world's children between the ages of six and seventeen are attending school. Moreover, on a global level, education has improved more dramatically in the last sixty-five years than it did in the more than twenty-three centuries between the establishment of Plato's Academy and 1950.[2] Numerous studies report that children around the world are learning more than ever before, especially in math, reading, and writing.[3] This is all good news.

On the other hand, in some regions of the world, many children are still not receiving any formal education. In sub-Saharan Africa, almost one-quarter of primary-aged children do not go to school. While most Asian nations have made impressive educational progress in recent years, 34 percent of Pakistan's primary-aged children do not attend school.[4] In sub-Saharan Africa, less than 50 percent of secondary-school-age children are enrolled, and, therefore, millions of young people enter the work force without vital academic and life skills. Moreover, a large number of fifteen-year olds in dozens of countries are not proficient in either reading or numeracy.[5] In many locales education is substandard or even abysmal because facilities are inadequate, resources are meager, teachers are poorly trained, and hunger, disease, and stress inhibit student learning. In India and numerous other nations, more than half of fifth-grade students read only at a second

1. "Millennial Development Goals"; "Percentage of Children," http://www.unicef.org/factoftheweek/index_50244.html.

2. Kristof attributes this argument to Lant Pritchett in "Those Girls."

3. White, "Educating the World."

4. Lomborg, "To Educate Children."

5. "Four Out of Five Children," http://data.unicef.org/education/secondary.

grade level.[6] UNESCO reports that 92 percent of second graders in Mali cannot read a single word and that 61 percent of second graders in Iraq cannot correctly answer a single subtraction question. Only 3 percent of impoverished students in Malawi complete primary school and the average first grade class has 130 students.[7] Their lack of schools and teachers forces numerous developing countries to use split-shifts that permit students to attend only for half a day. Teachers in many of these nations have only an eighth grade education, and the high school dropout rate is very high.[8]

Many children in developing nations do not have adequate nutrition, basic services, access to healthcare, or decent employment prospects. Why, therefore, should these countries make education a priority? They should do so because education reduces fertility rates (a smaller family size generally benefits children), improves people's health, increases political participation and resourcefulness, equips individuals to get better jobs, strengthens nations' economies, and builds stronger societies.[9]

Educating girls is especially critical. Female education "is powerfully correlated with increased economic productivity, more robust labor markets, higher earnings, and improved societal health and well-being." More highly educated women have fewer children because they often delay marriage and childbearing, use contraceptives, and work outside the home. In addition to gaining greater power in their marriages, exercising more control over how many children they have, and earning more income, educated women have more influence in society. Educating females also significantly reduces child mortality rates, child malnutrition, and HIV/AIDS. Studies conducted in numerous African and Asian nations show that when women have substantial control over family resources, they allocate more money to feed, educate, and provide medical care for their children than their husbands do. Educated women are also more likely to aspire to improve their lives, leave abusive partners, and refuse to participate in injurious cultural practices such as female genital mutilation.[10]

6. White, "Educating the World."

7. Kristof, "Those Girls."

8. Nordland, "Afghan School Woes."

9. E.g., King and Hill, *Women's Education*; Bruns, Mingat, and Rakotomalala, *Universal Primary Education*.

10. Phumaphi and Leipziger, "Forward," xvii (quotation), xviii; Sundararaman and Hazarika, "Education, Hunger and Malnutrition," 114.

Education usually increases people's productivity, likelihood of voting, political advocacy, support for human rights, and commitment to social justice, which substantially benefits their nations. One study found that each additional year of schooling increases the earnings of residents of developing nations 6 to 10 percent.[11] Their higher income and social status typically enables educated individuals to live longer, receive better healthcare, eat more nutritious food, and move to improve their job prospects.[12] When citizens of developing countries receive additional education, they generally adopt better farming and business practices, which significantly aids both their own families and their national economies.[13]

Numerous obstacles thwart efforts to increase student attendance and improve school quality. Financial impediments are especially important. Upgrading education is expensive, and in the world's poorest nations, funding for schools competes with developing the infrastructure, expanding energy production, supplying medical care, reducing crime, providing jobs, and sadly sometimes fighting wars. Most government officials give priority to measures such as building roads and hospitals, drilling for oil, and creating jobs that deliver immediate results rather than those like improving education that have long-term benefits. Other factors that inhibit children, especially girls, from attending school include war, terrorist intimidation, school violence, sexual harassment, epidemics like the Ebola crisis, and long-standing cultural practices. Moreover, many parents in developing nations are reluctant to send their children to school because attendance prevents children from working for wages or doing household chores; many parents also think that education has little value. In addition, "free" public schooling costs money. Students must provide their own uniforms, textbooks, notebooks, pencils, lunches, and transportation. Many parents also pay tutors to help their children prepare for exams and pass national standardized tests. Finally, political corruption hurts education by reducing the funds nations allocate to their education budget, individual schools, and school supplies. Foreign donors are understandably reluctant to fund education in nations that do not spend money responsibly.[14]

11. Besley and Burgess, "Halving Global Poverty," 3–22; Krueger and Lindahl, "Education for Growth," 1101–36.

12. Cohen et al., "Introduction," 8; Ahu-Ghaida and Klasen, *Gender Equity*, 2–13.

13. Hicks, "Education and Poverty Alleviation," 24. See also Herz and Sperling, *Girls' Education*, 21–39; Psacharopoulos and Patrinos, "Returns to Investment," 111–34.

14. Cohen et al., "Introduction," 11–12; Gillard, "Good Education."

Potential Solutions

So how can we help more children around the world attend schools and receive a better education? Accomplishing this requires furnishing medical assistance to children, convincing parents that educating their sons and daughters has many advantages, increasing funding to schools, improving the quality of teachers, and providing schools with more resources and technology. Because of their limited funds, developing nations need the assistance of rich countries to expand and enrich their schools. As the next chapter discusses in more detail, receiving proper nutrition when their brains are developing between birth and age two greatly increases children's ability to learn. Supplying nutrient supplements and anti-parasitic medicines and iodizing salt (iodine deficiency inhibits children's intellectual development) costs very little. Deworming a child (intestinal worms impede children's physical and intellectual growth) typically requires only $3.50. Hookworm, whipworm, roundworm, and schistosomiasis infect about one quarter of the world's people. Heavily infected children suffer from protein malnutrition, anemia, and stomach aches. Most cases are much milder; they cause a persistent lethargy and slight queasiness to which most children become accustomed. Children contract these parasites by contact with contaminated water, eating without washing their hands, or walking barefoot though infected puddles. Thankfully, a single deworming pill, costing a mere 20 cents, kills 99 percent of the worms in a child's body and protects her for four months thereafter. Anemia also plagues many poor children in developing nations; it can be treated for pennies with iron supplements, but unfortunately it rarely is. School absence rates decline by about 20 percent when children receive deworming, vitamin A, and iron pills at school three times a year.[15]

Several steps can help increase the attendance of girls in schools in developing nations. One is making female education a primary national goal. Studies show that providing scholarships, stipends, and conditional cash transfers, recruiting female teachers, and using materials targeted to girls increases their school enrollment. Ensuring girls' physical safety and privacy, discouraging gender stereotypes, celebrating their achievement, and providing female role models are also all important. To increase their attendance, schools need to provide private latrines to help girls

15. Karlan and Appel, *More Than Good Intentions*, 205–9; Miguel and Kremer, "Worms," 159–217; Bobonis, Miguel, and Puri-Sharma, "Iron Deficiency Anemia," 692–721.

manage menstruation.[16] Working to change social practices that prevent women from frequenting public places and interacting with males is also imperative.[17]

Other measures can boost the attendance of both boys and girls and increase how much they learn. Persuading parents of the advantages education has for their children (and consequently themselves), supplying scholarships to students who earn good grades, providing breakfasts and lunches at schools, and even paying poor parents to send their children to school can all raise attendance rates. Giving teachers better training, higher pay, and smaller classes and providing computer-assisted learning are likely to improve student learning.[18] All of these suggestions, of course, require more funds. Moreover, as discussed in earlier chapters, eradicating poverty in developing nations involves other essential changes, including giving people more access to markets, better transportation options, higher prices for agricultural products, and better-paying jobs. Without these changes, producing more highly educated individuals is likely to lead to greater unemployment, frustration, and brain drain.[19]

Obtaining an education must produce tangible benefits, especially helping their children procure better-paying jobs, to convince indigent parents to allow them to complete primary, and especially, secondary school. If children do not master basic concepts and skills in school and if finishing fifth grade or even tenth grade does not significantly improve their job prospects, then few poor parents will allow them to stay in school. While it is important to increase the number of colleges and the jobs in developing nations that require post-high school education, the current dearth of higher education and opportunities to work as professionals requires a different kind of schooling in these countries. Rather than emulating Western models of education that emphasize math, science, language, and social studies, students are better served by helping them develop financial, health, entrepreneurial, management, and administrative skills, including teamwork, project management, and problem solving. Innovative educational programs, most notably BRAC, a Bangladesh NGO that operates 32,000

16. Tembon, "Overview," 3–6; Herz and Sperling, *Girls' Education*, 9, 11, 45–74.

17. Bellew and King, "Educating Women," 292.

18. Lomborg, "To Educate Children"; Cohen, Bloom, Malin, and Curry, "Introduction," 21; Kristof and WuDunn, *Half the Sky*, 172–75; White, "Educating the World"; Kwansah-Aidoo and Djokoto, "Swaziland," 167.

19. Folson, "Ghana," 141–42.

primary schools; Pratham, which furnishes various educational support programs to 33 million children in India; and Escuela Nueva, a Colombian program that includes 20,000 schools, are promoting this shift.[20]

Two American professors have developed a "school for life" model that focuses on improving the social and economic welfare of students and their communities rather than on mastering standard academic content. Its health curriculum teaches students how to prevent disease, care for the sick, and procure medical care. Its entrepreneurship curriculum adopts ideas from successful financial and entrepreneurial programs devised by such associations as the International Labour Organization and Junior Achievement. In this educational approach, students practice what they study—such as washing their hands, wearing shoes when they are near latrines, and boiling water. They identify market opportunities with monetary value such as creating a school garden or a community recycling center. Students also learn and practice such skills as negotiation, delegation, planning, and collaboration that are helpful in the workplace. This model focuses on critical thinking skills and enables students to identify problems, assess relevant information and resources, and design and implement plans to solve these problems. This, in turn, teaches children "to take the initiative and responsibility for their own learning."[21]

Two international organizations are playing a major role in improving education in the developing world—the Global Partnership for Education (GPE) and the United Nations Girls' Education Initiative (UNGEI). Organized in 2002, the GPE helps developing countries, especially fragile and conflict-ridden ones, devise and implement sensible plans to upgrade their education systems by creating Local Education Groups (LEGs). Led by national government officials, LEGs typically include the leaders of development agencies, teachers' organizations, civic associations, and private education providers. These groups strive to raise the rate of school attendance, improve the quality of education, and increase funding for education in the developing world. Their leaders lament that many children in low-income nations learn very little because schools are deficient and inefficient. Numerous factors reduce the quality of the education that children receive. Especially important are developmental delays caused by the lack of early childhood interventions, overcrowded classes, insufficient textbooks, poorly prepared teachers, misuse of classroom time, the inability of parents

20. Epstein and Yuthas, "Redefining Education."

21. Ibid.

to supervise homework, not using children's mother tongue, and inappropriate assessment of learning. To remedy these problems, LEGs seek to furnish early childhood education, especially for impoverished children, recruit more qualified teachers, train them how to better instruct students in reading, math, and life skills, and provide beneficial reading materials.[22]

Established at the World Education Forum in Senegal in 2000, the UNGEI works to help all children finish primary school. This partnership of institutions includes donor agencies, international financial institutions, civil associations, and private enterprises. Its primary goals are to aid marginalized and excluded groups, eliminate gender-based violence in schools, improve learning outcomes for girls, and help girls finish elementary school and succeed in secondary education and the work force. Like the Global Partnership for Education, the UNGEI strives to eradicate barriers to learning including school fees and other educational costs as well as sexual harassment and violence in schools and to enable schooling to continue when countries experience natural disasters, armed conflict, or external shocks.[23]

Model Programs and Success Stories

While the obstacles to improving education for impoverished children are huge, success stories abound in developing nations. Consider two remarkable schools, one Christian and one secular, in two of Africa's largest slums, both in Nairobi, Kenya. Mathare packs 600,000 people into a mere two square miles filled with garbage, ramshackle dwellings, and mud streets. Extreme poverty, disease, gangs, crime, prostitution, and drug and alcohol abuse are all widespread. Because Mathare has only three public elementary schools (and no high schools) for its 300,000 school-age children, countless youth are uneducated, have little to do, and are easy prey for gangs and pimps. Soon after graduating from Eastern College in Philadelphia in 2005, Adam Gould interned with a Nairobi Chapel church plant. This internship, coupled with his previous experiences with child sponsorship and mission trips, college courses, a Youth Specialties conference, the study of scripture, and prayer, led Gould to sense God's call to minister to the residents of Mathare. He was especially motivated by Matt 25:31–46 (the parable of the sheep and goats), Luke 4:14–21 (Jesus' announcement that his public

22. "Education Empowers Girls," http://www.globalpartnership.org/.

23. "United Nations Girls' Education Initiative," http://www.ungei.org/index.php.

ministry would focus on aiding the poor), Isaiah 58 (which asserts that the true fast involves breaking the chains of injustice and setting the oppressed free), and Luke 10:25–37 (the parable of the Good Samaritan).[24]

Gould had little experience, educational expertise, or money, but he had a tremendous faith in God and a deep desire to enrich the lives of some of the poorest people on earth. Partnering with Believers Centre Mathare Church and Life in Abundance, he created the Kenya Children's Project in 2006 to start a primary school. Four years later Gould and Bob Kikuyu established eduKenya "to break the chronic cycle of poverty" for children and their families in Mathare by providing sustainable, holistic, and Kenyan-led development programs that center around operating schools. Kikuyu earned an MA degree in mission at Nairobi Evangelical Graduate School of Theology. Before helping establish eduKenya, he served as the worship pastor at Nairobi Chapel and as the senior pastor of its church plant Lifespring Chapel. In 2010 Gould married Njeri Ndiho who had worked in human rights advocacy, advertising, television, and youth ministry in Nairobi.

EduKenya operates the Mawewa School where 265 children in preschool through eighth grade receive an exceptional education, nutritious meals (a child can be fed for an entire month for $8), frequent medical check-ups, and enrichment programs. For several years its test scores ranked the highest among all schools in a regional consortium. Its teachers are essential to Mawewa's success; they serve not only as educators but also as role models, mentors, and even surrogate parents.[25]

EduKenya seeks to meet the needs of entire families by educating children, teaching their parents how to generate income, and caring for community members with HIV/AIDS and other life-threatening conditions. The competition for admission is rigorous (200 children typically apply for twenty-five available spaces), and the parents whose children are accepted pay a small fee ($3.50 or $5.50 a month per student depending on their level—about 10–15 percent of the average monthly income in Mathare) to increase their stake in their children's education. While eduKenya is currently funded in part by churches and individuals in the United States (it costs about $50 per month to educate a student), it has purchased rental properties in Nairobi (it owns a building with thirty-two apartments and a medical clinic) to enable its school and other programs eventually to be

24. Email from Adam Gould to author, March 25, 2015. See also "eduKenya," http://www.edukenya.org/about/.

25. "About eduKenya"; email from Gould.

self-sustaining. By financing all eduKenya's programs with money earned from these investment properties, Gould hopes to evade the snare of dependency that international aid often produces. Moreover, buying properties in Mathare supports the local economy and supplies better housing for some of its residents, most of whom currently live in makeshift structures that lack running water and electricity. EduKenya also trains adults in sewing, tailoring, hairdressing and making earrings, necklaces, mats, and baskets to increase their income and improve their life circumstances.[26]

In addition, eduKenya works to change the culture, practices, and physical appearance of Mathare. Children who are idle and uneducated are vulnerable to being recruited by violent gangs or forced into slavery, while those who finish school are more likely to fulfill their dreams. Instead of toiling for less than $2 a day, adults can learn skills to generate more income and furnish better food, clothing, shelter, and medicine for their families. EduKenya seeks to replace trash and sewage-filled streets with sanitation systems and community gardens. Gould and his coworkers want to see violence, conflict, and despair give way to tranquility, cooperation, and hope. They plan to open additional elementary schools in Mathare by partnering with local congregations to bring "love, peace and reconciliation" to its residents and to transform this impoverished community.[27]

Fifteen-year-old Mwaura began attending Mawewa School seven years ago. Like most of its students, he has had to overcome great obstacles. His father abandoned his family, and his mother is working in the Middle East. Consequently, Mwaura lives with his grandmother who pays his school fees, furnishes food for him and his five-year-old twin brothers, and provides some clothing and school supplies.

Mwaura's grandmother, however, is elderly and depends greatly on him at home. He cooks for his brothers, does their laundry, feeds and helps them bathe, and supervises their homework. Burdened by this huge responsibility and having little guidance, support, or nurture from adults, Mwaura performed poorly in school for several years.

During these years, Mwaura's behavior caused problems for his teachers. He was consistently late for school. He rarely completed his homework or in-class assignments. Mwaura often came to school wearing a dirty, tattered uniform and without bathing. His teachers eventually recognized

26. Email from Gould.

27. Ibid.; "Mission and Vision," http://www.edukenya.org/about/mission-and-vision/; "edukenya Documentary," https://www.youtube.com/watch?v=S6P3V7qAXCU.

how difficult his home situation was. After one teacher, Elijah Muli, began to affirm and encourage him, Mwaura's school work slowly improved.

Although Mwaura's circumstances at home remained the same, he realized that obtaining an education could enable him to have a better life and improve conditions for his mother and brothers. He continues to take care of his twin brothers, but his approach to his studies is much more positive. For the past two years, Mwaura has come to school on time. His grooming is better, and, although his uniform is still threadbare, it is cleaner. He completes all his homework assignments and does his work in class well. His relationship with his classmates has greatly improved. No longer the boy everyone avoids, Mwaura now has friends and feels like he belongs.

Mwaura explains his transformation: "I used to be stubborn . . . and very difficult [to deal with] before I understood that they [my teachers] were trying to help me. I didn't care about school very much because I saw it as just adding to the many things I was being forced to do. But later on I realised that education is [for me] not for my teachers or grandmother and that . . . I am the one who stands to lose my future. I have seen the value of education and the way my teachers work very hard for me to learn. . . . When my performance improved, I got [the] courage to work even harder, and every time I improved I saw [that] I can be [even] better." Muli prodded him to excel in school to help lift his family out of poverty. "So I worked very hard," "prayed to God," and "believed in myself." His academic standing in his class has risen from the bottom to the middle, and he is working diligently to be the top student in his class.[28]

In 2009 Kennedy Odele founded another school that is also transforming the lives of children in Nairobi. Odele was born to an illiterate, fifteen-year-old mother in Kibera, another Nairobi slum. At age ten, he left his mother and abusive step-father and lived on the streets. Noticing his passion for learning, a Catholic nun gave him a place to live and taught him to read. Inspired by a biography of Nelson Mandela and the speeches of Martin Luther King Jr., Odele, in his late teens, created an organization called Shining Hope for Communities. Because the first sexual experience for half of the women in Kibera is rape, Shining Hope initially focused on stopping the sexual abuse of girls. Odele and his friends found aiding others to be therapeutic and being a force for positive change to be empowering. Rather than escaping from Kibera, they stayed to help remedy its ills.

28. Adapted from an account provided by Ajema Kikuyu-Ngumba via email to the author on April 24, 2015.

Odele's relationship with Jessica Posner, a Wesleyan University student who spent her junior year in Kenya working with Shining Hope's street theater program, led to his receiving a scholarship to attend Wesleyan, an elite university in Connecticut. Odele and Posner founded Kibera School for Girls to educate females and increase their life opportunities. After Odele graduated from Wesleyan in 2012, they married and returned to Kibera.

Funded primarily by American-based foundations and individual Americans, their school is free. However, parents must agree to work five weeks each year to aid the school and to attend monthly meetings. The school admits Kibera's poorest and brightest children, with almost 500 children competing for the twenty places in each year's kindergarten class. A $130,000 donation from The Mother's Day Movement led to the construction of a building with twenty classrooms to educate pre-K to eighth grade students. Scores of Americans pay $1,200 a year to sponsor girls, which covers their educational costs and health care for their entire families. Meanwhile, every summer numerous college students go to Kenya to work with the school's students. Aided by an eight to one student-teacher ratio and a fifty-week program, the girls are thriving. In a recent assessment, 86 percent of Kibera students exceeded US standards for their grade levels in English, even though it is the third language for most of them. The Odeles seek to prepare the girls to attend the best high schools in Kenya, and, in some cases, the United States. In addition, they established a clinic to provide prenatal care, help deworm children, and teach mothers how to breast-feed their infants. To improve the community, they also opened a public library, started a newspaper, created a job training program, and helped residents establish microsavings accounts. They plan to construct schools in many other East African communities to educate children and give them a better future.[29]

Similar inspiring stories could also be told about schools in Zimbabwe, Mozambique, Sierra Leone, Pakistan, and many other destitute nations.[30] If recent college graduates with an amazing vision and great zeal but extremely limited experience and resources can establish and operate schools in one of the world's worst slums to lift children out of poverty, surely major progress can be made in other impoverished communities.

29. Kristof and WuDunn, *Path*, 130–40.

30. Kristof and WuDunn, *Half the Sky*, 179–83; Stafford, "Miracles in Mozambique."

What Can Christians Do to Help?

Christians can take several steps to help improve education for low-income children in the developing world. Those of us who live in wealthy countries can encourage our governments to fund education in poorer nations more generously. This aid can help build more schools, add classrooms, hire and train more teachers and pay them better, provide student scholarships, increase the use of technology in instruction, and purchase more school supplies. The governments of affluent nations must hold countries accountable for the aid they receive and continue to fund educational enterprises only if they produce tangible results such as constructing more facilities, supplying additional teachers, and helping students read, write, and compute better. Christians can urge businesses to use their charitable gifts to underwrite these same ventures. We can sponsor more children in developing nations to enable them to attend school rather than have to work to support their families. Christians can give generously to organizations that are working to educate impoverished children in developing nations. Some organizations such as eduKenya exist primarily to educate indigent children. Many other Christian organizations make this a part of their mission. Christians who are primary or secondary teachers or college professors can teach short courses during the summer or spend a semester or a year instructing children in the schools of poorer countries. One summer my wife and I taught in a summer school program operated by a mission in Belize, which was a wonderful experience for us and hopefully for our middle school students. Finally, we can also pray fervently for educational endeavors in developing nations, especially ones run by Christians that include biblical teaching and spiritual formation as well as instruction in basic academic subjects. By doing these things, Christians can help millions of poor children grow intellectually, socially, emotionally, and spiritually.

6

Improving Education for Low-Income Children in the United States

I hated being poor, but I knew it was transitory.
Education would lift me from the poverty I hated.

BEN CARSON

The educational performance of many American students, especially low-income ones, is deplorable. In 2013, almost 60 percent of all fourth and eighth grade public school students and more than 80 percent of black and nearly 75 percent of Latino children in those grades could not read or compute at their grade level.[1] In the United States meager income, low social status, and race are highly correlated with lack of education. Poverty has "an enormous physical, emotional, and economic" impact "on families, neighborhoods, and communities," Sue Books argues, "and therefore on children and schools."[2] Most students from middle- and upper-class homes start school equipped with a solid foundation for success. They are prepared by their socialization at home and preschool experience to

1. Edelman, "Who Are We?"
2. Books, *Poverty and Schooling*, 134.

work effectively at the kindergarten level. Many of the children raised in impoverished homes, by contrast, are ill-prepared for, inattentive in, and chronically absent from school.[3]

Moreover, public schools in poor communities receive much less revenue than those in affluent neighborhoods because school funding depends on state disbursements and local property taxes. As a result, "savage inequalities" exist among American schools.[4] The quality of teachers, facilities, and resources, amount of learning, preparation for work and life, and test scores are superior in schools largely attended by middle and upper-class students. Deplorably, thousands of low-income students drop out of school, and many others find school to be unwelcoming, irrelevant, or frustrating. Children who spend half or more of their childhood in poverty are almost 90 percent more likely not to complete high school by age twenty than those who have never been poor.[5] Educational reformer Nicole Baker Fulgham labels the huge gap in achievement between high and low-income students "a nationwide epidemic." The very different prenatal, early childhood, nursery, primary, and secondary school experiences of these two groups of children produces this chasm.[6] The cycle of poverty will continue for most low-income children unless their socialization and education are substantially improved.

Conception to Age Two

What occurs in the womb and during the first two years of life is critical to the physical and cognitive development of human beings. When pregnant women consume alcohol, smoke cigarettes, or have high levels of stress (all of which are more prevalent among poor women), their children often suffer severe negative consequences. Prenatal smoking contributes to premature births, low birth weight, attention disorders, and mild learning disabilities. Children whose mothers drink or smoke during their pregnancies frequently have lower IQs, less ability to reason and focus, and poorer memory skills. These children generally are more hyperactive and aggressive and less socially competent. They engage in more disruptive behavior

3. Rebell and Wolff, "US Schools."

4. Kozol, *Savage Inequalities.*

5. "Ending Child Poverty," http://www.childrensdefense.org/library/PovertyReport/EndingChildPovertyNow.html.

6. Fulgham, *Educating*, 15. See also Reardon, "Academic Achievement Gap," 91–116.

and commit more crimes as juveniles. These intellectual and behavioral problems often contribute to lower academic achievement.[7]

The socialization impoverished children receive frequently compounds these negative prenatal consequences. Eric Jensen contends that to grow up emotionally healthy, children under age three need "a strong, reliable primary caregiver who provides consistent and unconditional love, guidance, and support," a secure, stable home, and ten to twenty hours of pleasant, reciprocal interactions each week. This process helps young children develop beneficial emotions, especially compassion, gratitude, and forgiveness. Because poor mothers are more likely to be teenagers, single, depressed, and poorly adjusted socially, their children are less likely between birth and age two to have opportunities for positive learning and exploring their environment that foster optimal brain development.[8] Moreover, many of these infants and toddlers are weakly or anxiously attached to their parent(s), which later contributes to deep feelings of insecurity.[9] Reducing the stress low-income mothers experience, changing the behaviors of pregnant women, improving prenatal care, and equipping parents to nurture their children more effectively, therefore, are all essential.

Another way to help low-income children is to make books available to them. The work of First Books and Imagination Library is especially impressive. Created in 1995, First Books has distributed 115 million books to 90,000 organizations, accounting for 2 percent of all children's books distributed in the US.[10] That same year, singer Dolly Parton started a program to send free books to children age five and younger. Today 1,600 communities in the United States, Canada, and the United Kingdom provide her Imagination Library books to more than 750,000 children every month.[11]

Early Childhood Education

Attending preschool before kindergarten is crucial to the intellectual and social development of low-income children. Early educational experiences help children significantly improve their cognitive abilities and

7. Rothstein, "Health-Related Causes."

8. Jensen, *Teaching*, chapter 2.

9. Ibid., 16. See also Shonkoff and Phillips, *From Neurons to Neighborhoods.*

10. Kristof and WuDunn, *Path*, 298. First Books supplies 15 million books every year to organizations serving two million children, but 32 million children need books (300).

11. "Dolly Parton's Imagination Library," http://www.imaginationlibrary.com/.

self-control.[12] Abundant research indicates that early education programs are "the best way to address American economic inequality, poverty and crime."[13] By age three, most children who grow up in poor families are substantially behind their middle- and upper-class peers in verbal and intellectual development, and the gap normally widens if they do not go to a preschool.[14] By age four, children in low-income families have typically heard 30 million fewer words than children in affluent families.[15] Poor preschoolers are less likely than their wealthier peers to be able to identify letters, write their first names, or count to twenty.[16] By age five, a two-year achievement gap exists between many rich and poor children.[17] This "inequality at the starting gate" is later amplified by many low-income students attending schools with more crowded classrooms, fewer resources, and less gifted teachers and by their regression during the summers.[18]

United States Department of Education Secretary Arne Duncan argues that creating a national early education program focusing on birth to age five could "transform the life chances of children and strengthen families in important ways."[19] Currently, low-income parents are forced to choose between Head Start and low quality private preschools, and many of them do not send their children to any preschool.[20]

Since its inception in 1965, Head Start has been the principal preschool option for low-income families. Currently serving one million of the nation's poorest children, Head Start provides early childhood education and supplies nutritional advice, food, immunizations, and dental and health care for low-income children.[21] Continually underfunded, Head Start has never enrolled more than half of children who qualify and has had substantial turnover among its teachers. A 2012 federal evaluation "concluded that children who participated in Head Start were not more

12. Dawson, Ashman, and Carver, "Role of Early Experience," 695–712.

13. Kristof, "Preschools or Prisons?"

14. Halle et al., "Disparities in Early Learning and Development."

15. Hart and Risley, *Meaningful Differences*.

16. O'Donnell and Mulligan, "School Readiness."

17. Layton, "Poor Children."

18. Lee and Burkam, "Inequality."

19. Quoted in Kristof, "Preschools or Prisons?" See also Duncan and Murnane, *Restoring Opportunity*, 53–69.

20. Fulgham, *Educating*, 25.

21. Books, *Poverty and Schooling*, 126.

successful in elementary school" than their low-income peers who did not. Other scholars counter that many Head Start graduates begin to thrive as teenagers, perhaps because of its emphasis on social skills and character in addition to the three R's.[22] Providing free preschools for all children, as we have done at the primary and secondary level for almost two centuries, would greatly benefit low-income children.[23]

K-12 Education

Their inadequate socialization before age six and frequent health problems make it more difficult for low-income students to perform well in school. Lacking good nutrition and regular medical care, they often come to school hungry or sick. Many of them have visual, hearing, and dental problems that make academic work more difficult.[24] Poor children also experience more anxiety, fatigue, and exposure to violence. Their chronic stress leads poor children to miss more days of school, reduces their concentration and memory, weakens their social skills, and diminishes their motivation and effort.[25] Making matters worse, low-income students generally attend schools with less qualified and capable teachers, higher teacher turnover, poorer facilities, fewer books, guidance counselors, and nurses, and less extracurricular activities.[26] In addition, high-poverty schools typically have "higher rates of delinquency, truancy, disorder, and transience than low-poverty schools" and much less peer pressure to achieve academically.[27]

How can we help them perform better in school and prepare more effectively for life as adults? Schools whose impoverished students achieve at high levels usually have dedicated, gifted teachers who understand their backgrounds and needs and design instruction and develop relationships accordingly. Successful schools have high expectations for academic achievement and a curriculum that focuses on basic skills in literacy and

22. Kristof, "Preschools or Prisons?" See also "Head Start Impact Study."

23. Kirp, "Rich and Poor."

24. Rothstein, "Health-Related Causes."

25. Jensen, *Teaching*, chapter 2.

26. Books, *Poverty and Schooling in the U.S*, 135; Jensen, *Teaching*, chapter 2; Rogers and Mirra, *It's About Time*; Boyd et al., "Short Careers," 166–71; Farb and Matjasko, "Recent Advances," 1–48.

27. Putnam, *Our Kids*, 166–70; quotation from 169; Jeynes, "Parental Involvement," 82–110; Robinson and Harris, *Broken Compass*; Crosnoe, *Fitting In, Standing Out*.

mathematics. They also typically have prudent administrators, foster collaboration among teachers and staff, offer opportunities to improve teaching methods, provide additional instructional time, engage in continual diagnostic assessment, and demand high levels of parental involvement.[28]

Hiring talented teachers, equipping them to work effectively with poor children, and compensating them well is critical to improving schools. Many teachers, however, have neither shared the life experiences of low-income students nor been specifically trained to help them.[29] Teachers can help low-income children succeed academically and socially by understanding their life experience and culture, alleviating the factors that cause their stress, establishing high expectations for them, earning their trust, and helping them develop positive self-esteem.[30]

Administrators, teachers, and staff in high-performing schools assume that all children can succeed academically. These schools promote their students' "self-control, self-reliance, and self-esteem."[31] They ensure that students master basic reading, writing, and math skills and help them develop higher-order thinking skills. Teachers and staff regularly discuss how to improve teaching techniques. High-performing schools usually give their students additional instructional time through longer school days or after-school, weekend, and summer programs. Some of them use volunteers to provide extra tutoring or arrange for aides, parents, and older classmates to assist struggling students.[32]

Teachers and staff at high-performing schools consider parents to be "critical partners" in the learning process and encourage them to actively participate in their children's learning by reading to their children, helping them with their homework, taking them to libraries, and regularly conversing with their teachers.[33]

28. Hayes, "Successful High Poverty Schools"; Barone, *Literacy Gap*, 176–78.

29. Templeton, *Understanding Poverty*, xi, 53.

30. See Templeton, *Understanding Poverty*, 53–65; Haberman, *Star Teachers*.

31. "High-performing, High-poverty Schools," http://www.centerforpubliceducation.org/. See also Carter, *No Excuses*.

32. Dean et al., *Classroom Instruction*; Smyth and Wrigley, *Living on the Edge*; Eric Jensen, *Engaging Students*.

33. Ragland et al., "Working Memory," 370–79; Carter, *No Excuses*; Templeton, *Understanding Poverty*, 91–92.

Post-High School Education

Experts estimate that by 2020, almost two-thirds of jobs in the United States will require some sort of education or training beyond a high school diploma. Unfortunately, today 5.5 million Americans between the ages of sixteen and twenty-four are neither attending school nor working.[34] Therefore, to ensure that the offspring of today's poor children are able to reach their potential, we need to provide more post-high school educational opportunities for low-income teenagers. To do this, we must make colleges and technical schools more affordable and better prepare impoverished youngsters to graduate from their programs. Universal high school education and increased college attendance in the early twentieth century helped make the United States the most educated and prosperous nation in the world. However, since 1985 most other post-industrial countries have outstripped our nation in educational achievement, making it more difficult for many of our citizens to procure highly skilled, well-paying jobs. Compared with their peers, Americans between sixteen and twenty-four rank near the bottom among affluent countries in literacy, numeracy, and technological skills.[35] To earn a livable wage in a globalized, high-tech economy, individuals need some sort of postsecondary education.[36]

Since 1978 the cost of college has increased 1,225 percent, and the average student now graduates with $33,000 in loan obligations, while their parents often borrow even more money.[37] Consequently, wealth, rather than national origin, race, or ethnicity, has the highest correlation with attending and graduating from college.[38] In response, many educational experts and politicians have called for establishing programs to help low-income Americans earn a college degree. In 2014 Tennessee created a free community college program, which is available to all students who graduate from high school. The first year almost 90 percent of the state's high school seniors applied to the program. In 2014 Chicago established an initiative that pays for tuition, fees, and books at the city's seven community colleges

34. Editorial Board, "Drift"; Lewis and Burd-Sharps, "Place and Race."
35. Leonhardt and Quealy, "American Middle Class."
36. See Goldin and Katz, *Education and Technology*.
37. Cohen, "How to Make College Cheaper."
38. Sparks and Adams "High School Poverty."

for all Chicago Public School students who graduate with a 3.0 grade-point average or higher.[39]

Providing more assistance to help students attend college is essential. About a third of community college students are members of families with annual incomes below $20,000. Many of them work long hours at jobs to pay for their education and other living expenses, contributing to a dropout rate of nearly 80 percent. To help students graduate from community colleges, we must help cover their living expenses (tuition is only about a fifth of their total cost), ensure that they are better prepared to do college work, and provide guidance counselors, mentors, and child care.[40]

Our personal experiences reinforce our support for these measures. For several years, I taught as an adjunct at a branch of a local state university. A significant percentage of my students were single mothers who worked full-time and took four courses, the minimum required to be eligible for financial aid. Predictably, many of them felt overwhelmed as they struggled to fulfill all their responsibilities. The excessive demands on their time led some of them to earn low grades, and numerous students eventually stopped taking courses. My wife recently taught an introductory distance education course for one of the nation's largest providers of on-line college courses. Most of the students in her class grew up in poverty, have battled addictions, and are the first in their families to graduate from high school. They want to improve themselves, but their inadequate academic preparation makes it difficult for many of them to complete very basic college courses.

Potential Solutions

What else can we do to improve the education of low-income children? One remedy is to create more high-quality after-school programs that provide classes, tutoring, and help with homework to enable poor children to improve their school performance.[41] For every child in an after-school program today, two more would participate if facilities were available and their parents could afford to send them.[42]

39. Davis and Lewin, "Obama Plan."
40. Brooks, "Support Our Students." See also Perry, "Low Cost College."
41. Halpern, *Making Play Work*, 90–99, 164.
42. "America After 3 PM."

Reducing "summer slide" is also important. Because of their lack of books and intellectual enrichment at home, many low-income children regress during the summer. "Summer slide" typically accounts for two of the average three-year gap that exists between low- and high-income children by eighth grade. To remedy this problem, Alexandro Gac-Artigas, the son of a Chilean playwright, created Springboard Collaborative in Philadelphia. It sponsors a summer camp to improve reading skills and prods parents to teach their children during the summer.[43]

Providing more role models, counselors, and big brothers and sisters for low-income children to help them deal with developmental, relational, and academic issues is also essential. Many businesses have created programs that enable current or retired employees to work in schools and mentor children. Each Michelin facility in South Carolina, for example, has adopted a local school that has a high percentage of low-income children. Thousands of Michelin employees volunteer in these schools, serving as lunch buddies, tutoring students in science, math, and reading, performing scientific experiments, hosting job fairs for parents, and helping raise funds.[44]

Recruiting and retaining better teachers by paying them higher salaries (especially to teach in schools in low-income areas) and elevating their status is also imperative. Finnish and Canadian students score higher on standardized science and math tests than American students because their nations prepare teachers better, value education much more highly, and devote more resources to schools with the largest numbers of indigent students.[45] In the United States, by contrast, "teachers are poorly paid, poorly prepared and generally disdained" and "the richest schools and students get by far the most money."[46] Some complain that teaching has been more vilified than any other profession.[47] Experts recommend making education programs more selective and demanding, basing the retention and pay of teachers on their effectiveness, and designing the first three years of teaching

43. Kristof and WuDunn, *Path*, 84–88; "Impact," http://springboardcollaborative.org/what-we-do/the-impact/; Alexander, Entwisle, and Olson, "Summer Learning Gap," 167–80.

44. Mann, "Michelin Challenge Education," 10.

45. Firestone, "Failing Schools"; "High-Quality Teaching Profession," 11, 55.

46. Firestone, "Failing Schools." See also Green, *Better Teacher*, and Klein, *Lessons of Hope*.

47. Ibid.

to be more like a medical residency to improve classroom performance.[48] The key to attracting the best and brightest to the profession, the chancellor of the Washington, DC school system maintains, is to increase respect for teachers. To do this, she argues, we must establish high expectations for teachers, give them the resources (excellent training, a rich curriculum, and ample supplies) necessary to meet those expectations, pay them well, and publicly commend their achievements.[49]

To elevate the quality of teaching, experts propose ensuring that teachers have a mastery of their subjects, compensating them on the basis of their performance, and eliminating tenure. Joel Klein complains that removing an incompetent teacher is "virtually impossible." While he served as the chancellor of New York City's public schools, firing a teacher "took an average of almost two and a half years and cost the city over $300,000."[50] A Los Angeles County trial-court judge recently ruled that by making it harder to fire teachers, tenure effectively keeps poor ones in the classroom. These inept teachers, the judge argued, "substantially undermine" students' education and violate their right to receive the equal educational opportunity the California constitution mandates.[51] Numerous states are taking actions to make tenure harder to earn and retain or to eliminate tenure.[52]

Since 1990 Teach for America (TFA) has supplied thousands of teachers to low-income schools; in some cases, it furnishes one-fifth of the instructors in impoverished urban and rural districts. Half of TFA teachers are minorities, and half of them grew up in poverty. Two school networks that work successfully with low-income students—KIPP (Knowledge Is Power Program) and YES (Youth Engaged in Service) Prep—use substantial numbers of TFA recruits. Critics, especially some teachers' union officials and education professors, contend that TFA's mere five weeks of training is inadequate to prepare even the most gifted and enthusiastic college graduates to work effectively in the country's poorest communities. They also complain that because participants are required to make a two-year commitment, many low-income students continually have inexperienced

48. Ripley, "Teacher Colleges"; Hanushek, "Evaluation System"; Mehta, "Teacher Education"; Hanushek, Peterson, and Woessmann, *Endangering Prosperity*; Mehta, *Allure of Order*; Mehta, Schwartz, and Hess, *School Reform*.

49. Henderson, "Great Teaching." See also Bruni, "Teaching."

50. Bruni, "Better Teachers."

51. Sweetland, "Teacher Tenure."

52. "Teacher Tenure Rules."

teachers and their schools have substantial turnover and instability. Defenders of TFA counter that studies of teacher effectiveness in several states have consistently rated TFA instructors "at or near the top" on their impact on student achievement and principals have "overwhelmingly reported satisfaction with corps members."[53]

Another promising approach is the federally-funded Talent Transfer Initiative. This experiment gives outstanding teachers in urban schools an additional $20,000 in salary if they agree to teach for two years in a high poverty, lowest-achieving school in their district. Between 2007 and 2014, the highest rated teachers in ten large, diverse school districts in seven states filled almost 90 percent of the targeted vacant positions. The math and reading scores in these schools significantly increased, and most of these teachers remained after their bonuses ended.[54]

Some individuals do not have the aptitude or interest to succeed in college. Their talents are more mechanical and technical in nature. Technical schools offer programs in dozens of fields including culinary arts, computer technology, graphic design, hospitality, information technology, massage therapy, medical technology, nursing, plumbing, automotive repair, real estate, and welding. People with skills in these areas contribute greatly to society, typically enjoy their work, and can adequately provide for their families. Welders, for example, are in great demand in the Gulf Coast Region, and community colleges are helping to train them.[55] Making these programs more available, affordable, and desirable can help reduce the poverty of adults and their children.

School Choice: Vouchers

Since 2000 Minneapolis has allowed low-income urban students to attend suburban schools and magnet schools instead of only the school closest to their homes.[56] More recently, Cleveland has made all public, charter, and private schools available to all students.[57] The fierce competition among

53. Rich, "Fewer Top Graduates"; "What the Research Says," https://www.teachforamerica.org/sites/default/files/what-the-research-says.pdf.

54. Glazerman et al., "Transfer Incentives."

55. Cohen, "Welders."

56. "'Choice is Yours': Minnesota Program," https://schoolrequest.mpls.k12.mn.us/the_choice_is_yours_minnesota_program.

57. "The Cleveland Plan," http://www.clevelandmetroschools.org//site/Default.aspx?PageID=532.

American colleges has long made them the best ones in the world. The same type of competition is needed to improve our K-12 schools. As long as the public system enrolls 90 percent of all students, many administrators and teachers lack the incentive to upgrade them. However, if their low quality threatens their existence, schools will be compelled to improve. Supplying vouchers or tuition tax credits to parents could enable all children to attend first-rate schools and force schools to become better or go out of business. Numerous examples exist of private schools educating students of similar ability as those who attend public schools for about one-third the cost and obtaining substantially higher results on standardized state tests. They have typically been able to accomplish this because of their focus on student learning, the innovative leadership of their principals and board members, the dedication and high-quality of their teachers, and the willingness of parents to partner with teachers to help their children learn.[58] Currently few low-income parents can afford to send their children to private schools. Ideally all children would be able to attend excellent local schools, but the ones in their own neighborhoods are often substandard.[59] A voucher system could help change this.

Model Programs and Success Stories

Many schools are educating low-income students effectively. Renaissance High School in Detroit has a "culture of excellence" and "remarkably high" expectations. Almost all of its 700 students, many of whom are low-income, take several Advanced Placement courses and go to college, primarily at leading universities. Founded in 2000 in a rough neighborhood in North Philadelphia, Esperanza Academy High School is part of a faith-based network of more than 12,000 Hispanic churches and parachurch organizations. About 90 percent of its students graduate, and 85 percent of them attend college right after graduation. YES Prep, a charter school system in Houston, with 5,400, mostly low-income, students, was recently named the nation's best public charter school. Since 2007, all of the graduating seniors at IDEA Public Schools located in an impoverished, rural section of south Texas have been accepted into college. In 2014, YES Prep was ranked the

58. E.g., Webster, "Achievement Gap." See also Lareau and Goyette, *Choosing Schools*; Jeynes, *School Choice*.

59. Fulgham, *Educating*, 14.

fourth best high school in Texas and IDEA was ranked the fifth.[60] All of these schools have rigorous academic standards and give students individualized attention. The students at YES Prep, for example, have an extended school day and school year, take educational trips, participate in stimulating extracurricular activities, and engage in service learning projects. YES Prep students receive personalized college counseling and guidance later while they are attending college.[61]

The nation's 183 KIPP academies are especially impressive. Founded in 1994, this "national network of free, open-enrollment, college-preparatory public schools" is based on the premise that a school's high expectations, extended classroom time, and emphasis on hard work can enable all students to achieve. KIPP schools operate in twenty states and the District of Columbia and serve approximately 70,000 students. About 87 percent of KIPP students have low-income parents, and 96 percent are Latino or African American. More than 94 percent of KIPP middle school students have graduated from high school, and 82 percent of KIPP's alumni have attended college.[62]

KIPP stresses "five pillars": high expectations, choice and commitment, more time, the power to lead, and results. Teachers, staff, students, and parents "create and reinforce a culture of achievement" through a variety of "formal and informal rewards and consequences for academic performance and behavior." Parents pledge to ensure that their children arrive at school on time every day, enhance their children's learning, and regularly check their children's homework. Students promise to complete all their homework every night, ask questions in class if they are confused, follow teachers' instructions, and respect their classmates. KIPP's extended school day, week, and year gives students more time to obtain the knowledge and skills necessary to succeed later in competitive high schools and colleges and more opportunities to participate in varied extracurricular activities.[63] Numerous independent investigators testify to the substantial gains KIPP students have made in science, social studies, reading, and math.[64] KIPP

60. Ibid., 7–9 (all quotations), 155–57, 62; "Best High Schools in Texas," http://www.usnews.com/education/best-high-schools/texas?int=9abb08; See also Kearney, *Cristo Rey Story*.

61. "YES Prep," http://www.yesprep.org/.

62. "KIPP Schools," http://www.kipp.org/schools.

63. "About KIPP," http://www.kipp.org/about-kipp#sthash.oSdv33j1.dpuf.

64. See "Independent Reports," http://www.kipp.org/results/independent-reports; "Mathematica Research," http://www.kipp.org/results/mathematica-study.

schools also seek to develop seven attributes in their students: "zest, grit, optimism, self-control, gratitude, social intelligence, and curiosity."[65]

D. C. Virgo Preparatory Academy

Although it is a public school, the mission of D. C. Virgo Preparatory Academy in Wilmington, North Carolina, is very similar to that of KIPP schools. Located in a low-income, almost exclusively African-American community with few resources, it seeks to create a "community of responsible and contributing citizens that values academic rigor, strong moral character, community leadership, and twenty-first-century skills and that prepares students for future academic and personal excellence."[66] The middle school's predecessor, the graduates of which include basketball superstar Michael Jordan, closed because of its students' abysmal academic performance.[67] Wilmington's Blue Ribbon Commission on the Prevention of Youth Violence (BRC) identified the school's neighborhood as the city's most troubled area because of its high crime rate, extensive drug problems, and numerous gangs. The BRC partnered with the Wilmington School Board to reopen D. C. Virgo in 2012 on a stronger academic platform to provide a better education for neighborhood children. Since being reconstituted, D. C. Virgo has focused on writing, reading, mathematics, public speaking, and ethics. All students receive a free iPad, have both an academic counselor and a personal counselor, and meet in small groups with a teacher every day.[68]

Eric Irizarry, the school's principal, grew up in a rough part of Newburgh, New York. His parents divorced when he was in elementary school, and he moved with his mother to near Camp Lejeune in rural North Carolina. The oldest of five children, as a teenager Irizarry helped take care of his siblings and did odd jobs to supplement the family's income. While in middle school, Irizarry often got into fights and was disciplined by the principal. Academically gifted, he majored in education at the University of North Carolina at Wilmington. While teaching for several years at an elementary school in a low-income neighborhood in Wilmington, Irizarry completed a principal's degree at UNCW and then worked for three years

65. "About KIPP." See also Gladwell, *Outliers*, 250–52, 260–69; Angrist et al., "Who Benefits from KIPP?" 837–60.

66. "D. C. Virgo," http://www.nhcs.net/virgo/.

67. Green, "Superintendent Recommends"; Green, "Virgo Middle to Close."

68. "History of D. C. Virgo."

as an assistant principal at a charter school near Wilmington. Impressed by his vision, passion, and administrative talent, the school board chose him to be the principal when D. C. Virgo reopened.[69]

The challenges the school faces are immense. About 90 percent of its students are low-income. Only a quarter of them have a father who is actively involved in their lives. Moreover, most students are at least two grade levels behind when they arrive. Recruiting and keeping excellent teachers is difficult. Irizarry assesses both their academic expertise and their ability to relate effectively with D. C. Virgo's students. He looks for teachers who can handle students' frequent defiance of authority and the other classroom and interpersonal challenges they will face. Many applicants who look good on paper are not able to manage their classroom effectively, discipline students appropriately, or develop good rapport with them. Irizarry seeks to hire teachers who will be exceptional role models, mentors, and counselors, not simply exemplary instructors.

Many of D. C. Virgo's teachers have advanced degrees. About 50 percent of them are minorities, but only a few of them grew up in impoverished neighborhoods or attended a low-income school. Working at D. C. Virgo, Irizarry contends, is "high risk, high reward"; "students will challenge you in every way possible." To better equip its teachers, the school holds workshops to discuss the backgrounds and problems of destitute students and strategies and techniques for teaching.

To help students catch up to their grade level, the school provides extended time, tutoring, and a summer program. Students can receive individual tutoring during or after school hours. About a third of D. C. Virgo's students receive academic and cultural enrichment during a five-week summer initiative.

D. C. Virgo emphasizes both academic subjects and values. Its staff strive to develop a trusting relationship with students, identify their talents, celebrate their successes, and boost their self-confidence. Twice a year students display their gifts through dance, singing, instrumental performances, and works of visual art at an evening showcase. Each morning students verbally pledge to live by the school's motto of PRIDE—pride, respect, integrity, determination, and excellence. When they misbehave, Irizarry and the teachers require students to identify which principle(s) they have violated and why they need to change their behavior.

69. The remainder of the material about D. C. Virgo is based on an interview with Eric Irizarry at the school, February 16, 2015.

D. C. Virgo seeks to partner with the parents of their students. Irizarry stresses that gaining the commitment of parents to help their children succeed is critical, but hard to do. For many of these families, poverty is multigenerational. The demands of being single parents, stressful lives, or lack of responsibility lead many parents to renege on their pledge to support their children. D. C. Virgo offers workshops for parents on practical subjects such as helping children succeed in school and cooking nutritious meals.

School staff also work to help students avoid gangs and drugs and cope with the effects of violence in their neighborhood. Many students have older siblings who are gang members and/or have been incarcerated. Drugs are prevalent in their neighborhood, and numerous students have parents and older brothers and sisters who are dealers and/or users. Irizarry reports that few D. C. Virgo students have joined gangs, in part because of their increased academic success, greater sense of hope, and feeling that they are valued.

D. C. Virgo is making progress. For many of its students, school is a very positive experience. Moreover, many of them have improved their academic performance. A major measure of success will be whether their graduates succeed in high school, which the principal plans to carefully monitor. Eric Irizarry and D. C. Virgo's teachers and staff are working diligently and effectively to improve the lives of their students, the reputation of their school, and the quality of their neighborhood.

Career Academies

Another approach that has helped low-income students is establishing career academies within high schools. Begun in 1980, these academies presently function in about 8,000 high schools and serve one million students. Academy students take demanding academic and career-oriented courses and gain practical work experience. Studies show that career academy students, especially at-risk ones, perform better academically and are better prepared for both college and careers than members of control groups. Moreover, their graduates have more sustained employment and higher earnings than controls.[70] Youth can also attend vocational high schools to prepare for careers in such areas as automotive technology, finance, cosme-

70. "Career Academies," http://www.mdrc.org/project/career-academies-exploring-college-and-career-options-ecco#overview; Peck, "Middle Class," 72–73; Kemple, "Career Academies."

tology, culinary arts, dental assisting, and digital design. Hundreds of these schools operate across the nation, and many programs enable graduates to earn an industry certification. Eliminating the false assumption (and the negative stigma) that only low-performing and misbehaving students attend these schools is critical.[71]

What We Can Do to Improve America's Schools

Schools that are successfully educating low-income students share several common traits. Most importantly, they design their teaching practices, curriculum, and school rules to promote student learning. Teachers in schools where low-income students perform at high levels usually work collaboratively. They discuss student achievement data, design curriculum, and devise lesson plans, benchmark assessments, and grading rubrics. In addition, outstanding teachers mentor less effective ones. The principals of these schools believe that all students can learn at high levels, strive to improve classroom instruction, and seek to determine which practices produce success.[72]

Christians have long played a pivotal role in improving American education, and we must continue to do so regardless of where and how we choose to educate our own children. The Catholic Church, numerous Protestant denominations, and associations of Christian parents operate thousands of schools across the United States. Nicole Baker Fulgham urges Christians to publicize the problems low-income schools face, work to remedy them as teachers, parents, and volunteers, and engage in "faith-based advocacy." She exhorts churches to discuss the issues confronting schools in impoverished communities and host public education forums.[73]

Christians can also improve education for poor children by teaching in public schools and donating to organizations that assist low-income students. Congregations can found or support high performing schools. In addition, congregations can partner with one of the nation's 45,000 public schools that has a high percentage of low-income students to supply food, tutor students, collect books, or hold literacy classes for parents.[74]

71. Bidwell, "Vocation High Schools."

72. Chenoweth, "It Can Be Done," 38–43; Chenoweth and Theokas, "High-Poverty Schools," 56–59.

73. Fulgham, *Educating*, 132–46.

74. Ibid., 148–67. See also Becker, "School Choice," 22.

Christians can also eliminate educational inequity by providing better early childhood education, striving to improve the quality of teachers, working to empower parents, increasing funding for schools, and providing more school choice. They can join or financially support organizations that labor to upgrade public schools in low-income communities and prepare their students effectively for college, work, and life. Finally, they can formally and informally mentor low-income children. Robert Putnam urges America's religious communities to greatly increase their mentoring activities. Children from wealthy families are two to three times more likely to have such informal mentors as coaches, youth group leaders, family friends, and teachers than are children from low-income families.[75]

Conclusion

Schools impact their students tremendously. Their interactions with teachers, other school personnel, and peers "indelibly impress upon children certain perspectives of who they are and what they can do in the world."[76] Schools can inspire hope or crush dreams. Schools can give low-income children the knowledge, interpersonal skills, and confidence they need to become productive, caring adults or do little to overcome their liabilities.

Numerous factors play a major role in better educating low-income students: belief that they can learn effectively, diligent efforts to improve local schools, greater educational competition, creative administrators and teachers, organizations that furnish helpful ideas and resources, philanthropists who fund educational reform, and exemplary schools that function as paradigms.

Most Americans agree that reforming education is essential. In a 2013 poll, 85 percent of respondents said that "improving the quality of our public schools" is either extremely or very important.[77] Their intellectual gifts and hard work, family support, dedicated teachers, committed mentors, and scholarships enable many children who grow up in impoverished homes to excel in elementary school, high school, and college and gain the knowledge and skills to obtain good jobs and contribute to society.[78]

75. Putnam, *Our Kids*, 259, 214–15. See Erickson, McDonald, and Elder, "Informal Mentors," 344–67.

76. Maholmes, *Fostering Resilience*, 9.

77. "Key Findings," http://images.politico.com/global/2013/07/30/130730_hart.pdf.

78. Books, *Poverty and Schooling*, 139.

They can also serve as role models for other children who are raised in low-income communities.

Improving schools that low-income students attend will help them immensely, but it is not a panacea. As Putnam contends, the achievement gap between high and low-income children "is created more by what happens to kids before they get to school, by things that happen outside of school, and by what kids bring (or don't bring) with them to school" than "by what schools do to them."[79] The economic problems and social pathologies of destitute children, James Traub asserts, are "too deep to be overcome by school alone."[80] We must also create more jobs, improve health care, ensure public safety, eliminate institutional racism, and give the poor greater political power.[81] Only by attacking all these problems simultaneously can we substantially reduce childhood poverty.

79. Putnam, *Our Kids*, 182.

80. Traub, "What No School Can Do," 54.

81. Books, *Poverty and Schooling*, 137.

7

Abolishing Human Trafficking

Governments cannot bear the burden of responding to modern slavery alone.

ANDREW FORREST

The Magnitude of the Problem

I have read—and, while volunteering in both developing nations and at home, witnessed—countless stories of children tragically affected by poverty. Among those that haunt me the most, however, are those in which children, whose lives should be devoted to education and play, are instead enslaved by ruthless pimps, warlords, business owners, and others who traffic these innocents for their own gain. I first realized fifteen years ago that slavery was no longer buried in the past, but remained alive and well. Since then I have learned all I could about this evil practice and have spoken in my community and on local university campuses to raise awareness and encourage advocacy. I have written editorials and encyclopedia articles about human trafficking and traveled to my state capital and Washington, DC to advocate with elected officials. While I recognize that modern-day slavery is still flourishing, I am encouraged that we are making some progress. When I first started telling people about human trafficking, they typically responded in disbelief; now my listeners usually recognize that it exists, and many of them are interested in learning more and working to eradicate it.

The Trafficking Victims Protection Act of 2000 (TVPA) defines human trafficking as "modern day slavery" that involves "force, fraud, or coercion for the purpose of commercial sex, debt bondage, or forced labor." Although more than 90 percent of nations have abolished slavery, millions of people around the globe are still being illegally bought and sold.[1] Estimates, given the clandestine nature of the slave trade, vary, but a recent report from the Global Slavery Index determined that as many as 45 million people are "working" against their will as sex slaves, as domestic servants, in various hazardous jobs in forced labor camps and quarries, as beggars, or in such illicit activities as burglary.[2] According to the US State Department, as many as 820,000 men, women, and children are trafficked across international borders every year. Countless others are trafficked within their native countries. Approximately two-thirds of those victimized are female; one in three victims is a minor.[3]

Examples of this heinous victimization of children abound. Global anti-slavery activist Kevin Bales, in *Disposable People: New Slavery in the Global Economy*, describes the lives of boys held in slavery in the fishing industry on Lake Volta in Ghana. These boys, some as young as five, spend up to nineteen hours a day working on fishing boats. They labor in mind-numbing conditions on poorly-constructed, rickety vessels, haul in several backbreaking catches each day, and are often forced to dive into dangerous waters to disentangle nets, which are more valuable to their masters than are the lives of these young workers. Malnourished, unwashed, and frequently ill and exhausted, these boys quickly become shells of their former selves; many disappear into the lake, only to wash up, unmourned, on shore days later. To their captors, they are no more than replenishable commodities: as cheap and easily replaced, Bales says, as a styrofoam cup.[4]

On the other side of the globe, Julian Sher, in his book, *Somebody's Daughter: The Hidden Story of America's Prostituted Children*, details another odious way in which children are victimized by traffickers: the sex trade. "Maria," whose story Sher recounts, is representative of thousands of other adolescents, many as young as eleven or twelve, who are forced

1. UNODC, *Global Report.*
2. "Global Findings," http://www.globalslaveryindex.org/findings/.
3. "Trafficking in Children."
4. Bales, "Modern Slavery." See also Bales, *Disposable People.*

to sell their bodies online and by walking the streets or being hustled at truck stops or clandestine brothels. "Maria," who was shipped to Las Vegas by a pimp, is one of many girls available for sale in what one of the city's detectives calls "the mecca for child prostitution."[5] A recent article in the *Pittsburgh Post-Gazette* chronicles another victim's story. "Kate," like many others who fall into the hands of pimps, was removed by authorities from her drug-addicted mother as a young girl and later sexually and physically abused. After running away from foster care at age fourteen and becoming homeless, she was easy prey for a pimp, who, like others in his "profession," was adept at exploiting her vulnerability.[6]

One critical attribute that these—and the majority of other victims—have in common is their poverty. Poor children, both in the developing and developed world, are vulnerable to be victimized by those who prey on and commodify the defenseless. Parents in developing nations who are struggling to provide for their children are often willing to entrust them to a fraudulent recruiter who offers them a fee in order to apprentice their son or daughter. Once the child is removed from home, however, the apprenticeship quickly dissolves into the sham it is. Countless other poor children in developing nations end up on the streets—utterly alone. Sometimes the ravages of disease leave them without a caregiver; in other cases, natural disaster strikes and traffickers swoop in and gather up young victims. Once trafficked, these children face unspeakable horrors. Many become domestic servants—modern-day slaves who work long hours, live in brutal conditions, and often suffer abuse. Others work equally long days in hazardous or backbreaking jobs in rice fields, brick kilns, gold and diamond mines, or farmers' fields. Many girls, some as young as seven or eight, are exploited sexually—coerced into servicing a dozen or more customers a day.

Poor children in the United States are also the most likely to be trafficked. According to the National Human Trafficking Resource Center (NHTRC) poverty is one of the leading circumstances that place American children at risk; other factors, such as homelessness, prior abuse, and child welfare involvement are either directly or frequently related to poverty.[7] The US Department of Justice maintains that "involvement in commercial sex activity is a problem of epidemic proportion" for children and teens

5. Sher, *Somebody's Daughter*, 2.

6. Grytsenko, "Troubled Young Life."

7. National Human Trafficking Resource Center, "Child Sex Trafficking."

who live on the streets in the United States.[8] The National Center for Missing & Exploited Children (NCMEC) further avers that, in 2014, one in six reported runaways was a victim of the sex trade; 68 percent of those victims "were in the care of social services or foster care when they ran."[9]

Many of these child victims are also unprotected. Whether they live on the streets or in an orphanage in the developing world, or are a runaway, a throwaway, or a placement in substandard foster care in the West, these children fly under the radar. No one is truly watching out for them. An unprotected child is a vulnerable child—and few act on that vulnerability faster than traffickers who use violence, forced drug addiction, threats against families, and brainwashing to coerce their victims. In an interview in the *New York Times*, an imprisoned former pimp admitted that he trawled bus stations and malls looking for a "younger female with a backpack" who was likely a runaway. He approached his potential victims knowing that, after a "seasoning" that starts by offering them a safe place to stay, food, and "friendship" but quickly escalates to sexual and physical violence, and often drug addiction, he would have a new conquest for his "stable," a moneymaker to enhance his wealth.[10]

For these criminals, trafficking is nothing more than a business. Their victims are simply commodities, chattel that they use, abuse, and discard at will in order to maximize their profits. John Ashe, president of the UN General Assembly, stressed the lucrative nature of trafficking in 2014. "With annual profits as high as 36 billion dollars per year," he declared, "it ranks as the world's third most profitable crime after illicit drug and arms trafficking."[11] Moreover, trafficking victims are unique in that, unlike drugs, they can be sold and resold, resulting in ongoing profits. This reselling is especially prevalent in the sex trade. Young victims often work seven days each week, servicing multiple customers a day. Testifying before Congress, "Inez" told of being brought to the United States from Mexico, ostensibly to work as a waitress. After she arrived, however, her handlers took her passport from her, threatened to harm her family at home, and forced her to work in a mobile brothel in Florida. Customers bought condoms to use as tickets. Each day she turned thirty-two to thirty-five condom wrappers

8. Walker-Rodriguez and Hill, "Human Sex Trafficking."

9. National Center for Missing and Exploited Children, "Child Sex Trafficking."

10. O'Leary and Iaboni, "When No One's Looking."

11. Ashe, "Remarks."

in to her bosses to prove how much she had "worked."[12] In developing nations, where sex with a virgin is widely believed to increase longevity and provide protection against or even a cure for AIDS, some young victims have their cervix sewn shut multiple times so that they can be offered as virgins over and over again.[13]

Strategies for Ending Human Trafficking

When I speak to individuals or groups, people often tell me that they feel helpless to stop trafficking. Many believe that the only way they can make a difference is by directly rescuing victims, which is beyond their capabilities. There are, however, other important ways we each can actively participate in the modern abolitionist movement. At a UN convention in Palermo, Italy in 2000, attendees were charged with identifying the best practices for reducing a variety of organized criminal activities, including human trafficking. The formal outcomes of that work are widely known as the Palermo Protocols, one of which is the Protocol to Prevent, Suppress and Punish Trafficking in Persons, especially Women and Children.[14] That protocol both defines human trafficking and describes a three-pronged approach designed to eradicate it. Experts across the globe have adopted that protocol, widely known as the 3Ps, as their foundation in the fight against trafficking. The 3Ps—prevention, protection, and prosecution—are each critical, interrelated elements in these efforts.

Prevention includes everything countries, non-governmental organizations, churches, parachurch organizations, and individuals proactively do to thwart trafficking. Education, raising awareness, reducing demand, protecting the vulnerable, and rewriting laws to address and define human trafficking are especially important in preventing the spread of modern-day slavery. Protection focuses on helping those who have already been victimized and includes work to rescue, rehabilitate, and reintegrate (another acronym, commonly referred to as the 3Rs) them into society. Protective work relies heavily on supplying more training for law enforcement and human services providers and changing public perceptions and institutional policies. It also includes providing such services for victims as shelters, education, health care, psychological and spiritual aftercare, and the vacation of their prior convictions. Prosecution refers to the legal penalties nations

12. U.S. Congress, *International Trafficking*, 26.

13. "Sex Trafficking Issue," http://daughtersrising.org/the-sex-trafficking-issue/.

14. United Nations, "Trafficking in Persons."

and states impose on those who traffic others. Experts argue that jail time, fines, and forfeiture of assets are the most effective punishments. Enacting appropriate deterrents and ending legal corruption is pivotal to prosecuting traffickers. Opportunities to participate in this work, from raising awareness to advocacy, abound.

How Christians Can Fight Against Human Trafficking

In the face of this assault on the marginalized, the "least of these," who are created in the image of God and deeply loved by him, what can we, as individuals and as churches, do? First and foremost, we can pray; second, we can educate ourselves; and third, we can work together to end contemporary slavery.

Unfortunately, the American church has a mixed history in relation to slavery. Before the Civil War, many southern Christian slaveholders and ministers used the Bible's admonition to slaves to obey their masters to justify the institution. Many other Christians, on the other hand, worked tirelessly to bring an end to slavery in the British Empire and the United States. For the most part, though, Christians in the United States have been leaders in the contemporary movement to eradicate human trafficking. The Salvation Army, for example, developed programs intended to eradicate sex trafficking early in the twenty-first century. The United States Conference of Catholic Bishops has long devoted resources to raising awareness and providing victim services. The Faith Alliance against Slavery and Trafficking, a collaborative effort on the part of several Christian churches and parachurch organizations, began its work in 2003. Concerned Christians founded and direct such leading anti-trafficking NGOs as International Justice Mission (IJM), A21, and Shared Hope International. Sara Groves and other Christian recording artists are working to raise awareness of trafficking among their fans. In 2012, the Passion Conference, an annual event devoted to helping college students live out their faith, focused on raising awareness of and fighting against human trafficking. In November 2014, religious leaders from around the globe gathered at the Vatican at the invitation of Pope Francis and subsequently released a *Joint Declaration of Religious Leaders against Modern Slavery*, which announced their goal of eliminating slavery globally by 2020.[15]

15. "Faith Alliance," http://faastinternational.org/; Joint Declaration," www.globalfreedomnetwork.org/declaration.

Abundant options are available to individuals, study groups, and churches who want to work to eradicate slavery. They can begin by learning as much as possible in order to recognize and report trafficking in their communities. Recently a massage parlor opened in a small town near my home. Several local women became concerned when a newspaper ad for the business claimed to employ "beautiful young girls" to provide massages. The women contacted the FBI, and the agents thanked them for calling. As I write this, federal officials are following up on the lead. While these women acted appropriately when they feared children were being prostituted, many experts urge us not to focus our efforts solely on the sex trade. While the sexual exploitation of children is particularly heinous, many other kinds of forced labor may be taking place in our back yards.[16] Learning more about all aspects of trafficking is critical as we work to eradicate it. Magazine and other door-to-door sales crews, for example, are often cited by experts as seedbeds of labor trafficking. A 2015 report by the Polaris Project reveals that crew managers "use psychological manipulation, violence, sexual harassment or assault, and abandonment in unfamiliar cities to pressure victims into working harder and to intimidate those who wish to leave their situation."[17] I often think of a young man who came to my door a few years before I started learning about modern forced labor. He was selling cleaning products and had a slick sales pitch. It was a hot day, and we had just finished our dinner. I invited him in for a sandwich and a glass of water, which he devoured. When he left, I noticed that other young people were working in our neighborhood. As they finished canvassing the streets, they climbed into a van parked nearby. I later realized that he and his travelling companions were undoubtedly victims of forced labor. Now I would call both the local police and the National Human Trafficking Hotline (888-373-7888) if such a person came to my door.

As mentioned earlier, I have noticed a huge improvement in the public's awareness of modern-day slavery during the last fifteen years. Being aware, however, is quite different from understanding trafficking and working to end it. The members of North Avenue Presbyterian Church in Atlanta learned that lesson in 2005 after a report on the sex trade of minors in the city was released. "Hidden in Plain View," which was commissioned by

16. International Labour Office, "Forced Labour." According to the ILO, those who are subjected to forced sexual exploitation represent about 25 percent of all trafficking victims.

17. "Labor Trafficking," http://www.polarisproject.org/human-trafficking/resources/labor-trafficking-sales-crews.

the Atlanta Women's Agenda, shocked church members with its evidence that children were being prostituted on the corner outside their sanctuary, where their church had stood since 1898.[18] Deeply disturbed by what he read in the report, senior pastor Scott Weimer decided to discuss the findings with his congregation in a sermon. In a 2009 interview, Weimer admitted that the delicate nature of this sermon concerned him. "I wasn't sure what kind of response I'd get, but it was immediate and powerful. Everyone, young and old, asked immediately 'What can we do?'"[19] Members of the congregation were initially dumbfounded, but went beyond awareness to quickly address the crime on their doorstep. After focusing on stimulating Atlanta's faith community to act, the church helped found Street Grace (Galvanizing Resources against Child Exploitation) in 2008. Street Grace works to eradicate the sexual exploitation of children in five ways: awareness raising, prayer, advocacy, provision of aftercare, and protection of the vulnerable. Volunteers spread the word, prod the state legislature to help trafficked children, and aid rescued victims. Street Grace also provides mentoring for children who are deemed to be at-risk. One of their initiatives, FACE: Fathers against Childhood Exploitation, focuses on reducing demand by mobilizing and empowering men to help stop the sex trade. Pastor Weimer, who inspired his congregation to act, has served on Street Grace's board since its founding; many church members also volunteer their time and provide financial support.[20]

Changing people's perceptions is a critical first step in the fight to protect victims. Before an individual can be rescued and cared for, his or her victim status must first be recognized. Sadly, many law enforcement officials and the public think that most victims "deserve" their fate. In the developing world, many suffer under a system that denies their human rights. In the West, especially for those exploited in the sex trade, victims, even those who are minors, are viewed as willing participants. In 2010, Rachel Lloyd, founder of GEMS (Girls Educational & Mentoring Services) testified before the Senate Judiciary Committee on her work with young victims of the sex trade. Many of the girls in her program, she told the senators, all of whom were struggling to put their sexual exploitation behind them, regularly "encounter social workers, cops, nurses in emergency rooms, judges and prosecutors, and community members who either treat

18. Priebe and Suhr, "Hidden in Plain View."

19. Montgomery, "Grace in the Streets."

20. "Street Grace," http://www.streetgrace.org/mission/.

them with scorn and disgust or simply look the other way. . . . Keisha from the Bronx will be seen as a 'willing participant,' someone who's out there because she 'likes it' and who is criminalized and thrown in detention or in jail."[21] Since her testimony seven years ago we have, thankfully, made progress. A 2015 campaign, jointly sponsored by the McCain Institute and the Human Rights Project for Girls has the slogan, "There's No Such Thing as a Child Prostitute."[22] Its goal is to help the public recognize that children do not have the mental and emotional capacity to choose a life of prostitution, but, instead, are victimized by those who sell them and should be provided with the same rights as victims of other crimes.

Volunteer opportunities to address the needs of those victimized are more readily available than they were a decade ago. Numerous services are needed to effectively rehabilitate and reintegrate victims. Such services, in the wake of increased government and public funding, are more plentiful. In Lloyd's congressional testimony, she also told committee members that fewer than fifty beds existed in shelters specifically designated for human trafficking;[23] by 2012, according to the Polaris Project, that number had increased tenfold to more than 500, which is still woefully inadequate.[24] In 2012, Elizabeth Echevarria founded Living in Liberty in the Pittsburgh area. This faith-based non-profit organization is dedicated to providing rehabilitative services including shelter, legal referrals, food and clothing, counseling, and health care to female victims of the sex trade. Some of its funding comes from Repurposed, a secondhand store it operates. Volunteers work in the store, help educate their communities, work on outreach to possible victims, and organize fundraising events. In Wilmington, NC, attorney Lindsey Roberson, who helped draft North Carolina's anti-trafficking legislation, was instrumental in founding A Safe Place, which provides a variety of services to female trafficking victims. This organization also relies on volunteers to act as advocates, teach life skills, and raise funds. Similar groups and ministries exist or are being formed in communities around the country. The National Human Trafficking Resource Center maintains a directory of anti-trafficking associations that can help individuals find local volunteer opportunities.[25]

21. US Congress, *Child Prostitution and Sex Trafficking*, 15.

22. "Child Prostitute," http://rights4girls.org/campaign/.

23. US Congress, *Child Prostitution and Sex Trafficking*, 16.

24. "Shelter Beds."

25. National Human Trafficking Resource Center, "Referral Directory," http://www.

Advocacy is another way we can contribute to the work to end slavery. It is critical that strong laws be in place to support these efforts. The 2000 TVPA was only a first legislative step in the United States. Each state also needs to pass legislation that defines and provides penalties for trafficking, funds training, and establishes services. The Polaris Project, a Washington, DC based NGO that focuses much of its work to end human trafficking on the legislative process, developed a model state law in 2004. The organization also developed ten categories of law that they use annually to assess each state's progress on this issue; the categories include defining trafficking, providing appropriate penalties for perpetrators, and supplying victim services among others. The first states to adopt trafficking legislation were Texas and Washington in 2003. By 2012, when West Virginia finally made trafficking a crime, all fifty states had begun to put appropriate laws on the books.[26] Even with these foundational laws in place, advocacy is still essential. Concerned citizens can alert their legislators to their concerns and urge them to sponsor and vote for relevant legislation. The Polaris Project website is one tool American advocates can use to learn more about this process.[27]

Ensuring that existing laws are enforced is also important. This is primarily a problem in developing nations where, as we discuss in the chapter on violence, the rule of law is often compromised. IJM has been a leader in the fight against human trafficking since its founding in 1997. Focusing primarily on the developing world, IJM's work to prevent trafficking and other forms of violence, rescue victims, and repair broken justice systems effectively combines every aspect of the Palermo Protocols. In *Terrify No More* (2005), IJM founder Gary Haugen recounts how IJM operatives and attorneys worked with Cambodian police and social workers to rescue young girls from brothels, give them secure aftercare, and prosecute the traffickers who had sold them to the highest bidders with seeming impunity. Though the prostitution of children was illegal in Cambodia, officials had long looked the other way, failing to provide the victims with the legal protection the law prescribed. The entire economy of Svay Pak, a section of Phnom Penh, rested on the sex trade, and IJM faced huge resistance in its work to end it. A successful rescue was possible only after years of arduous work earning the trust of and training local police and planning an intricate

traffickingresourcecenter.org/training-resources/referral-directory.

26. Polaris, "Human Trafficking Legal Framework," 2.

27. "Policy Advocacy," http://www.polarisproject.org/what-we-do/policy-advocacy.

operation to remove victims from the area's red light district.[28] IJM has repeatedly encountered this pattern of official indifference. In an April 2015 TED Talk, Haugen told his listeners that "the problem is not that the poor don't get laws; it's that they don't get law enforcement."[29]

Some congregations have made eradicating human trafficking a major part of their ministry. For example, members of A Jesus Church Family in Portland, Oregon, reach out to victims of sex trafficking by participating in three local ministries—Door to Grace (DTG), the Sexual Assault Resource Center (SARC), and Adorned in Grace. In addition, some members identify pimps by trolling through Craig's List, contacting them, and engageing with them to understand their life circumstances and motivations. They try to help these perpetrators understand the damage they are doing and encourage them to stop.[30] Eddie Byun, who pastors a large, English-speaking congregation in South Korea, first learned about human trafficking in 2010. In response, he devoted himself to prayer and "brainstorming sessions with God" to help him understand what he and his church could do.[31] The result was HOPE Be Restored, a freedom and justice ministry in his church. HOPE has formed six teams that focus on different aspects of the battle against trafficking. Members of their prayer team recognize that trafficking is an issue that must be fought with spiritual weapons. They pray together, create prayer guides, and lead regular prayer walks through Seoul. The other groups are an awareness team that supplies speakers to community organizations and hosts an annual justice conference; a research team that provides the data critical to the ministry's work; a networking team that joins with government officials, churches, and others to build partnerships; a restoration team that furnishes aftercare to victims; and an outreach team that tries to prevent the victimization of the vulnerable.[32]

While not every church can provide such a broad suite of services, churches can educate their congregations, both through classes and sermons, about trafficking. They can also organize prayer campaigns and fasts to engage, as HOPE does, in the spiritual battle to end the enslavement of people who are created in the image of God. Furthermore, church members and congregations can work to protect defenseless children. Many of

28. Haugen with Hunter, *Terrify No More.*

29. Haugen, "Hidden Reason."

30. "Anti-Sex Trafficking," http://www.hearthecry.org/portland/sex-trafficking/.

31. Byun, *Justice Awakening*, 103.

32. Ibid., 103–08.

the programs that we discuss in the next chapter on orphans—foster care, working with single mothers, and sponsoring children in developing nations—apply here as well. In developing nations, children who are being provided for are much less vulnerable to the wiles of a trafficker. In the West, when a poor child is being mentored, has quality after-school care, or is watched over by a concerned individual or group who can intervene, the same holds true. Churches can host child sponsorship events, fund ministries that provide services to victims, adopt inner-city school classrooms, and encourage members to volunteer in mentoring programs. A church tool kit available from the Faith Alliance Against Slavery and Trafficking (FAAST) is especially helpful. It includes Bible study materials for teens and adults, a prayer guide, and training resources and specific suggestions to enable churches to proactively work to end trafficking.[33]

Assessment of Anti-Trafficking Efforts

Despite the fact that today more people are enslaved than at any time in human history, the work of anti-traffickers across the globe is having an impact. Public awareness campaigns are educating millions; in 2014, for example, many airport terminals in the United States began to display educational posters that feature the National Human Trafficking Hotline number. Since 2000 most American states have passed laws criminalizing trafficking and mandating victim services. The US State Department, which is required by the TVPA to study and annually report upon the current status of trafficking globally in its *Trafficking in Persons Report*, highlighted several promising developments in 2014, including a global human trafficking hotline network that allows NGOs to coordinate their response to victims and new banking practices that help track suspicious financial activity.[34] Pressure generated as a result of this report has provided "a strong incentive for governments at every level to do all that they can to prosecute trafficking and to shield at-risk populations."[35]

Christians—as individuals and congregations—are critical to the work of abolition. As Pastor Byun noted, abolition is first a spiritual battle. Christians must join forces in prayer and fasting as we work to destroy modern-day slavery. We must also join forces with others—NGOs, government

33. "Resources," http://www.faastinternational.org/#/resources/church-toolkit.

34. *Trafficking in Persons Report*, 22.

35. Kerry, "Remarks."

officials, social service workers, and law enforcement—who participate in this battle in a practical way. By raising awareness, keeping our eyes open, volunteering with and financially supporting anti-trafficking ministries and organizations, and advocating with our legislators, Christians can make a difference in the lives of the vulnerable and the victimized. It seems abundantly possible that, with our Creator's help, these efforts will, as Gary Haugen, president of IJM argues, "mortally wound slavery in our lifetime."[36]

36. Haugen interview.

8

Caring for Orphans and Neglected Children

Defend the weak and the fatherless;
uphold the cause of the poor and the oppressed.

PSALM 82:3 (NIV)

Religion that God our Father accepts as pure and faultless is this: to look after orphans and widows in their distress.

JAMES 1:27 (NIV)

Orphans in the Developing World

For years, I have read about, prayed over, and wrestled with the knowledge that millions of children in the world are orphans and/or homeless. Gary and I have had countless discussions about the best way to help these little ones who weigh so heavily on my heart and mind. The problem is massive. According to UNICEF, nearly 13 million children in the developing world are "double orphans," children who have lost both of their parents. More than 100 million others have lost one of their parents and, undoubtedly, are impacted negatively by that loss.[1] Without help, the future for these children is bleak at best. Many will find themselves on the streets or trafficked. They will scrounge for food, receive no medical care, and be excluded from school. In *There Is No Me without You,* Melissa Fay Greene tells of Ethiopian sisters, ages seven and five, who lost both of their parents to AIDS. In part because of the stigma of AIDS, no family members were willing to take in the girls. Having no other options, they stayed alone in their family's one-room cinder block home. The local court ordered an uncle to provide supervision and financial support for them. Neighbors left them food when they could. Before long the uncle began to show up at night and rape the older girl. He threatened to evict them from their home and told her that her sister would be next if she told anyone what was happening. After months of abuse, she finally confessed to a neighbor who, with other local women, waited to confront the uncle the next time he came to the door. He ran away but was not punished. Thankfully, though, the girls were referred to a local home for abandoned children and are now thriving.[2]

Sadly, such a caring solution is not available to all who need it. Worldwide, between 8 and 10 million parentless children live in some type of orphanage.[3] While many of these institutions do their best to nurture their charges, others are brutal places that subject the babies and children in their care to sexual abuse, organ harvesting, and illegal adoptions. Because many of these orphanages operate unlicensed with little or no government oversight, running an orphanage in a developing nation has become big business. Subsidized by donations from the West and funds collected from volunteers or adoptive parents, some orphanages recruit "orphans" from parents by promising to take care of and educate them for a prescribed period of time. One study found that nearly 90 percent of the children living in orphanages in Ghana actually had a living parent; nearly all of the country's orphanages were unlicensed. Moreover, countless children are abused by those who have paid a fee to "volunteer," thereby gaining unsupervised access to the children in their care.[4]

1. "Orphans," http://www.charitywater.org/about/mission.php.
2. Greene, *No Me without You*, 171.
3. Ahern, "Orphanages."
4. "Protecting Children."

For a long time, I believed that adoption was one of the best ways to reach out to these unfortunate children and improve their lives, but I never found myself in the position to adopt. Instead, I have supported friends and acquaintances as they have walked through the process, rejoicing when their new family members arrived in the United States. On two return trips from overseas travel, we were blessed with the presence of several pairs of newly adoptive parents and their babies on our flight. My heart was full with happiness for these new parents and their children as they began to forge their new lifelong bond.

We have watched and prayed for friends as they successfully navigated their way through the morass of the application and approval process, raised finances, traveled overseas to meet their soon-to-be children, brought them home, and integrated them into their families. One family we know quite well adopted a little boy from Uganda several years ago, and he has adapted so well to his new life that he and his sister interact almost like twins. We also know people who have dealt with the sadness of a late process denial of their adoption by a foreign court and, perhaps even more heartbreaking, those who have struggled, or even failed, to connect with their new child. Several older children we know of have resisted their new lives and their loss of independence after they arrive; used to handling things on their own, they have a hard time becoming part of a family unit.

Gary, in his ever-practical way, was the first to raise questions that made sense to me about adoption. He reminded me that, for the $15,000 to $30,000 spent on each international adoption, countless children who remained in their home countries could experience marked improvements in their lives.[5] I also started to read stories of children who were adopted from unwitting and unwilling parents after their children were placed in an orphanage under false pretenses. As someone who has long worked to help end human trafficking, I know that we must stop this seamy side of international adoption. How, then, can we best help these children?

I still believe that international adoption plays an important role in providing for orphans in developing nations. I have, though, tempered my support for it. I have come to agree with one adoptive couple, who explained in a *Pittsburgh Post-Gazette* article that the only children they would consider for adoption were those who "didn't have better options"—those who could not find a home with biological family members or with

5. "Cost of Adopting," https://www.childwelfare.gov/pubpdfs/s_costs.pdf.

other parents in their home country or with those of their own culture.[6] I certainly do not intend to discourage those who feel called by God to adopt; I only suggest that prospective parents enter the process with caution. As Jen Hatmaker, a Christian author and blogger, and the mother of two children adopted from Ethiopia, says, "I am not anti-adoption, I am anti-unethical adoption."[7] Prospective adoptive parents should start by educating themselves thoroughly about international adoption. A myriad of excellent resources are available to provide guidance.[8] Parents also need to carefully select the country from which they hope to adopt. Nations that participate in the Hague Convention, an international agreement that strives to protect the interests of adopted children, will usually provide more control over the adoption process than will countries that have not agreed to convention guidelines. Parents should also use discretion when choosing an adoption agency. They should be sure that the agency is licensed both here and in the home country, and they should talk with others who have recently used its services. International adoption is one crucial way that Christians can make a difference in the lives of orphans. If you feel called to adopt, we pray that you are blessed in the process.

Child Sponsorship

Gary and I have concluded, however, based on our research, that child sponsorship is often a more effective way to positively impact the lives of poor children in the developing world. As child sponsors for nearly forty years, we have a long track record with such programs. Research published in 2013 affirms our belief in the effectiveness of sponsorship. Bruce Wydick, Professor of Economics and International Studies at the University of San Francisco, organized a team of scholars to study the long-term impact of children sponsored through Compassion International's program. The researchers collected data on thousands of adults who, as children, had been sponsored between 1980 and 1992, as well as on many others from the same area who had not been sponsored. They found that those who had been sponsored were much more likely to become church and community

6. Ward, "Ethiopian Adoptees."

7. Hatmaker, "Adoption Ethics."

8. For more information, see Chapman, "Adoption 101"; Davenport, *International Adoption*; Hatmaker, "Adoption Ethics, Parts 1 and 2"; "Intercountry Adoption," http://travel.state.gov/content/adoptionsabroad/en.html.

leaders, to hold white-collar, salaried jobs, and to complete secondary and university education than their non-sponsored peers.[9] These results make sense. A child who receives healthcare, a quality education, and a church family is going to have a better chance to improve his or her circumstances than those who do not have the same benefits. Sponsorship allows poor children to remain with their family of origin and removes some of the financial burden their parents would have struggled with as they raised them. Sponsored children can remain in school and are much less likely to fall prey to fraudulent offers from human traffickers. Globally, according to Wydick's research, nearly 9 million children are sponsored by donors to more than 200 organizations. Compassion International and World Vision are the two largest faith-based child sponsorship organizations.[10] They use different models of sponsorship—Compassion provides donations directly to the sponsored child; World Vision works from the assumption that helping the child's community become self-sustaining will positively impact not only the sponsored child, but all the children who live there. We believe that each model works—and we have participated in both.

To encourage sponsorship, churches can hold sponsorship Sundays and give congregants an opportunity to work together to sponsor a group of children. For its Hope Sunday outreach, World Vision provides congregations with resources, sermon outlines, videos and PowerPoint presentations, and sponsorship folders.[11] Compassion International furnishes similar materials for its annual Compassion Sunday program.[12] Some churches partner with smaller, local ministries to sponsor children. Port City Community Church in Wilmington, North Carolina, works with the Victorious Community Church in Nakuru, Kenya, to operate a home for children living on the street. Mama Hellen's Rehabilitation Center, which was founded by this Kenyan church when the pastor and his wife felt called to minister to local street children, provides a home, schooling, and spiritual nurture to the children in its care. Port City donations supplied the funds to build the center's facilities, and its members sponsor children financially and prayerfully. They also build relationships with their sponsored children by writing to them and even, on short-term missions trips,

9. Wydick, "Sponsor a Child."

10. Wydick, Glewwe, and Rutledge, "International Sponsorship," 393, 401.

11. "Hope Sunday," http://hopesunday.wvpartner.us/.

12. "Compassion Sunday," http://compassionsunday.com/.

meeting them.[13] An added benefit to child sponsorship can be experienced at home. By sponsoring children, families can teach their own daughters and sons about poverty and model ministering to a child in need. Children can learn about another culture and build relationships by writing and receiving letters, sending pictures, and helping choose small gifts for their sponsored "sibling."

Helping parents support and nurture the lives God blesses them with is another way Christians can aid poor children who might otherwise end up in orphanages or on the street. Most parents want to provide for their children, but the daily grind of poverty makes it overwhelmingly difficult. According to Tara Livesay, who works at a birthing center for poor mothers in Haiti, only one in 300 of the women to whom she ministered chose to give her child up for adoption. These mothers are poor, often young and single, and some of their pregnancies were the result of rape. Yet they deeply love their children and want to raise them.[14] In 2010 mom-blogger Kristen Welch joined other bloggers on a Compassion International sponsored trip to Nairobi. She went in order to reflect on what she saw and learned and report on it in her blog. Devastated by the poverty surrounding her, she was particularly upset when she learned that girls, often as young as twelve, were undergoing back-alley abortions. The pregnancies, usually caused by rape, left these girls believing that abortion was their only option. Feeling called to help, Welch and her husband sold their house and moved their family into a more modest one to raise seed money. Partnering with a Nairobi native who was a former sponsored child, the Welches opened Mercy House, a home for pregnant teens from the slums of Nairobi. Mercy House provides health care, counseling, parenting classes, and education. Not only do the residents stay during their pregnancy, they reside there with their babies for more than a year.[15] Funded by private donations, Welch's vision has thrived. By 2015, the Mercy House ministry included two residences that furnish housing for sixteen expectant and new young mothers and their children.[16] These children, who undoubtedly would have been sacrificed to abortion, and their young mothers now have a new chance at life.

13. "Hope 127 Kenya Project," http://portcitychurch.monkpreview2.com/hope127/kenyaproject/.

14. Hatmaker, "Adoption Ethics: Part One."

15. Tudor, "Rescued From Wealth."

16. "About Rehema House," http://mercyhousekenya.org/work/kenya/rehema.

Katie Davis, the author of *Kisses from Katie*, found her heart touched by the plight of poor children in Uganda when she and her mother participated in a short-term mission trip to an orphanage during her senior year in high school. The next summer she returned to teach kindergarten, ostensibly for a short time; she now makes Uganda her home. Her story is remarkable, and is detailed in her book. She has adopted several children and founded Amazima Ministries, which provides assistance to local children and families. Ministry supporters can sponsor a child's education, help furnish food and health care to those in need, or help birth mothers earn income by purchasing bracelets and necklaces that they make.[17] Amazima's work not only helps children improve their future, but gives them a chance to grow up in their families of origin.

Another ministry that provides a holistic approach as it assists children in need is Help One Now (HON), which works in Haiti, Peru, and several African nations. HON's mission is to work with local ministries that help orphans and vulnerable children. Its ultimate goal is to "break the cycle of extreme poverty." They do so by rescuing and providing homes for abandoned children, working with at-risk populations to prevent slavery and free those already enslaved, and caring for children who are likely to be orphaned.[18] They understand the way extreme poverty works and proactively endeavor to aid those in its clutches. Recently, for example, when staff realized that Haitian rice farmers were losing their livelihood because they could not compete with subsidized rice shipments from the United States, they offered temporary educational sponsorships for farmers' children. HON's leaders believed that, by paying for school fees and food, and thus relieving parents of these financial burdens, families would be more likely to remain intact and children would be safer from Haiti's restavek slave culture.[19]

Few of us are called to start a ministry or move to a developing nation. All of us, however, can help care for the world's orphaned and abandoned children. The ministries mentioned here are only a few of the many that care for such children. By sponsoring a child or supporting ministries that educate and care for children or assist birth families, we will make a difference in the lives of the "least of these."

17. "Katie's Story," https://amazima.org/about-us/katies-story.

18. "Help One Now," http://helponenow.org/.

19. Hatmaker, "Adoption Ethics, Part Three."

Foster Care and the Church

One bleak January afternoon six years ago, I watched as five-year-old MaKayla and her four-year-old brother, Jayden, slowly followed their caseworker, Linda, up our sidewalk. They both sported a threadbare, ill-fitting winter coat; MaKayla's stretched across her chest and barely reached her waist; Jayden's, on the other hand, nearly smothered him. Each of them carried a paper bag, and Linda struggled with a large plastic garbage bag. I soon learned that these bags held all of their belongings—a collection of tattered clothes that did not fit and a few dirty, but well-loved, toys. These children, whose sense of "normal" had been shattered a few days earlier when they were removed from the only home they knew, were coming to stay with us for a temporary foster placement.

After a few words of introduction and a quick farewell from Linda, they found themselves in the formerly empty-nest of two close-to-retirement academics. Everyone was a bit befuddled by this new situation. Gary and I did our best to acclimate them to a new routine—one that included regular baths, mealtimes, and bedtimes, storybooks and songs, daycare and kindergarten, and Sunday school. Alternately loving and defiant or sweet and sassy, they were clearly overwhelmed by their new "home" and its rules and regularity.

The children's father, who struggled with drug addiction and had frequent problems with the law, had been their sole provider after their mother moved to another city. He often left them at home alone. MaKayla was accustomed to being in charge; Jayden was timid and wanted to stay close to his sister. While we struggled with how best to love and discipline these two little ones, they responded quickly to routine and safety. In no time at all we were "Mommy" and "Daddy" to them. Within a few months, however, the courts returned them to their father. Less than a week later, they were once again removed from their home after his pregnant girlfriend, who had the children with her, passed out from a drug overdose during a late-night visit to a local fast food restaurant. Not one of the carload of clothes and toys I sent home with them was anywhere to be found when their caseworker went to their house to gather their belongings. In a sad post-script, their father's girlfriend gave birth to his fifth child while serving a prison sentence for possession.

MaKayla and Jayden's story, bleak though it may seem, has a happy outcome. Recently, after three long years of haggling in the courts and the children's erratic visits from their father, they were adopted, and Gary and

I had the privilege of attending the proceedings. The family who adopted them, the same couple who taught their Sunday school class when they lived with us, and who became their permanent foster parents after their second removal from their father's care, are now providing them with a stable, loving home. I have to look deep when I glimpse them across the sanctuary on Sunday morning to see the frightened, needy children I first met on that cold January afternoon. Yes, they still have their struggles. Numerous studies, some of which are discussed in our chapters on education, have shown that the early years are crucial in a child's emotional and intellectual development. But they are in a much better place and are progressing toward a much better future than they would have had with their biological father.

Unfortunately, however, MaKayla and Jayden's happy ending is not the norm. Many of the children under the care of the state never do find a permanent, safe family. Products of homes in which they are neglected and/or abused, these children are removed from their parents and placed in group homes or foster care. Many are shuttled back and forth from their parents' care to the state's until they finally age out of care, unsupported financially or emotionally, into a dismal future. According to CNN and the Dave Thomas Foundation for Adoption, less than 3 percent of those who age out of foster care will earn a college degree, one in five will become homeless, only half will be employed at age twenty-four, one in four will experience PTSD, and 71 percent of the young women, most of whom will be unmarried, will be pregnant by age twenty-one.[20]

In our two foster placements and in my several years of volunteer work as a court-appointed special advocate (CASA) for children in foster care, we witnessed a system that is understaffed and overwhelmed by the needs of the children in its care and judges who, because of state law and judicial precedent, cannot adequately consider the individual circumstances of the many children who enter their courtrooms. Given that, in 2014 more than 650,000 children in the US spent at least some time in foster care, more than 50,000 were adopted, and more than 100,000 were eligible for adoption, we can clearly do a better job of caring for these children.[21]

Churches and their members can certainly help by supporting and providing foster care. Recently, for example, Church at the Gates in Missoula,

20. Soronen, "Foster Care."

21. "Trends in Foster Care and Adoption," http://www.acf.hhs.gov/sites/default/files/cb/trends_fostercare_adoption2014.pdf.

Montana, held a meeting for members who are interested in foster care and adoption. More than one hundred attendees learned that, if only one in 250 Montana families who self-identify as Christians provided foster care, all of the children currently under the care of the state would have a home. The gathering, coordinated by Child Bridge, a Christian non-profit dedicated to "bridging the gap between churches, communities, and government" by raising awareness of foster care needs and recruiting families to provide care, included speakers from government agencies.[22] The church was encouraged to not only recruit families to furnish care, but to aid them by supplying clothing, toys, meals, and respite care.[23]

Another effective way Christians can reach out to boys and girls in foster care is by volunteering as a court-appointed special advocate. CASA volunteers are assigned to work with one or more children who are in care by getting to know them and advocating for them in court. My longest CASA placement was with a little girl who had been sexually molested by her mother's boyfriend. I met with her frequently, took her to movies and the playground, and attended court proceedings related to her care. She was in foster care for only part of our time together; the court returned her to her mother after about a year in a foster home. Although reunited with her mother, she remained under the care of the state, so my role in her life continued. I was expected to alert her caseworker if I saw something that concerned me. After one outing, I returned her to the apartment she shared with her mom. She wanted me to see her room, so despite her mother's half-hearted protest, I followed her back the hall. I learned that she was sleeping on a bare mattress on the floor of the room she was sharing with mom and her new boyfriend. I called her caseworker. I was overjoyed to learn recently that this girl has now graduated from high school; her older brother, who was assigned to my supervision for a while, is attending college. It looks as though they are headed to a better future than I had envisioned for them. I cannot claim to understand all of the factors that contributed to their situation; I do, however, believe that prayer and the continued intervention of an advocate helped. The CASA program is always in need of volunteers; to learn more and to find out if an office exists in your county, check its website: http://www.casaforchildren.org/.

Members of the Austin Stone Community Church in Austin, Texas, have committed to filling the gap between the large number of children in

22. "About Child Bridge," http://www.childbridgemontana.org/History.html.

23. "Everyone Can Do Something."

their city who need quality foster care and the number of homes available to them. They "prayerfully envision a day when there is not a line of children" in Austin waiting for care, but "rather a line of families, responding to God's call to care for the orphan, waiting for another child who needs a permanent home."[24] As they work to achieve that vision, the church is hosting foster care training, providing a support system for those who foster, developing opportunities for members to mentor children or become CASA volunteers, assisting families who are fostering to adopt, and financially supporting agencies that work with those in care. One church family trained to become foster parents now provides a home for two teenage boys. Friends in their small group provide respite care, give breakfast to the boys and take them to church on Sunday mornings when their foster parents teach Sunday school, and help love and mentor the boys in other ways.[25]

By coming together to provide care and support those who foster children, a church creates an extended family for them. Faith Bridge Foster Care in Atlanta has formalized that concept in its Community of Care model, a small group ministry "that surrounds foster families and foster children in loving, stable environments made up of trained volunteers."[26] Each small group furnishes wide-ranging support, including respite care, transportation, mentoring, tutoring, and clothing and toys. Each group also bathes its foster families in prayer. Fostering is hard. Children who have been neglected and abused by their biological parents typically have numerous emotional and developmental issues. As many as 50 percent of foster parents stop providing care within the first year because they become overwhelmed by its demands.[27] Having others to help is critical for those who are striving to provide a loving home to these children. When Gary and I fostered, we were fortunate that several of his students were education majors who were required to have state clearances. This enabled us to hire them as babysitters. The children loved spending time with the college students, and we reveled in a night or afternoon out. A retired teacher in our church volunteered to tutor MaKayla and Jayden, who both struggled academically. She still works with them, and they think of her as family. Without this kind of support, it is very difficult to effectively foster.

24. "Flip the Line," http://www.forthecity.org/fliptheline#.

25. "Salt and Light"; "Foster Care Initiative," http://www.forthecity.org/fostercare.

26. "Ministry Model," http://www.faithbridgefostercare.org/about-us/ministry-model/.

27. Esaki, Ahn, and Gregory, "Foster Parents' Perceptions," 679.

If your congregation does not already have an orphan and foster care program in place, prayerfully consider talking with church leadership about starting one. The Christian Alliance for Orphans, founded in 2004, is a network of Christians committed to working with "coordinated initiatives that grow effective adoption, foster care and global orphan care rooted in the local church."[28] They sponsor an annual Orphan Sunday in churches around the globe, host conferences, and provide webinar training. Faith Bridge provides links to books, white papers, and program guidelines on their website; they also offer training in the Atlanta area.[29] Rick Warren's Saddleback Church in California provides numerous resources to help develop such a program, including a prayer guide, a list of ways to help orphans and foster children, and opportunities to partner with its orphan care initiative financially. Leaders of the initiative remind Christians that orphan care is the responsibility of the whole church, not just of those who provide direct care. Certainly each of us can play a role in improving the lives of such local children in need.[30]

Refugee Children and the Church

As I write this chapter, the Western world is intensely focused on refugees and how best to respond to them. Galvanized in the early fall of 2015 to help Syrians fleeing the civil war at home by a photograph of a drowned toddler on a Turkish beach, many are now refusing to assist these same refugees after police discovered a Syrian passport on the body of one of the terrorists who killed 130 people in Paris just two months later. Proclaiming "je suis Paris," social media posters are vilifying those who are trying to escape the violence in their cities, and governors in half of US states have announced that they will not provide sanctuary for any Syrians. In Texas several people who protested outside a mosque carried semi-automatic weapons and wore face masks.[31]

For the first time since the end of World War II, more than 50 million people, about half of whom are children, have been forcibly displaced from their homes. More than 25,000 of the 1.1 million refugees who have formally submitted applications for asylum are minors who have been

28. "About Us," https://cafo.org/about/.

29. "Resources," http://www.faithbridgefostercare.org/resources/.

30. "Get Started," http://orphancareinitiative.com/getstarted/.

31. Moinzadeh, "Gun-Toting Protestors."

orphaned or separated from their parents.[32] How should the church respond to this crisis? Scripture is replete with commands to care for the outsider.[33] Jesus, in the Sermon on the Mount, exhorted us to pray for and love our enemies.[34] Christians who do not find their security in this world, but in their relationship to the Creator of the universe should be the first ones in line to help these women, children, and even men who are fleeing for their lives. Numerous ministries have stepped up to help. The Preemptive Love Coalition, for example, is providing food and other aid to displaced families.[35] In a recent campaign promoted on Facebook, they raised over $75,000 in five hours to provide food to starving children trapped near the front lines in Syria.

In Matthew 25 Jesus admonishes us to care for the "least of these." James argues that pure religion is evidenced by those who look after the orphans in their midst. Given the number of children who are orphaned, neglected, homeless, and unprotected, the problem can seem (as do the others we discuss) overwhelming. But if each Christian helps one endangered child, the difference will be pronounced.

32. "World Refugee Day."

33. For example, see Exod 23:9, Lev 19: 33–34, Deut 10:18, Zech 7: 9–10, Matt 25: 35, and Mark 12: 30–31 among many others.

34 See Matt 5:43–48.

35. "Emergency Relief for Families," http://www.preemptivelove.org/emergency_relief_for_families_victimized_by_isis

9

Living on Minimum Wage in America

Overcoming poverty is not a gesture of charity. It is an act of justice.

NELSON MANDELA

If the misery of our poor be caused not by the laws of nature, but by our institutions, great is our sin.

CHARLES DARWIN

As the twentieth century closed, journalist Barbara Ehrenreich left behind her house, friends, career, and ATM card to undertake an experiment. To experience the types of work millions of Americans perform and better understand the psychological and material hardships such employment entails, she labored undercover at several minimum wage jobs. On job application forms she presented herself as a divorced homemaker whose only work experience had been as a housekeeper in private homes. In Key West, Florida, she worked as a waitress; in Portland, Maine, she toiled as a hotel maid and with a cleaning service; and in Minneapolis she stocked shelves at Walmart. She lived in cheap, temporary housing and coped with the physical and mental exhaustion minimum wage work often entails. All her jobs required her to "master new terms, new tools, and new skills." During her experiment, Ehrenreich strove to display the traits that job training programs teach and employers value: obedience, cheerfulness, cleanliness, and punctuality. Most of her coworkers in these minimum wage jobs possessed these attributes, although the lack of reliable transportation and childcare made getting to work on time difficult for many of them.[1]

Ehrenreich experienced the financial challenges minimum wage workers face. They are forced to cope with a "host of special costs." Finding affordable housing is their principal problem. Since many of them do not have enough money for a security deposit and first month's rent to obtain an apartment, they pay "through the nose for a [motel] room by the week." Consequently, they do not have a kitchen, the meals they can prepare are very limited, and they often eat at fast food restaurants or snack on items from convenience stores. Because most of them have no health insurance, they pay full price for medications.[2]

Ehrenreich's meager income required her to eat lots of beans, cheese, chopped meat, and noodles, rarely purchase clothes, and forego entertainment. Her rent consumed 40 percent of her take-home pay. Ehrenreich concludes that something is "very wrong" in American society "when a single person in good health" who has a working car "can barely support herself by the sweat of her brow." People who do not own cars (especially those who live in places without public transportation) confront an additional challenge. They must depend on relatives or friends for rides to work and often also to a babysitter's home or childcare center. Some of her coworkers rode bikes or walked to their job sites, which greatly limited either where they could work or live.[3]

Ehrenreich also describes the struggle of low-wage job seekers to find employment. They rely primarily on help-wanted signs, newspaper ads, and word-of-mouth messages that rarely include information about wages. In a society that glorifies financial tycoons and multimillionaire athletes, she notes, making $7 or even $10 an hour often makes people feel inferior. Consequently, few individuals reveal how much they earn or learn that another business pays higher wages than their current employer.[4]

1. Ehrenreich, *Nickel and Dimed*, 193.
2. Ehrenreich, "Nickel and Dimed."
3. Ehrenreich, *Nickel and Dimed*, 196–97, 199 (quotation), 205.
4. Ibid., 206–7.

Like many other low-wage workers, Ehrenreich felt the sting of disrespect. When she served as a waitress, the management had the right to inspect her purse as she left work every day. She denounces the drug testing and pre-employment personality tests required of minimum wage workers as "demeaning intrusions." Company rules against "gossip" or in some cases all talking prevented workers from expressing their grievances to peers. Those who are treated as untrustworthy—as potential slackers, drug addicts, or thieves—sometimes begin to act less reliably. When managers and impersonal rules continually remind workers that they occupy a low position in the social hierarchy, they may accept this belittled status. During her experiment, Ehrenreich reports, she never met a shirker, a drug addict, or a robber. Instead, she was amazed by how much pride most people took in doing jobs well that provided such meager wages and little recognition.[5]

Sociologist Diana Kendall argues that if a journalist replicated Ehrenreich's experiment today, she would face even greater challenges because both the competition for minimum wage jobs and the cost of living has increased in many areas.[6] The Massachusetts Institute of Technology living wage calculator estimates that a family with two adults and two children living in my home county in western Pennsylvania needs to have a yearly income of $33,257 to pay its basic expenses. That requires an hourly wage of $16, which is more than double the current minimum wage. A typical American family of four, the MIT site reports, must "work more than three full-time minimum-wage jobs (a sixty-eight-hour work week per working adult) to earn a living wage."[7]

Consider the Nailors who live in Evart, Michigan, the kind of place that Norman Rockwell often featured in his paintings. Although they reside in a house "in a small town in Middle America," they struggle. The earnings of John Nailor, who operates a computer repair business, are less than the poverty level for a family of four. His two young daughters wear hand-me-down clothes and play with used toys. By the end of every month, the family has only a few coins left. They do not have cable television and rarely go out to eat. Without food stamps and income tax credit, Nailor declares, "We would be lost."[8]

5. Ibid., 208–12; first quotation from 208–9, second from 210.

6. Kendall, *Sociology*, 231.

7. "Living Wage Calculator," http://livingwage.mit.edu/.

8. "Nailor Family" (http://www.childrensdefense.org/policy/endingchildpoverty/children-of-hard-times/new-faces-of-poverty-the.html). As another example, see

Those who work in the fast-food industry especially struggle. This industry has long enjoyed high profit margins. Nevertheless, most American employees earn the national or state minimum wage. Most fast-food workers are not teenagers who are pocketing discretionary spending money. In reality, 70 percent of them are over the age of twenty, and more than two-thirds of them are women with children who are their family's primary breadwinner. More than half of fast-food employees, a rate that is higher than in any other industry, have one or more family member(s) who is receiving welfare.[9]

My wife and I have observed numerous examples of the situations and problems Ehrenreich describes through our volunteer work with a local ministry that aids individuals and families undergoing financial crises. Most of our clients earn less than $10 per hour and have no health insurance. We are constantly amazed by how well many of them manage their finances. They live in the least expensive housing they can find, rarely eat out, spend little on entertainment, and buy their clothes at thrift stores. Significant numbers of them do not own cars and walk or bike to work or pay others to give them rides. The cost of car payments, repairs, and insurance of our clients who do own cars often puts them behind on other bills. Since few of them have a vehicle to trade, money for a down payment, or a good credit history, they buy used cars from dealers at inflated prices and pay very high (sometimes predatory) interest rates.[10] Our clients working at minimum-wage jobs generally take advantage of government programs such as food stamps and LIHEAP, utility company programs that cap their payments, and local programs such as the town's food pantry. Many of them apologize for asking our organization for assistance; some are embarrassed and even ashamed.

My wife and I worked at various minimum wage jobs both as teenagers and adults. Except for a short period in her life, we saw these jobs as a temporary expedient, not a potentially permanent situation. As a young woman, she labored as a waitress and a secretary; later she worked for a temp agency. I trimmed Christmas trees as a teenager, had a part-time job as an orderly in two different hospitals while attending college and seminary, and as a seminary student worked one summer in a factory. These

---

Jamieson, "Life and Death."

9. Cuomo, "Fast-Food Workers."

10. See "Abusive Car Loans."

experiences exposed us to the monotony, boredom, and lack of respect many minimal wage jobs entail.

Unfortunately, many financially well-off Americans know little about the conditions and impact of poverty. Ehrenreich argues that middle and upper-class Americans typically view poverty as an austere, but sustainable, condition rather than as the "acute distress" it actually is. Not having enough money to eat lunch or being compelled to work while one is ill or injured because she cannot afford to miss a day's pay is an emergency situation, not a viable lifestyle.[11] The financially secure rarely recognize that those living in low-income communities have less access to grocery stores, discount retailers, and affordable housing. The documentary *A Place at the Table* vividly depicts the challenges of finding nutritious, inexpensive food in inner cities and rural areas.[12] Shopping trips to buy goods at lower prices often take several hours for low-income individuals who have to use public transportation.[13]

Bandwidth Poverty

Harvard economist Sendhil Mullainathan delineates three types of poverty: money poverty, time poverty, and bandwidth poverty. This third type—the percentage of our mental capacity available for making decisions—is an attention shortage fueled by monetary and time poverty. "Scarcity captures the mind," compelling a person to concentrate on his unfulfilled needs. Scarcity strongly affects how individuals think. It inhibits "the brain's ability to grasp, manage and solve problems," making people less efficient and effective. Those who are focusing on an immediate deadline are unable to consider later ones. People who lack the money to pay their bills often fixate on today's expenses and ignore future ones. Worrying about money reduces people's ability to plan wisely, solve problems, exercise willpower, and control their impulses. Because people are unable to think about anything but the immediate crisis, their decisions often make matters worse. The many deadlines and pressures the poor confront prevent them from planning for

11. Ehrenreich, *Nickel and Dimed*, 214 (quotation), 47.

12. "A Place at the Table," http://www.magpictures.com/aplaceatthetable/. See also Pringle, *Place at the Table*.

13. Barnes, *Cost of Being Poor*, 186, 165.

the future. Hoping for a quick fix, many unwisely spend money on lottery tickets or they buy alcohol to temporarily escape their problems.[14]

Linda Tirado who has two low-paying jobs, attends college full-time, and cares for her children, explains that her stressful schedule causes her to move from one responsibility to another without planning. Many bad decisions the working poor make about food, medical care, smoking, and other matters, Tirado claims, "make perfect sense" given their circumstances. Buying food that is tasty and cheap and keeps well rather than purchasing food that is healthier, harder to cook, and more likely to spoil is reasonable. Medical clinics provide little help because the indigent cannot afford the copays and the staff tell patients to see specialists. Tirado admits that her smoking habit is unhealthy and expensive. However, she argues that it is the only thing that "keeps me from collapsing or exploding."[15]

Their pressures and anxiety prevent many minimum wage workers from taking advantage of programs and opportunities that could improve their situation.[16] Many fail to sign up for assistance programs because they are preoccupied with everyday life, do not know about them, or do not recognize their value.[17]

Having a meager income often creates a vicious cycle. The poor frequently borrow money or postpone regular payments to cover emergency expenses. They procure high-interest payday loans, use installment plans to purchase products, and pay high credit-card fees and interest rates. Often low-income individuals make only the minimal payments on their credit cards, thereby accumulating large interest fees. Because they fall behind, the indigent also frequently pay their bills after they are due, which costs them late fees. Many simply do not have the funds to pay all their bills on time.

Recognizing the impact of bandwidth poverty helps us move beyond blaming the victim to deeper explanations of destitution. Poverty often thwarts long-term thinking. This concept helps elucidate why many low-income individuals do not try to get a better job, obtain more education or training, or leave an abusive partner. All of these actions require sophisticated planning, which a brain, plagued by stress, fatigue, depression,

14. Mullainathan and Shafir, *Scarcity*, 7–13, 27 (first quotation); Putnam, *Our Kids*, 130 (second quotation).

15. Tirado, "Bad Decisions."

16. Rosenberg, "Cycle of Scarcity"; Mullainathan and Shafir, *Scarcity*, 148.

17. Konniokva, "No Money, No Time"; Rosenberg, "Cycle of Scarcity."

excessive alcohol consumption, or drug use, cannot do. Consequently, the poor often need the assistance of caring individuals to improve their lives.

The Impact of Poverty

Being raised by low-income parents often adversely affects children. Many of them experience great stress when their families cannot cover their basic expenses. These children frequently eat poorly, wear inferior clothing, and move repeatedly. Some live in substandard housing or are homeless. Many low-income parents suffer from low self-esteem, lack of respect, depression, and even a sense of hopelessness, which reduces their ability to lovingly nurture their children. The poor often have low expectations, adopt a fatalistic outlook, and believe they cannot change their circumstances.[18]

Not surprisingly, numerous poor people eventually become apathetic. Their lack of social contacts, a meaningful job, and education leads many of them to feel powerless to improve their lives. When people fail to keep their promises to them, their plans repeatedly fail, and their needs outstrip their resources, many low-income individuals understandably become resigned to their fate.[19]

Tirado conveys the hopelessness plaguing many poor Americans. "We have learned not to try too hard to be middle-class." It does not work and "makes you feel worse for having tried and failed yet again." None of the poor financial decisions matter in the long run. "I will never not be poor, so what does it matter if I don't pay" all my bills? Making sacrifices, she maintains, will not improve her circumstances. The poor, she contends, feel pressured to enjoy life when they have a little money, "because no matter how responsible you are you will be broke in three days anyway."[20]

"Poverty," Tirado laments, "cuts off your long-term brain." It explains why some women have children with several different men. They try to establish connections wherever they can. The affluent, Tirado declares, "have no idea how strong the pull to feel worthwhile is." Most poor women recognize, she maintains, that they are "probably not compatible" long-term with their sexual partners, but their lovers make them "feel powerful and valuable." Poor women, Tirado asserts, seldom think about "what will

18. Todd, *Hope Rising*. See also Myers, *Working with the Poor*, 63.

19. Bartle, "Factors of Poverty. See also Maholmes, *Fostering Resilience.*

20. Tirado, "Bad Decisions."

happen in a month." Many poor people, she insists, just seize simple pleasures whenever they can.[21]

Helping the indigent develop hope is pivotal to improving their lives. People who have hope, Valerie Maholmes argues, can think, plan, and act to achieve their desired outcomes. Hope inspires individuals to persevere despite adversity. It helps people overcome disappointments, pursue goals, and perceive the future as promising rather than fruitless. Their neglectful parents, inferior housing, clothing, and food, interpersonal problems, and a lack of respect cause many poor children to view the world as stacked against them.[22] One study found that by age three, the children of working professionals typically hear 500,000 messages of encouragement compared with 75,000 for children of parents on welfare; on the other hand, children of professional families hear 80,000 discouraging remarks by age three, while children of families on welfare hear 200,000.[23] To develop hope, a sense of security, and the confidence that they can conquer obstacles and achieve goals, children need to have a nurturing, positive relationship with a caregiver.[24] Other supportive individuals—relatives, family friends, teachers, coaches, and mentors—can also help children become more optimistic and achievement-oriented.[25]

Ways to Help the Working Poor

Making it easier for the poor to establish bank accounts, furnishing more options to automatically pay bills, and providing opportunities for financial counseling and borrowing are critical.[26] The poor have trouble getting a bank account and, therefore, "spend a lot of time figuring out where to cash a check and get money orders to pay bills."[27] The Chalmers Center's Faith and Finances training courses offer valuable instruction to individuals who

21. Ibid.

22. Maholmes, *Fostering Resilience*, ix, 2, 14, 18. See also Snyder, *Psychology of Hope* and Blair and Raver, "Child Development," 309–18.

23. Hart and Risley, *Meaningful Differences.*

24. Snyder et al., "Hopeful Choices," 1061–70; Evans, "Childhood Poverty," 77–92.

25. Kenny et al., "Achievement Motivation," 205–12; Roesch et al., "Dispositional Hope," 191; Gillham and Reivich, "Cultivating Optimism," 146–63.

26. See, for example, "Neighborhood Trust Financial Partners," https://neighborhoodtrust.org/employer-solution/.

27. Tirado, "Bad Decisions."

want to learn how to help the poor with budgeting and financial issues.[28] Mullainathan and Eldar Shafir post ideas derived from behavioral economics on a website to benefit the indigent and those who partner with them.[29] Single Stop operates 113 sites across the country where the poor can apply for benefits, receive help to complete their taxes, and obtain legal and financial advice.

Consider the case of Maria, a twenty-eight-year-old who has a full-time job but struggles to feed herself and her daughter and pay their bills. Out of her monthly income of $1,360, she pays $500 in rent and $300 for child care. At a Single Stop facility, Maria learned how to gain $20,000 a year in resources, finance a college degree, and greatly improve her life circumstances. Maria discovered that she qualified for an earned income tax credit and child care credit of almost $5,400. She was also eligible to receive food stamps and health insurance worth $7,000. Finally, Maria found out that she could get $5,730 a year in financial aid to help her attend college and significantly increase her earning potential. Single Stop has helped more than a million American households acquire almost $3 billion in resources.[30]

As discussed in chapter 6 on education, neuroscience and other academic disciplines have explained the critical role that parents and other caregivers play in establishing an intellectual, social, and emotional foundation for children in early life. Unfortunately, however, many public policies thwart the efforts of low-income families to provide this foundation. For example, instead of helping many adults who conceive children and then drift apart, our legal system often increases the animosity between them. Most indigent fathers become resentful when they are ordered to provide child support that exceeds their ability to pay. Moreover, if they fail to pay the full amount, authorities withhold as much as 65 percent of their paychecks, seize their bank deposits or tax refunds (if they have any), suspend their driver's licenses, and eventually put some of them in jail. Knowing that most of his money will go to child support lowers a father's incentive to work; losing his driver's license makes it much harder to get to work, and imprisonment takes away his pay check.[31]

28. See "Chalmers Center," https://www.chalmers.org/.

29. Rosenberg, "Cycle of Scarcity'; "Ideas 42," http://www.ideas42.org/.

30. "Single Stop," http://singlestopusa.org/meet_maria/. See also Marr et al., "EITC and Child Tax Credit."

31. Robles and Dewan, "Skip Child Support."

Several other factors, including the lack of paid parental leave, the erratic scheduling of part-time work, and the meager paychecks many jobs provide, limit the time parents can bond with their newborn, compel them to scramble to find quality childcare, and force them to work more than one job. Contentious relationships, unpredictable work schedules, and long hours on the job inhibit parents from spending time with their children and engaging in activities that further their cognitive development.[32]

To improve conditions for parents with minimum wage jobs, we could emulate the example of the Australian government, which offers parents who are separating free or low-cost, community-based mediation to facilitate their transition from one household to two. Fortunately, the US Office of Child Support Enforcement is helping low-income fathers obtain job training and greater access to their children, which has increased both their earnings and their child support payments. In addition, a substantial increase in the earned-income tax credit could greatly improve the lives of low-income children.[33]

Increasing the Minimum Wage

An obvious but controversial way to enrich the lives of low-income parents and their children is to increase the minimum wage. Supporters contend that justice demands it, the current minimum is woefully inadequate and has not kept pace with inflation since the early 1980s, increasing it would benefit the economy, and it would help employers by reducing turnover and the need for on-the-job training. Today's federal minimum wage of $7.25 is only about one-third the nation's median hourly wage of $20.35. For many years, it was one-half of the average hourly wage. Some economists argue that the minimum wage would be $17 an hour if workers were fairly compensated for their increased productivity instead of channeling the money to corporate profits, the salaries of CEOs, and shareholder dividends.[34] Moreover, of the thirty-four Organization for Economic Cooperation and Development countries, the United States' minimum wage is the third lowest as a percentage of its median income.

Higher minimum wage rates do not generally prompt employers to lay off workers or refuse to hire new ones. Instead, businesses typically

32. Huntington, "Help Families."

33. Ibid.

34. "No Jobs, No Benefits."

benefit by having less labor turnover and compensate by reducing the wage increases of higher paid workers, modestly raising prices, or improving their efficiency. Higher wages can help companies recruit and retain workers and decrease their turnover and are likely to make their employees more satisfied and effective. Several large companies, including Facebook and Walmart, and two Republican-leaning states—South Dakota and Alaska—have recently raised their minimum wage. Numerous cities have established a "living wage" for public sector workers and private city contractors without increasing unemployment or hurting the local economy. In 2015 Los Angeles voted to raise its city-wide minimum wage to $15 an hour by 2020, which will increase the pay of about 50 percent of people who work in the city.[35]

Others counter that companies cannot remain viable if they pay workers more than the value they add to their firms. Raising the minimum wage will lead companies to hire fewer workers and prevent many low-skilled individuals from obtaining a position and receiving "on the job" training.[36] Journalist David Brooks asserts that poverty is widespread because many Americans either do not work fulltime or have a job. He argues that low income is caused primarily by dropping out of high school, having children at a young age, not marrying, abusing alcohol, using illicit drugs, the decline of manufacturing jobs, and "the fraying of the social fabric." Therefore, to improve the condition of the poor, he maintains, we need to create better schools, help parents stay together, provide more job training, and create neighborhoods with mediating institutions.[37]

Numerous economists dispute these objections to raising the minimum wage. They contend that boosting the minimum wage by 30 percent would lift almost five million Americans out of poverty.[38] They also challenge the claim that raising the minimum wage causes the loss of jobs. More than 600 economists signed a letter to President Obama and congressional leaders in January 2014 urging them to raise the minimum wage to $10.10. "The weight of evidence," they argued, showed that previous increases in the minimum wage had not produced greater unemployment.[39] In fact,

35. "Higher Minimum Wage"; Medina and Scheiber, "Minimum Wage."

36. Dunkelberg, "Minimum Wage."

37. Brooks, "Inequality Problem."

38. Dube, "Minimum Wages."

39. "600 Economists Sign Letter," http://www.epi.org/minimum-wage-statement/. See also Dube, Lester, and Reich, "Minimum Wage Effects"; Allegretto, "Minimum Wage Studies."

twelve of the thirteen states that raised their minimum wage in the last few years increased the number of jobs.[40] Many also contend that raising wages for the nation's lowest-paid workers helps the economy by increasing consumer spending. Moreover, paying them higher wages would decrease the amount of public funds needed to subsidize their income.[41]

Raising the minimum wage to at least $10.10 an hour and indexing it to future cost of living increases is a sensible and just policy. It would make the minimum wage about half the median pay for full-time workers, which would be close to the standard of other high-income nations and to the American norm during the 1960s and 1970s. It would also improve the physical and psychological wellbeing of low-income workers and help reduce our nation's glaring inequality. Three-fourths of Americans, including more than half of Republicans, favor raising the minimum wage to either $9 or $10.10 an hour. In referenda, voters in both blue and red states have repeatedly approved proposals by large margins to increase the minimum wage.[42]

A Radical Approach

Dan Price, the founder and president of Gravity Payments, illustrates what business owners can do to help financially-struggling workers. After reading about the relationship between happiness and money, Price decided to increase the salary of all his firm's 120 employees over the next three years to at least $70,000. To fund this increase, Price will reduce his own salary from almost $1 million to $70,000 and use most of his company's anticipated profits during this period. This will double the salaries of about thirty workers and significantly increase the paychecks of another forty.

Price launched his Seattle-based credit-card payment processing company in 2004 as a nineteen-year-old student at Seattle Pacific University. He adopted this policy after hearing numerous stories about how tough many of his employees found it to pay their bills even with salaries that were considerably above the federal minimum wage. Hearing many accounts of how his employees struggled to cover rent increases or make

40. Cuomo, "Fast-Food Workers."

41. Editorial Board, "$15 Minimum Wage."

42. Dugan, "Raising Minimum Wage."

credit card payments deeply disturbed him. Price wants his employees to be able to purchase a house and send their children to college.[43]

Price's small, privately-owned company is unlikely to serve as a bellwether, but his magnanimous plan did capture significant media attention and may inspire other CEOs, including those who have many minimum-wage employees, to increase their pay. Tim Kane, an economist at the Hoover Institution, predicted that it would "reduce turnover, increase morale and help him build an even greater company." A senior lecturer at Harvard Business School asserted that this policy would enable Gravity Payments to retain talented workers. Other business professors, however, warned that this move would damage the firm's long-term viability.[44]

Applauding Price's plan, Tim Weinhold contends that "overpaying" workers "makes biblical and business sense." He highlights the Apostle Paul's argument in 1 Corinthians 9:9–10, which states in part that "whoever plows and threshes should be able to do so in the hope of sharing in the harvest." "According to this principle," Weinhold asserts, "workers deserve not merely (market-dictated) wages, but an appropriate share in the rewards of business success—the harvest—they help create." He praised Southwest Airlines for giving one-third of its total profits to its employees in 2014. Similarly, Costco pays its employees almost triple the compensation Walmart does, including sizable profit-sharing bonuses. Despite this "higher cost structure, Costco dramatically outperforms Wal-Mart" in almost every "category of business performance."[45]

Location, Location, Location

Real estate agents quip that the three most important considerations about property are "location, location, location." Where people live has a tremendous impact on their lives and prospects. Research demonstrates that schools, sense of community, relationships with other residents, local amenities, social norms, and neighborhoods' economic opportunities greatly shape children's outcomes. Both black and white children who grow up in predominantly black neighborhoods have little chance of attaining middle-class standing. Studies reveal that children whose families move

43. Cohen, "$70,000 a Year"; Dimon, "Why We're Giving."

44. Cohen, "Praise and Skepticism." See also Cohen, "Company Copes with Backlash" and Moon, "$70,000 Minimum Wage."

45. Weinhold, "'Overpaying' Workers."

from poorer neighborhoods into more affluent ones do better in numerous ways. Moreover, the younger children are when they move, the better consequences they experience. Children who spend time in middle-class neighborhoods are less likely to later be single parents and are more likely to attend college and to have higher-paying jobs.[46]

These studies lead some economists to call for a new housing policy. Instead of giving tax incentives to developers to build complexes in low-income areas, they argue, the government should help construct affordable housing in neighborhoods that provide better living environments. Making it easier for low-income parents to move to more prosperous neighborhoods can significantly aid their children. However, because most poor parents cannot afford to live in these areas, we must also work to improve the neighborhoods where they currently live.[47]

How Can We Help Minimum-Wage Workers?

Commenting on the riots that plagued Baltimore in 2015 after the death of Freddie Gray at the hands of city police, Nicholas Kristof complained that Americans ignored "the systemic catastrophe of broken schools, joblessness, fatherless kids, heroin, oppressive policing—and, maybe the worst kind of poverty of all, hopelessness." If the children of wealthy white parents were "damaged by lead poisoning, consigned to dismal schools, denied any opportunity to get ahead, more likely to end up in prison than college, harassed and occasionally killed by the police," millions would be outraged.[48]

To change these circumstances, we need to help low-income Americans take advantages of public and private resources that are available to them and increase the minimum wage. Christians should show greater respect for and appreciation to waitresses, motel maids, shuttle drivers, sales clerks, and other minimum-wage employees, recognizing how hard many of them work and how important their work is to our society. Christians should tip generously to increase their income. A good guideline is 20 percent of restaurant bills, 2 percent per day of the cost of motel rooms, 10

46. Leonhardt, Cox, and Miller, "Upward Mobility" (quotation); Walters, "Research on Mobility." See also Briggs, Popkin, and Goering, *Moving to Opportunity*; Sampson, *Great American City*; Massey et al., *Climbing Mount Laurel*; and Darrah and DeLuca, "'Escaping Inner-City Poverty,'" 350–84.

47. Leonhardt, Cox, and Miller, "Upward Mobility."

48. Kristof, "When Baltimore Burned."

percent of the cost of a haircut, and $2 per ride. Anecdotes abound about stingy Christians who tip woefully and about waitresses who lament that when people pray before their meals, they know their tips will be lousy.[49] Christians should support various public and business policies that can improve the wages, benefits, healthcare, childcare, and housing of minimum-wage workers and their offspring.

Christians must help the working poor by developing personal relationships, mentoring adults and children, encouraging them to participate in churches and community organizations, including them in public decisions that affect their lives, and improving their educational and economic opportunities. Although they are vital, good mentoring relationships are hard to develop. The poor often resist them because they see them as paternalistic and they have been hurt too many times to trust even well-intentioned mentors. Many middle and upper-class individuals are reluctant to serve as mentors because they do not feel properly qualified or equipped to do so. Training mentors to work effectively with low-income families and convincing them that they will benefit from these relationships is critical to improving the circumstances of the working poor and their children.

As Michael Katz argues, "poverty remains a national disgrace in part because of the way we define and think about it—which, in turn, shapes the energy we put into its eradication."[50] Understanding the challenges minimum wage workers face can inspire us to improve their circumstances and those of their children.

49. See, for example, Prior, "Bad Tippers?"; "Sundays Are The Worst."

50. Katz, *Undeserving Poor*, xiii.

10

How Businesses Can Help Impoverished Children

Remember the Lord your God,
for it is he who gives you the ability to produce wealth.

DEUTERONOMY 8:18

In 2012 Jay Gould, who shares the name of the nineteenth-century American railroad magnate, took control of the bankrupt, 136 year-old American Standard Company. Seeking to rejuvenate the firm, he accentuated its longstanding purpose: to provide plumbing and sanitation in locales where hygiene is a matter of life and death. Company engineers invented a plastic toilet pan that people could easily attach to a latrine pit to provide a tight seal to keep out flies and prevent hazardous cross-contamination. The firm also initiated a Flush for Good program that donated one latrine cover to a family in a developing nation to reduce disease for every Champion brand toilet it sold. When Gould announced this program at a company meeting, employees responded with a standing ovation. The sale of Champion toilets increased 62 percent in 2013, and American Standard's profits quadrupled during a twenty-month period. Moreover, employees' drive and sense of mission increased substantially. Gould is not alone. Other businesses, large and small, have demonstrated that a concern for social welfare positively impacts not only indigent people, but company morale and profits.

Companies can play a major role in alleviating the poverty of children around the world. They have the resources, talent, incentive, and opportunity to do so. Businesses can aid underprivileged children by paying their parents a living wage, supplying valuable products and services, implementing social programs, donating generously to philanthropic organizations and projects, and encouraging their employees to volunteer.

Thankfully, many businesses are already doing one or several of these things. Hundreds of companies of all sizes now sell their products in the developing world. Numerous firms are specifically designing products to make the lives of the poor healthier, easier, and more pleasant. Meanwhile, thousands of firms are devising and implementing initiatives to improve society, a practice known as Corporate Social Responsibility (CSR) that benefits the destitute, customers, stockholders, and companies themselves. As American Standard illustrates, both altruism and self-interest motivate businesses to work to remedy social ills and aid the poor. These endeavors boost companies' public image, expand their consumers, and enhance nations' economic development.[1]

In their efforts to reduce poverty and aid indigent children around the world, businesses have many advantages over nonprofits and government organizations. Large firms especially have valuable assets. Their distribution networks often extend into impoverished areas. They have substantial expertise in marketing and communications. Corporations have the economic and political clout to combat entrenched interests and develop partnerships with other for-profit companies, NGOs, and community groups. Major firms have huge financial resources and tremendous research capability. Their widely recognizable brand names help them promote their products and services among the destitute. Their large volume often enables them to sell products slightly above their costs. Their financial strength permits corporations to take risks to reach the huge market at the bottom of the economic pyramid (the more than four billion people who earn less than $1,500 a year). Nonprofits that assist poor children do not create wealth, depend on capricious donors, have questionable sustainability, and often regard aid recipients as hapless, helpless victims. Businesses,

1. See Kotler and Lee, *Corporate Social Responsibility*; Kotler, Hessekiel, and Lee, *Good Works*. For an alternate perspective, see Markley, "Corporate Social Responsibility."

by contrast, generate capital, are more stable, and treat the poor as customers and employees.[2]

Companies that strive to supply goods and services to the bottom half of the world's earners face great challenges. Firms typically have to invest money before receiving any revenue. If they are successful, other businesses are likely to imitate their products or services. Companies may have trouble finding enough workers who are motivated by their mission. Determining what products and services the poor desire and truly need is often difficult. Businesses also face major distribution challenges, including making products affordable, reducing packaging costs, providing credit to customers, and coping with inadequate infrastructures. These problems, coupled with their failure to realize the pecuniary potential of this market, recognition that serving the poor will require major changes in their operating procedures, and financial risks, discourage many large companies from pursuing economic enterprises that could aid the impoverished.[3]

Nevertheless, serving the poor frequently benefits businesses. It typically increases their revenue, profit, and reputation. The innovations companies devise for one developing nation can usually be adapted for use in other ones. To succeed in the low-income global market, firms must operate very effectively and competitively by making high quality, durable, low-cost products, reducing their marketing and distribution costs, and using less skilled people to manufacture and disseminate their products.[4]

While hundreds of companies provide goods and services to the poor, many more engage in CSR. This involves varied activities, including funding nonprofits, providing training and resources to enable the poor to become more productive, donating merchandise or services to the impoverished for every sale a business makes, treating their employees in developing countries ethically and fairly, or using company resources to remedy such social ills as contaminated water, malnutrition, subpar education, and youth crime.

Some companies make CSR fundamental to their operations. Ben and Jerry's, for example, "uses only fair trade ingredients" and has created a dairy farm sustainability program. Starbucks evaluates "the economic,

2. Mech, "For-Profits"; Mech, "Two Basic Solutions."

3. Mech, "For-Profits."

4. Ibid.

social and environmental aspects of coffee production" to ensure that its establishments use only "sustainably grown and processed coffee."[5]

Ten Thousand Villages, Tegu, and Soapbox Soaps

Numerous businesses exist to market products made in developing countries. In 1946, Mennonite Edna Ruth Byler was deeply moved by the dire poverty she encountered on a trip to Puerto Rico. To improve the lives of indigent women, she bought their handicraft and sold it to friends and church members in the United States. Her organization today is called Ten Thousand Villages and sells $27 million in products from more than thirty developing nations. Byler also helped launch the fair-trade movement that today involves certification processes, international governance, and multiple networks and generates more than $4 billion in sales per year.[6]

Other companies are created specifically to alleviate social ills. Their mission trip to Honduras when brothers Chris and Will Haughey were in their mid-twenties changed their lives. Appalled by Honduras' social conditions and lack of opportunity, they decided to create a for-profit company using one of the nation's principal resources—timber—to aid some of its residents. Building on their education in engineering and management and their business experience, they founded Tegu in 2007. Using funds from family and friends, the brothers built a manufacturing facility near Tegucigalpa, the capital of Honduras.[7]

Tegu makes magnetic wooden blocks that children can stack and stick together in countless combinations. The company has enjoyed remarkable sales and is fast becoming a competitor of Legos. Its 150 employees earn livable wages. Tegu financially supports a school that educates children whose families survive by scavenging food and recyclable materials from the Tegucigalpa trash dump. Before the school opened, these children worked alongside their parents. For every toy a customer purchases, he or she can

5. Fallon, "Corporate Social Responsibility?"; "Improving Lives," http://www.toms.com/improving-lives.

6. "Ten Thousand Villages," http://www.tenthousandvillages.com/; "Brighter Futures," http://www.tenthousandvillages.com/media/2013–2014AnnualReport.pdf; "Fair Trade USA," http://fairtradeusa.org/tags/fair-trade-movement.

7. "Tegu," http://www.tegu.com/our-story/; Lee, "Tegu's Magnetic Blocks."

choose to fund one day of education for a child who attends this school or to have Tegu plant twelve trees.[8]

Soapbox Soaps was created to prevent childhood diseases and deaths that result from the deplorable hygiene that plagues many regions in developing nations. Its founders were convinced that regular use of soap could save children's lives. Only later did the company develop various health and beauty products. For every bottle of liquid soap a Westerner buys, the firm provides a needy child with a month of clean water. Our "mission came first," its CEO declares; "we only figured out how to sell soap afterwards."[9]

The HealthStore Foundation

The HealthStore Foundation uses an innovative microfinance approach to reduce the spread of infectious diseases in the developing world. These diseases, especially malaria, respiratory infections, and dysentery, which account for about 80 percent of the illnesses and deaths of children in the world's poorest countries, can be treated with inexpensive generic drugs. Every day about 21,000 children die worldwide, and two-thirds of these deaths occur because children have no access to competent medical care or basic drugs. The cost of these life-saving drugs is frequently less than a cup of coffee in the West. Unfortunately, supplying these drugs in an inexpensive, convenient way is difficult. Millions of the world's most vulnerable people live many hours or even days away from facilities that furnish these medicines. The present distribution system in low-income nations is ineffective because supplies are inadequate, quality control is abysmal, counterfeiting is rampant, and the poor cannot afford even the small cost of the drugs.[10]

In 1997 Scott Hillstrom, an American entrepreneur and attorney, founded the HealthStore Foundation to decrease the suffering and death of African children. Using a micro-franchising model, his foundation created a network of small clinics and pharmacies to provide essential medicines to marginalized groups in Kenya. Under the umbrella of the Child and Family Wellness Shops network, community health workers own and operate drug stores and nurses own and operate clinics. These clinics diagnose,

8. "Tegu FAQs," http://www.tegu.com/tegu-faqs/; "Tegu Is Growing"; Shellnut, "The Toy Makers."

9. Thorpe, "Why CSR?"

10. Militzer, "BoP Needs Drugs"; "CFW Clinics," http://www.cfwshops.org/.

treat, and help prevent respiratory infections, malaria, diarrheal diseases, and sexually-transmitted infections and provide family planning, pediatric care, and instruction in parenting.[11]

The HealthStore Foundation is a nonprofit, but like successful for-profit franchises, it requires all its shops to use uniform training and operating procedures, locate in market centers, and follow strict quality controls, which it carefully monitors. The foundation furnishes a common brand and supply network as well as professional development opportunities for owners and staff. Because people in the twenty poorest developing nations spend an average of only $33 per year on health care, the foundation leverages the network's combined buying power to purchase quality medicines at rock bottom prices and subsidizes franchisees to keep costs low. The foundation also requires every outlet to carefully keep patient records and vital health statistics and evaluates their financial performance.[12]

The HealthStore currently operates sixty-five drug stores and micro-clinics in Kenya. Since its first store opened there in 2000, the nonprofit has provided drugs and primary healthcare to about five million people. In 2013 a sister organization began opening clinics in Rwanda.[13] The foundation's facilities principally serve subsistence farmers and their children. The HealthStore's success demonstrates that micro-franchising has a pivotal role to play in improving the health of impoverished children and adults in developing nations.[14]

Clean Cook Stoves

In developing nations, cooking food over open fires causes many problems. Their lack of access to electricity or natural gas forces nearly half the world's people to use wood, coal, or animal dung to fuel fires they build to prepare their meals. Burning wood involves many hardships and dangers. Because women do most of the cooking, they expose themselves, their unborn children, and their infants and toddlers to the equivalent of forty cigarettes a day. Every year four million children and women die from smoke-related

11 Militzer, "BoP Needs Drugs"; "Scott Hillstrom"; "CFW Clinics."

12. Militzer, "BoP Needs Drugs"; "CFW Clinics"; "CFW Shops."

13. "Scott Hillstrom."

14. "CFW Shops." See also "Health Care Franchise," http://www.pbs.org/now/shows/321/index.html; Rangan and Lee, *CFW Clinics in Kenya*.

respiratory diseases, especially pneumonia, caused by indoor cooking. In fact, pneumonia kills more children under five than any other disease.[15]

Cooking over open fires has many other physical, economic, and social costs. The World Health Organization estimates that indigent people around the world, mostly mothers, typically spend more than thirty hours per week gathering wood. Their quest to find wood reduces mothers' time to take care of their children, work in the fields, or earn money. Moreover, poor families use about 35 percent of their income to buy fuel, which significantly reduces their ability to purchase food and other basic necessities, buy seeds for planting crops, or pay school fees. In Africa many women walk fifteen miles a week to find wood for cooking and carry fifty-pound loads home. Tragically, women who gather firewood in war-torn areas often fall victim to rape. Extensive use of wood for cooking also contributes to deforestation.[16]

These dangers to people's health and safety, coupled with the damage to the environment, have evoked worldwide concern. In 2010 the United Nations established the Global Alliance for Clean Cook Stoves, which pledged to provide cleaner, safer, more efficient stoves to 100 million homes in developing nations by 2020. Championed by actress Julia Roberts, the alliance has raised millions of dollars to devise, market, and distribute clean-burning stoves in Africa and Bangladesh.[17]

Several creative companies seek to supply these stoves. Especially notable is the Paradigm Project, which aims to sell 5 million cleaner-burning, fuel-efficient rocket stoves to poor families by 2020.[18] Established by Neil Bellefeuille and Greg Spencer in 2007, Paradigm sponsors a for-profit company. Noting that Americans invest almost ten times as much in private equity funds than they give to charity, these entrepreneurs seek to channel some of that money into social enterprise in developing nations. Bellefeuille and Spencer insist that many people are willing to invest in businesses that help reduce poverty and improve the environment while also earning a profit.

Alarmed by the health, financial, and environmental problems making meals indoors over open fires causes, Bellefeuille and Spencer decided

15. "Paradigm Project," http://www.theparadigmproject.org/#intro.

16. Mok, "Bringing 5 Million Rocket Stoves."

17. "Rocket Stoves for Developing Countries," http://www.impacthound.com/energy-rocket-stoves-developing-countries/.

18. "Innovative Social Enterprise."

to produce and market clean cook stoves. They gain tax credits for their stoves because they decrease carbon emissions. After certifying the 40 to 60 percent reduction of CO_2 emissions their stoves achieve, they sell these "certified offsets" to large corporations in Europe and the United States that want to reduce their carbon imprint. This revenue enables them to subsidize poor Kenyans' purchase of affordable, safer, healthier cooking stoves while also paying dividends to investors.[19]

To learn firsthand about African conditions and identify with their customers, Paradigm Project's staff endured attacks by giant camel spiders, ate meals cooked over open fires, and walked many miles carrying heavy loads of wood on their backs. Impressed by their actions, some tribes selected them to be honorary elders. Partnering with Food for the Hungry, World Vision, and the World Food Program, the company began selling cook stoves in Kenya in 2008, which are priced 30 percent below cost.[20]

Their remarkable success in Kenya (demand has been four times what they expected) has prompted Paradigm to manufacture and sell stoves in other East African nations and in Guatemala and Haiti. Bellefeuille and Spencer claim that families who use their more efficient stoves each year spend $280 less in fuel costs, devote 260 fewer hours to collecting wood, and save seven trees. In addition, Paradigm pays Kenyans good wages to sell and repair stoves. Most significantly, mothers and children are now less likely to die from smoke inhalation or severe burns.[21]

RBC Wealth Management-USA and Coca-Cola

Some companies whose primary mission has nothing to do with helping poor people in developing nations, nevertheless work to alleviate particular social ills. Both RBC Wealth Management-USA and the Coca-Cola Company, for example, provide uncontaminated water in developing nations. RBC recently pledged to spend $50 million to ensure that people around the globe have access to clean water. For the last seven years, in conjunction with the annual Blue Water Day, RBC employees have worked on various projects to preserve fresh water in urban areas throughout the world.[22]

19. Bellefeuille, "Stoves."
20. Ibid.
21. Ibid.
22. Thorpe, "Why CSR?"

Coca-Cola is setting up Ekocenters—modular, solar-powered units that provide water-purification technology, internet connections, and power to charge phones and do banking—in poor communities in six developing nations. The company plans to establish 150 functioning Ekocenters in Africa and Southeast Asia, all managed by local residents. Coke's goals are not purely altruistic. The firm also hopes to improve its "reputation in untapped communities" and will eventually sell its products in these centers.[23]

Investing in Education

Other companies aid the poor by heavily investing in education and vocational training; they help nations with inadequate resources give adults and children tools to succeed in the global workplace. IT giant Infosys trains thousands of its Indian employees in communications, management, and technical skills. The Dangote Group, which refines sugar and manufactures cement, teaches Africans how to drive trucks. After logging 186,000 miles for the company, drivers are given their vehicles and can work as independent contractors. Aviva, a United Kingdom insurance company, has paid for 800,000 children in seventeen nations, to learn vocational skills through its Street to School program.[24]

Varied Business Approaches

Still other firms seek to remedy a wide array of social ills. The US-based Hershey Company, well known for its chocolate products, supplies malnourished children in Ghana with "peanut-based, nutrient-rich, ready-to-use therapeutic food" to help them regain their health. Hershey's Project Peanut Butter aids Ghana's economy by creating jobs and buying ingredients from local farmers.[25] Similarly, DLA Piper, one of the world's largest law firms, provides pro bono services in the United States to improve education, relieve hunger, decrease juvenile delinquency and domestic violence, and assist veterans.

23. *Sohn*, "Case for Aiding World's Poorest."

24. Pota, "Education."

25. "Responsibility," http://www.thehersheycompany.com/social-responsibility/shared-goodness/goodbusiness.

Meanwhile, some businesses have established non-profit affiliates that directly work to alleviate social ills. California-based Gaia Development, for example, helped create Collective Solutions to combat poverty and climate change. The firm donates a percentage of its profit to Collective Solutions and encourages its employees to use their time and expertise to aid the poor. Among other activities, Gaia employees work with Collective Solutions in Nicaragua to help families build solar ovens from scrap materials, thus diminishing their dependence on dwindling supplies of wood.

Other companies provide technical, financial, and material assistance to low-income farmers in developing countries. SVAgri operates 125 stores in India that sell supplies to farmers and helps them find markets for their crops. Similarly, KK Foods connects Ugandan farmers with buyers and assists them to grow the commercial crops most in demand. TechnoServe helps cocoa farmers obtain pesticides, fertilizers, and credit from local banks in West Africa. To be successful, these companies must offer products and services poor farmers can afford, and their employees work closely with smallholders to help them make wise agricultural decisions.[26]

Umbrella Organizations

Two large organizations promote Corporate Social Responsibility—the World Business Council for Sustainable Development (WBCSD) and CSR Europe. Created in 1998, WBCSD provides companies with practical guidance and useful tools, including its book *Corporate Social Responsibility: Making Good Business Sense*, to help them improve social conditions in diverse political, cultural, and religious settings. The organization prods companies to guarantee human rights, alleviate persistent poverty, teach skills, furnish jobs, increase access to primary healthcare, and fund education.[27] CSR Europe, founded in 1996, is the principal European business network working to motivate and equip companies to combat social ills. It furnishes a venue for more than 10,000 companies to share best practices for advancing social welfare.[28]

26. Shemkus, "Poor Countries."

27. "WBCSD"; "WBCSD—Social Impact"; "WBCSD—About," http://www.wbcsd.org/about/organization.aspx.

28. "CSR Europe," http://www.csreurope.org/about-us.

Regal Springs Tilapia

The philosophy and activities of Regal Springs Tilapia further illustrate what companies can do to aid impoverished children and their families. One of the world's largest producers of farm-grown tilapia, Regal Springs operates facilities in Indonesia, Honduras, and Mexico. We interviewed Magdalena (Leni) Lamprecht Wallhoff, its head of global sales, about Regal Spring's social philosophy and efforts to improve conditions and the lives of children in the communities where the company works. Her father Rudi Lamprecht, an agricultural engineer who worked for the UN Food and Agricultural Organization, started the company in 1988. Wallhoff grew up in Indonesia, Sweden, and Switzerland, graduated from Germany's Black Forest Academy, and earned a BA in political science and communications at Northwestern University. After teaching for a year in health centers in Mongolia, Wallhoff completed a master's degree in public health at the University of Minnesota. In her work for Regal Springs since 2003, this mother of three has primarily overseen its global sales and directed its social responsibility endeavors.[29] In 2013 Wallhoff was named the Aquaculture Person of the Year by *Fish Farming International*, and a year later she spoke to an FAO meeting about the importance of providing jobs in rural areas that pay a living wage.[30] She argues that Micah 6:8 and Jesus' command to care for the poor compel Christians to passionately promote social justice. Wallhoff's faith motivates her to harness Regal Springs' resources to help its employees improve their circumstances and to aid destitute children in the three countries where the company operates.[31]

Regal Springs' corporate philosophy accentuates "integrity, generosity, teamwork, stewardship of resources, and respect for life."[32] The company "offers thousands of individuals the chance to earn a stable income, learn skills, and contribute directly to the development of their families and communities." Its executives want to end the cycle of poverty in locales where they produce fish. Regal Springs hires managers who care deeply about their employees and works to create more stable communities. Its managers seek to give their workers hope for a better future. Numerous

29. Phone interview with Magdalena (Leni) Lamprecht Wallhoff, Jan. 24, 2015.

30. Nadkarni, "Aquaculture Person."

31. Interview with Wallhoff.

32. *Regal Springs Employee Handbook*, 5.

teams of company volunteers devise and implement plans to improve their communities.[33]

Regal Springs has more than 9,000 employees and provides indirect income for another 20,000 people. The company invests substantially in housing, health care, education, and the infrastructure of the communities where it produces fish.[34] When children in developing nations finish elementary school, they have the prospects of a brighter future; when their families are more stable and healthy, employees are happier, experience less stress, and are more productive. Regal Springs provides well-paying jobs, and it funds education and public health services in the communities where it operates to enhance their residents' quality of life.[35]

Regal Springs also strives to be environmentally responsible. It is the "first aquafarm in the world to meet" "a rigorous set of standards that ranks fish farms on seven principles of environmental and social impact."[36] Concern about rapid deforestation in areas where it operates led the company to start a Fish for Trees program to encourage local residents to establish their own fish farms and stop cutting down trees. Regal Springs also promotes better nutrition by supplying a low-fat, high protein seafood product.[37]

Regal Springs employs 1,600 people in a mountainous, impoverished region in north-central Honduras who work in a hatchery and feed and processing operations. The company provides livable wages, health care, education, and nutrition to improve people's lives in Honduras and to decrease the flow of children who flee to the United States to escape poverty and gang violence. Regal Springs offers classes in responsible parenting and ways to prevent domestic violence. In addition, the company furnishes free day-care facilities for workers and helped found more than sixty free preschools to prepare students to succeed in elementary school. Regal Springs also pays teachers' salaries and buys curricular materials. Honduran children who attend preschools are much more likely to complete primary school, and those who finish sixth grade have substantial advantages in life. Regal Springs also helped establish high schools and created an adult literacy program, which during a nine-year period, reduced one

33. Interview with Wallhoff.

34. Ibid.; Boyd, "Tilapia Fish Tacos."

35. "Regal Springs," http://www.regalsprings.com/wp-content/uploads/2014/05/RegalSprings_Newsletter_Nov13_LowRes.pdf.

36. See "Regal Springs Tilapia," http://www.megafishnet.com/news//20981.html

37. Boyd, "Tilapia Fish Tacos"; "Regal Springs."

community's illiteracy rate from 80 percent to 1 percent.[38] Moreover, the company funded constructing roads, supplying clean water, and spraying to wipe out dengue fever, a serious public health threat. It also installed 2,000 eco-stoves, which are more economical, safer, and less destructive to the environment.[39]

Regal Springs has 6,000 employees in Indonesia and 1,500 in Chiapas, Mexico.[40] In Indonesia, Regal Springs is replicating the preschool programs that it has established in Honduras. The company supports its employees in direct, personal ways, including by providing financial aid for their weddings, funerals, and religious events.[41] As in many other parts of Mexico, gangs and political corruption are major problems in Chiapas, the nation's poorest region where 82 percent of children under age eighteen live below the poverty line. Regal Springs helped establish schools and pays teachers' salaries in Chiapas. It also provides day-care facilities for its workers' children and funds community health campaigns. The company partners with a local program to offer free dental check-ups, physicals, vaccinations, nutritional supplements, eye exams, and lice treatments. Moreover, Regal Springs promotes the long-term well-being of its employees by making their mortgage payments, providing health and life insurance for them, and teaching them about their legal rights.[42]

The Benefits of Business Endeavors to Aid the Poor

While helping to improve the lives of the poor, endeavors to upgrade social conditions benefit companies in numerous ways. Their productivity, sales, profits, and customer loyalty often increase and their reputation improves. Companies are able to attract and keep employees who derive satisfaction from aiding the needy.[43] Susan Cooney, who founded the crowdfunding philanthropy platform Givelocity, asserts that many of today's most talented individuals choose to work for companies with a strong commitment

38. Interview with Wallhoff; "Honduran Children," http://www.regalsprings.com/picture-of-the-day-honduran-children/.

39. *Handbook*, 12.

40. See "Poverty in Mexico," http://www.explorandomexico.com/about-mexico/6/107/; "20 Million Mexican Children."

41. *Handbook*, 14.

42. Interview with Wallhoff.

43. "Corporate Social Responsibility," https://www.iisd.org/business/issues/sr.aspx.

to CSR. They want to join firms that focus on the "triple bottom line" of "people, planet and revenue."[44] Using company products and profits "to do good in the world" helps to attract shoppers and clients.[45] One CEO maintains that "employees gain a sense of pride and accomplishment" through their CSR endeavors and "often engage in additional charitable actions" in their free time.[46] In a recent global survey, 55 percent of respondents claimed that they would pay more for the products and services of businesses that have a positive social and environmental impact.[47] Speaking for many corporate leaders, an executive of a consulting firm contends that "our CSR policy is at the core of our daily operations" and aids the company in several ways. "Our clients want to work with us because we are focused on [creating] a healthier and more productive world." Moreover, by "setting a good example," "we inspire other organizations, companies and individuals" to work more vigorously to improve social and environmental conditions.[48]

As noted, social enterprise activities can energize companies, inspire their employees, and improve their productivity. When Meg Whitman became CEO of Hewlett Packard in 2011, the company seemed rudderless. One key component of her efforts to strengthen the company's sense of purpose was establishing the Matter to a Million program—a global partnership with Kiva, a nonprofit microlender. HP gave all of its 270,000 employees a $25 Kiva credit they could loan to any aspiring entrepreneur in a developing nation they chose. Expressing the views of many, an Australian wrote, "I am so excited that, through the generosity of this program, we are able to make a difference." Matter to a Million, like Flush for Good, illustrates how the efforts of companies to "build a better world" often improve their own performance and esprit de corps.[49] Journalist Nicole Fallon calls CSR "a win-win" enterprise. It enables companies to appeal to socially-conscious employees and consumers and to "make a real difference in the world."[50]

44. Fallon, "Corporate Social Responsibility."

45. Ibid.

46. Thorpe, "Why CSR?"

47. "Doing Well by Doing Good," http://www.nielsen.com/us/en/insights/reports/2014/doing-well-by-doing-good.html.

48. Thorpe, "Why CSR?" See also Bishop and Green, *Philanthrocapitalism*.

49. Lueneburger, "Company's Good Deeds."

50. Fallon, "Corporate Social Responsibility."

How Can Christians Encourage Businesses to Do More to Help the Poor?

Christians can urge the companies for which we work to invest more resources to establish or fund policies and programs that advance the welfare of destitute adults and children. Some of us can volunteer with company programs that aid indigent children. Others can use our expertise or talents to directly assist the poor through our jobs. Business people can teach individuals in the developing world how to launch or expand businesses in bookkeeping, accounting, marketing, management, and other enterprises.

Christians can investigate whether their firms could earn a profit while providing goods or services to enrich the lives of the destitute. We can also prod companies to promote humanitarian causes by explaining how doing so could enrich the lives of the poor, improve workers' sense of purpose and morale, and garner favorable publicity. Businesses can make their facilities, marketing expertise, and web design capabilities available to under-resourced humanitarian organizations that are working to help children. Employees could also identify social ills that are important to themselves and customers and collaborate with aid organizations to remedy them.[51]

In deciding where to donate their charitable funds, business executives should evaluate to what extent aid organizations develop various kinds of capital—resources that generate wealth without being depleted in the process. These include natural capital such as arable land, livestock, and fishing; material capital such as better tools and technology and fishing nets; human capital such as improving people's ability to be more productive through education or job training; and social capital by connecting individuals with business opportunities and promoting greater cooperation. Company leaders should also give to humanitarian organizations that view beneficiaries as partners. Finally, they should help fund organizations that provide poor people with greater access to services and markets, generate revenue that can help businesses grow, and are financially accountable and efficient.[52]

Christians with entrepreneurial skills can start businesses to help the poor at home and abroad. One organization that can aid their efforts is Praxis. It works to train and supply resources to faith-motivated entrepreneurs who seek to have a social impact. Each year, Praxis provides the

51. Interview with Timothy Mech, Grove City College, April 21, 2015.

52. Ibid.

leaders of businesses and non-profits with the "knowledge, network, and personal discipleship" to create organizations to aid the poor. College students who aspire to be entrepreneurs can participate in the Praxis Academy, a summer program that can deepen their faith and teach them about starting companies and global culture.[53]

Finally, we can carefully choose where we spend our money. Whenever possible, we can buy from companies that are helping the world's poor through their various operations and activities. We can support firms that are supplying clean water, combatting preventable diseases, funding education, and undertaking other endeavors to aid impoverished children. Women have the principal role to play in this endeavor because they make 85 percent of Americans' decisions about buying products and services.[54] Collectively, these activities can greatly advance the welfare of the world's impoverished children.

53. "Praxis," http://www.praxislabs.org.

54. "I Am Woman."

11

How Microfinance Can Help Impoverished Children

The Lord Jesus . . . himself said, "It is more blessed to give than to receive."

ACTS 20:35

And let our people learn to devote themselves to good works,
so as to help cases of urgent need, and not be unfruitful.

TITUS 3:14, ESV

Since 1945 Western nations have dispensed an estimated $2.3 trillion in foreign aid. Nevertheless, in part because much of this money has been misspent or squandered, 3 billion people, or more than 40 percent of the world's population, still live on less than $2.50 a day and remain mired in poverty. While the health, education, sanitation, and nutrition of the poor has improved, extensive poverty persists. What economic strategies can best alleviate destitution and give the next generation a more materially and spiritually fulfilling life? Numerous strategies have been employed—microloans, microsavings, microinsurance, conditional and unconditional cash transfers, and a wide array of government and private programs.

Determining which policies, programs, and interventions most effectively alleviate poverty and then actively marketing and funding them is critical.[1]

Imagine what your life would be like if banks refused to accept your deposits. Or if the fees for depositing funds outweighed the benefits of doing so. If you could not open a bank account, you could put all your savings in a coffee can, but a thief could wipe out your stash in a minute. Or you might choose to buy gold or animals to sell when a need arises; the value of these assets, however, fluctuates. What if you also could not borrow money to pay your bills, survive a health or weather crisis, or start or expand a business? What if government programs provided no assistance to you during times of unemployment, disability, or old age? Because most of the world's three billion poorest people have no bank accounts, ability to borrow money, or safety net, their lives are financially precarious.[2]

As I write these words, I receive an email declaring your "car needs repair, the sink springs a leak, or the furnace goes kaput—what next?" The ad describes a "back-up plan" that can provide peace of mind "whatever your emergency." The ad is appealing because many Americans lack the savings to pay for major unexpected expenses. Whether or not we download and read *Ten Simple Ways to Boost Your Emergency Fund*, though, most Westerners can find ways to pay such bills. The poor in the developing world rarely can.

Microloans

Ndeye Sarr of Senegal has carved out a niche in the competitive West African clothing market. Using the money from a microloan, she purchased an electric sewing machine, hired an employee, and filled as many as a dozen client orders at a time, much more than the two she previously could handle at once. Her income grew dramatically, and she became the primary breadwinner for her extended family of thirty people. Subsequent loans enabled her to buy two more sewing machines and create more intricate clothing designs. Collaborating with two local tailors, Sarr now produces substantially more clothes and sells some of them in neighboring countries. "I am blooming thanks to you," Sarr wrote to her lender. She can pay for her

1. Karlan and Appel, *More Than Good Intentions.*

2. Collins et al., *Portfolios*; Kristof, "Microsavings"; Shifflett, "Savings Groups"; Ashe and Nelson, "Introduction," 1–2; quotations from 1.

three children to attend school. Her story illustrates how microloans are improving the lives of some citizens of developing nations.

Opportunity International began making tiny loans in 1971, and Accion International coined the term "microenterprise" in 1973.[3] A few years later Muhammad Yunus, an economics professor in Bangladesh, popularized microloans, and for the next quarter century they were widely hailed as a magic bullet that could greatly decrease poverty. Advocates claimed that they could help millions enlarge their agricultural production or create small profitable businesses to escape poverty's horrors. Yunus's Grameen Bank project, which today has six million borrowers in 80,000 villages, was the shining star in the microlending galaxy; its success persuaded many international development specialists to view microloans as a potential savior. In 2006 Yunus and Grameen were awarded the Nobel Peace Prize for their impressive results in reducing poverty.[4] Microcredit helped dramatize the plight of the poor. The pleas of celebrity promoters like Irish rock star Bono of U2, countless stories of transformed lives, and the innovative marketing schemes of various microlenders have prompted millions in affluent nations to go online to choose individual entrepreneurs to fund.[5]

Microfinance institutions (MFIs) use money that is supplied either by donors (if they are nonprofits) or commercial lenders (if they are for-profit-organizations) to provide loans of $50 to $1,000 to individuals who typically earn no more than $2 per day. Varying greatly in size and assets, some MFIs supply loans in single communities, while others dispense hundreds of millions of dollars in numerous nations. In addition, some well-established and highly respected NGOs such as CARE and Catholic Relief Services have added microcredit endeavors to their portfolio of services. To reach more clients and deliver their funds more effectively, many MFIs use group (rather than individual) liability, door-to-door-services, village banking, and cell phone and internet transactions.

Many financial institutions, economists, and aid organizations tout microloans as the key to improving the lives of the destitute. They are a "sustainable 'bottom-up' development" that create jobs, increase income, and strenghten community solidarity. Microfinance is a $70 billion industry

3. "1970s: Microlending Begins," https://www.accion.org/content/1970s-microlending-begins; "History," http://opportunity.org/about-us/history.

4. See Yunus, *Banker to the Poor*; Yunus and Webber, *World Without Poverty*; Dowla and Barua, *Grameen II Story*.

5. Karlan and Appel, *More Than Good Intentions*, 139.

involving more than 10,000 institutions that serve 150 million people around the world.[6] The poor generally borrow money to deal with life-cycle needs (expenses related to childbirth, education, weddings, funerals, homebuilding, or old age), to cover personal emergencies (injury, sickness, unemployment, or theft), to cope with disasters (floods, fires, or tornadoes) or war, or to invest (starting or expanding businesses or purchasing equipment or property).[7]

Their proponents insist that microloans reduce poverty by helping recipients expand their farms and start businesses. Microloans provide poor communities with new goods and services and recirculate money throughout them. Microloans often stimulate the poor to spend money more wisely and to save. They can enhance the self-esteem of impoverished individuals and equip them to be better parents and citizens.[8] Microloans enable poor entrepreneurs to buy in bulk, reduce their travel to obtain supplies, stock more inventory, purchase more equipment to decrease their labor costs, increase their output, and better serve their communities. The children of borrowers can eat better and go to school. Microcredit also often empowers women. Philanthropist Phil Smith contends that microfinance "works for one simple and indisputable reason—the vast majority of the poor" are "willing and able to lift themselves" out of destitution if they have an opportunity. The fact that many borrowers apply for additional loans, he adds, proves that they are beneficial.[9]

Despite their numerous benefits, microloans are under sharp attack. Critics argue that microloans are rarely available to the world's most destitute people, sometimes involve predatory lending practices, harm recipients who cannot repay them, and can create dependency. The high interest rates the indigent pay for loans (typically 30–40 percent) often drives them deeper into poverty. Moreover, many borrowers use funds to buy durable consumer goods or simply to survive instead of investing them in productive enterprises. Finally, critics contend, microcredit has neither empowered women nor significantly improved the health or education of borrowers and their children. Recent studies of microloan recipients in Hyderabad, India and rural Morocco by MIT professors found that only 5 percent of these individuals started new businesses and that loans did little

6. Duncan, "Crowdfunding Development."

7. Rutherford, *The Poor.*

8. Mech, "Microfinance."

9. Greer and Smith, *The Poor Will Be Glad*, 102–3, 101, 113.

to improve people's financial welfare, increase education, or give women greater power in their homes or communities. Critics also complain that the "over-inflated expectations" of microloans divert attention from other potentially fruitful ways to reduce poverty.[10] The high interest rates on loans and the alarming default rate in some countries leads many development experts and some nonprofits to advocate microsavings rather than microloans.[11]

Although criticism abounds, some microfinance organizations claim to have very high rates of success. Opportunity International, for example, assists more than five million clients in twenty-two developing countries. Founded in 1971 by American businessman Al Whittaker and Australian entrepreneur David Bussau, it seeks to obey "Jesus Christ's call to love and serve the poor." Opportunity International contends that because of its policies, support, and focus on accountability clients repay 98 percent of their loans. Almost all its staff are citizens of the countries where they work and, therefore, understand the local culture. More than 90 percent of Opportunity International's loans go to women who primarily use them to improve the nutrition, healthcare, and education of their children. Women are more likely than men to operate small household businesses, repay loans, and save money. Men often squander money on alcohol and other nonproductive activities that hurt their families. Opportunity International organizes loan recipients into "trust groups" of ten-thirty members. These groups meet regularly to receive financial counseling and share business and personal advice.[12]

To address the problem of high interest rates, numerous microcredit organizations, including Opportunity International, Kiva, and Zidisha, arrange many of their loans though a web-based, "person-to-person lending platform that eliminates intermediaries completely." Zidisha uses this approach exclusively. It also allows clients to reschedule repayments (with certain limitations) and permits lenders to forgive loans for humanitarian reasons. Zidisha's founder reports that it charges only 8 percent for its loans and claims that 98 percent of its more than 11,000 borrowers have repaid

10. Mech, "Microfinance"; Banerjee et al., "Miracle of Microfinance?"; Dichter, "Introduction," 2, 4; Hulme, "Microdebt"; Bateman, *Microfinance*.

11. Bateman, *Microfinance*, vi (quotation); Mui, "Microsavings Programs."

12. "Partnerships Provide Tools and Training," 2; Greer and Smith, *The Poor Will Be Glad*, 110. See also Bearden, "Microfinance."

their loans.[13] Many donors like microloans because they can choose the clients they fund, which enables them to establish a personal connection with the individuals they select.[14]

Microloans improve many poor people's lives. Dorothy Kanjausto lives in a destitute village near the capital of Malawi. After her husband died, she struggled to provide for her three children. She used a loan of $133 to open a nursery and primary school to educate impoverished local children. Additional loans enabled her to hire teachers and add classes. Her school currently employs seven teachers and educates 200 students. Dorothy is now providing for her own children and three AIDS orphans.[15] Like most other yucca farmers in Nicaragua, Don Antonio Orozco found it difficult to grow a high quality product and market his crops. The funds, training, and technological assistance he received from Opportunity International enabled his farm to become more profitable. Moreover, Opportunity International's processing plant purchases most of Antonio's yucca, giving him a reliable market. He now owns 1,900 acres and employs thirty-two members of his community.[16]

Microloans, however, are not a panacea for poverty. Only about 5 percent of the world's poorest three billion people have obtained them. In some locales where microloans are readily available, only 20 percent of those who meet the eligibility requirements apply. Several factors account for this. Some lenders allow the money to be used only to finance business enterprises. Allowing borrowers to pay off debts and buy clothes, food, and medicine would make microloans more attractive. Another impediment is that many poor people do not have the talent or drive to use microloans effectively, especially to start entrepreneurial enterprises.[17] Microloans will be more effective if providers improve their quality and flexibility, better understand how their clients make financial decisions, and coach their

13. "Statistics," https://www.zidisha.org/statistics; Kurnia, "Microfinance."

14. Bare, "Millennials Will Reinvent Charity."

15. Greer and Smith, *The Poor Will Be Glad*, 111.

16. "Don Antonio Orozco," http://opportunity.org/in-action/entrepreneurs/don-antonio-orozco.

17. Karlan and Appel, *More Than Good Intentions*, 72–74, 78–81, 85–107. Similarly, gifts by organizations to create new businesses have typically been unsuccessful for three reasons: the enterprises that were funded were not financially viable; the recipients did not value the gift; and recipients' lack of discipline encouraged mismanagement and fraud. See Befus, "Discovering a Role," 87–88.

recipients. Despite their limitations, microloans have enabled millions of families to escape poverty.[18]

Microsavings

The problems with microloans lead many development scholars to argue that microsavings are more effective means of alleviating poverty. Saving is imperative for families whose daily consumption needs are constant but whose income is intermittent. Savings enable families to send children to school, cope with emergencies, and make investments. Their lack of access to formal financial services leaves half of the world's people with few efficient and inexpensive ways to save money. Despite these barriers, "the poor can and do save."[19] After conducting interviews with destitute villagers and slum dwellers in South Africa, India, and Bangladesh, the authors of *Portfolios of the Poor: How the World's Poor Live on $2 a Day* concluded that few poor households spend all they earn to simply survive. Instead, many of them put aside money as a reserve (often by participating in saving clubs).[20]

Because the poor cannot open bank accounts, various mechanisms have recently been devised to help them save money—programs operated by NGOs, international organizations, microfinance institutions, and different types of savings groups (SG). The latter category includes rotating savings and credit associations (ROSCAs), accumulated savings and credit associations (ASCAs), which exist in two forms—savings groups and self-help groups—and credit unions. The size of these savings groups vary greatly from ones with one hundred clients to some with more than 6 million clients. ROSCA members contribute a small fixed amount of money at regular intervals. They all receive the same payment in a predetermined order. ROSCAs are very simple and transparent. They require little bookkeeping and minimal trust among participants. However, ROSCAs have several liabilities: members usually must wait their turn to receive their payout regardless of when needs arise; they cannot contribute any more or less than the specified amount; the fund does not increase in value; people who are last in line will not receive their payout if the group disbands; and

18. Roodman, *Due Diligence*, 6.

19. "Yale Savings," http://www.poverty-action.org/microsavings.

20. Collins et al., *Portfolios*, 31–32, 46–52, 61.

after they receive their payments, people have less incentive to continue to contribute to the fund.[21]

ASCAs do not have these problems. Since being introduced in Niger in 1991, they have improved financial services and economic opportunities for millions of poor people. Members deposit small sums of money into a joint fund, from which they can borrow to pay for their consumption, educational, or healthcare needs or to invest in business ventures. At the end of a cycle (typically a year), the fund is distributed to members in proportion to the amount they contributed plus whatever interest their money has earned from loans the fund dispersed (usually 20–40 percent). Consequently, members of saving groups do not need to sell an animal or crops at a substantial discount or borrow from their families or village money lenders to pay for emergencies. Savings groups give the indigent "a convenient, flexible, affordable financial service," promote mutual assistance, accountability, and self-discipline, and reduce stress. They involve "minimal risk, maximum transparency," an opportunity for loans, and an annual cash payoff.[22]

Numerous nonprofits, including CARE, World Vision, and HOPE International, have established savings groups initiatives. Today more than six million people in sixty countries, primarily in Africa, belong to an estimated 312,000 ASCA groups. Savings groups provide low-cost financial services to impoverished residents of rural communities, teach them how to manage money, and supply cash to meet vital needs.[23]

Self-help groups (SHGs) began in India in the 1980s. Like members of savings groups, SHG participants deposit their savings in a general fund, can borrow from it, and pay interest on loans they receive. However, the SHG's fund is not distributed annually to its members and continues to grow over time. In addition, most SHGs also receive loans from banks, some of which are guaranteed by international organizations. Today about 60 million self-help groups operate around the world.[24]

Called by various names in different regions, credit unions furnish savings accounts and loans to the members who own them. About 200

21. Interview with Mech; Ashe and Nelson, "Introduction," 2–3.

22. Ashe and Nelson, "Introduction," 1. See also "Forget Microcredit," http://oxfamblogs.org/fp2p/forget-microcredit-microsavings-work-much-better/.

23. Ibid., 1–2; quotations from 1. See also Wilson, Harper, and Griffith, *Financial Promise.*

24. Ibid., 5.

million members belong to 53,000 credit unions in one hundred nations. Members share a common bond through their local communities, religious bodies, places of employment, or social organizations. Credit unions provide higher interest on savings, offer lower rates on loans, and have fewer fees than do commercial financial institutions.[25]

Many development experts argue that these various types of savings groups significantly alleviate poverty. They are inexpensive to establish (training and supporting groups until they become self-sufficient cost about $25 per member). Second, the hundreds of agencies that work to improve literacy, agriculture, sanitation, and health in developing nations can also help increase the number and effectiveness of savings groups. Third, savings groups can increasingly cover their own start-up costs because training materials can be disseminated through the Internet and record-keeping and transactions can be done electronically.[26] Most savings group programs recruit women because they are usually responsible for the well-being of their families and are more likely than their husbands to make payments regularly and use loans wisely.

Savings groups are dramatically improving the lives of many poor people in developing nations.[27] Consider two examples: after Rwandan Judith Nyirantarama's husband deserted their family in 2002, grinding poverty prompted five of her seven children to leave home and live on the streets. She spent several years begging before community members chose Nyirantarama in 2009 to participate in a savings group. A small loan enabled her to establish a business selling tomatoes and fish, and, with the help of additional loans, she began to sell other vegetables and bananas. Today her business is thriving, her children have returned home, she can adequately feed and clothe them, and they all have medical insurance.[28]

The massive earthquake that struck Haiti in 2010 destroyed Mireille Henry's home. Losing everything forced Henry and her children to live in a field. A microsaving initiative enabled Henry to rebuild her life. She is one of 5,000 Haitian participants in a program whose members belong to savings groups of twenty to thirty. Participants receive rigorous financial training and contribute about $2 per week to the group's general fund.

25. Ibid., 6; "World Council of Credit Unions," www.woccu.org/membersserv/intlcu-system; Bateman, *Microfinance*, 168.

26. Ashe and Nelson, "Introduction," 9.

27. Johnson and Storchi, "Savings Group," 42–43, 47, 57.

28. Baklimah and Umoh, "Sustainable Access."

Members can borrow money at low interest rates to start a business, buy seeds, or pay for doctor's visits or school fees. Henry and her children now live in a small home with an aluminum roof. Her friendship with other group members and improved economic circumstances have made Henry more determined and hopeful.[29]

Savings groups provide a variety of personal and social benefits. Participants chastise and encourage one another, offer gentle counsel, and demand that members "shape up or ship out." Members actively work to reduce domestic violence, curb alcohol use, end harmful dowry practices, and bring water taps, roads, and buses to their communities. Savings groups improve members' problem-solving skills, teach people how to manage money, and motivate individuals to claim their rights.[30] Helping manage their savings groups gives women experience and confidence and encourages them to take leadership positions in the community. Participation in savings groups also increases women's self-respect, ambition, and independence as well as their decision-making power in their households.[31]

Many groups create profitable ventures to increase their loan funds or to distribute more money to members. They often supply valuable services their communities lack such as shuttles and convenience stores. Inspired by a savings group, more than 500 families in an Indian village created a pickle business. Participating families earn much more than the country's average farm income.[32] Some SG members also collaborate to grow crops. By pooling their resources, one group in Uganda was able to buy a tractor, expand their agricultural production, and open small shops and granaries.[33]

Some nonprofits also help the destitute save money. Their work has previously been hampered by lack of funds and the cost of managing accounts. However, the increasing use of cell phones (which greatly reduces transaction costs) and the infusion of cash from the Bill & Melinda Gates Foundation has helped expand their endeavors. Explaining the foundation's action, Melinda Gates insisted that savings enables people "to marshal their resources to build something better for themselves and their children." It

29. "Haiti Earthquake."

30. Wilson, "Thrift-Led Development," 85–88 (first quotation from 85; second from 86).

31. Gash, "Pathways to Change," 101–25.

32. Wilson, "Thrift-Led Development," 89; "Self Help Groups in India," http://www.microfinancegateway.org/.

33. Wilson, "Thrift-Led Development," 97.

helps families move "from reacting to events to planning for a healthier, happier future."[34]

By reducing the costs of transactions, technological developments permit nonprofits to provide more financial services to the indigent. For example, staff who work for Cashpor in India use clients' cell phones to establish savings accounts. Clients can use their phones to make additional deposits to their accounts or give cash directly to Cashpor personnel who regularly visit account holders.[35]

As noted, some faith-based organizations have created savings programs to combat poverty. A prime example is HOPE International, whose savings groups and credit associations operate in seventeen countries. This ministry strives to help people overcome both physical and spiritual poverty by providing discipleship programs, biblically-based business training, savings opportunities, and small loans. HOPE also works to improve health care and increase literacy in impoverished communities. Its programs have enabled more than 575,000 people to start or expand a business, and it has a 96 percent loan repayment rate. Believing that true transformation comes only from developing a personal relationship with Jesus Christ, HOPE hires committed Christians who engage in "culturally appropriate evangelism" in the countries where they work.[36]

Microinsurance

Many development experts also view microinsurance as a valuable tool for aiding poor families, but thus far it has not been widely available or appealing to the indigent. The income of the poor is unpredictable and precarious. An illness or injury to a family's principal breadwinner or weather-related problems such as flooding or drought cause expenses to rise rapidly and earnings to plunge. This often forces the destitute to sell their productive assets—their land, animals, tools, and, tragically, even their children. Although loans and savings can help them during these difficulties, insurance can provide greater assistance. Insurance also provides people with access to preventative health and dental services. Only about 3 percent of those

34. "Create Savings Accounts."

35. "A Better Mattress"; Davis, "Microsavings."

36. "Hope International," http://www.hopeinternational.org/; Barnes, "Families in Poverty."

living in the world's one hundred poorest nations, however, have insurance of any type.[37]

Two basic impediments prevent most poor families from purchasing insurance: companies have great difficulty earning a profit through selling adequate insurance policies to the indigent and most poor are unwilling to buy insurance when it is available. To successfully sell small insurance policies, companies need to have a high volume and low administrative costs, which have been hard to achieve. Moreover, companies must deal with the "moral hazard" issue: people often "change their behaviour (farm less carefully [or] spend more money on healthcare)" if they do not have to "bear the full consequences." Insurers also confront the problem of "adverse selection": those who are the most likely to have a particular problem in the future are more likely to purchase that kind of insurance. Finally, clients submitting false claims or clinics overcharging patients often prevents insurers from making a profit.[38]

Although the World Bank, the Gates Foundation, and other organizations have spent millions to develop insurance programs for the indigent, companies thus far have not been able to provide either health or crop insurance at affordable rates without losing money. Various strategies are being employed to cope with these challenges. Adding life insurance to cover the remaining loan balance if a borrower dies is inexpensive, so many microlenders do offer this insurance as well as coverage for funeral expenses and payments to survivors. Development leaders urge all members of savings and self-help groups to purchase insurance to increase the number of policy holders and make insurance more profitable for companies and affordable for clients.[39] Some economists prod governments to cover part of the cost of the insurance premiums for the destitute.[40] MicroEnsure offers a promising model. Launched by Opportunity International in 2002, it insures ten million people in developing nations, 80 percent of whom have never previously been insured, against crop failure, illness, death of family members, and political violence.[41]

37. Greer and Smith, *The Poor Will Be Glad*, 121.

38. Banerjee and Duflo, *Poor Economics*, 148–49.

39. Roodman, *Due Diligence*, 94–98, 116–18

40. Banerjee and Duflo, *Poor Economics*, 154–55.

41. "MicroEnsure," http://microensure.com/products.asp.

Alternatives to Conventional Microfinance

Some development experts argue that providing conditional cash transfers (CCT) and unconditional cash transfers (UCT) and working to improve the education and health of children is a better approach to alleviating poverty than microloans.[42] Since 2000, CCTs have been giving money to indigent households that meet particular behavioral requirements, typically connected with children's schooling and healthcare. Effectively designed and implemented CCT programs have produced many positive outcomes, especially increasing food consumption and school enrollment.[43] The two largest CCTs—Brazil's Bolsa Família and Mexico's Oportunidades—have decreased poverty, boosted literacy, and reduced child labor in Latin America's two most populous countries.[44] Oportunidades, for example, gives families cash payments to provide preventative care and immunizations for children and pre- and postnatal care for mothers if parents attend nutritional, health, and hygiene classes. One study found that 97 percent of eligible families enroll and that their children's illnesses have been significantly reduced.[45] CCTs work better in rural areas where people primarily need more food, clean water, elementary schools, and basic health care than in urban areas where family breakdown, violence, and drugs compound poverty.[46] After their initial success in Latin America and South Asia, CCT programs are now operating in more than thirty nations.[47]

One day Gabriel Otieno Anoche, a twenty-five-year-old Kenyan carpenter came home from work to find that strangers had given his wife a mobile phone. It was linked to a bank account that contained $1,000, which they could spend as they wished. This money came from Give Directly, a charity that dispenses no-strings-attached cash to the extremely poor. The Anoches used half of their windfall to buy a tin roof for their house and the other half to purchase chickens and timber to start two businesses that now produce a monthly income of $90. Having "the money and the mindset," Gabriel declares, "can change your life." The Anoches are one of several

42. Bateman, *Microfinance*, 204–9. See also Maluccio and Flores, *Impact Evaluation*.

43. "World Bank," http://web.worldbank.org/.

44. de Hoop and Rosati, "Cash Transfers."

45. Karlan and Appel, *More Than Good Intentions*, 232; Gertler, "Conditional Cash Transfers," 336–41 (Progresa is the original name of Oportunidades); Gertler and Boyce, "Impact of Progresa"; Skoufias, "Impact of Progresa," 37–61.

46. "Give the Poor Money."

47. Simmons, "Case for Conditional Cash Transfers."

hundred randomly selected poor households in sixty-three villages who have received this bonanza.[48]

This program is an example of an Unconditional Cash Transfer. Both charitable organizations and governments have recently begun to dispense unrestricted funds. So far recipients of unconditional cash in Kenya are not blowing it "on booze and brothels," as some critics warned. Instead, most households are using their money to buy food and livestock. Another program that gave one-time handouts to 550 households in a Vietnamese community reported that its poverty rates fell 20 percent in two years. In 2009 the Ugandan government began dispensing grants of about $10,000 to groups of twenty young people who submitted well-designed business plans. Recipients spend the money to learn a trade and buy tools and stock. Thus far this program has produced better results than job training classes or additional years of secondary education do.[49]

Many warn that the poor will not use UCTs to improve their farms, educate their children, or start businesses. Instead they will increase their creature comforts, or worse, squander the money on alcohol, tobacco, and drugs. When members of our local aid organization stress that we only pay the bills of clients and never give them cash, professionals, business people, and church leaders applaud. But are we being too paternalistic and pessimistic? Additional evidence suggests that the indigent use cash handouts wisely. Randomized cash grants to destitute Mexican families, Malawian schoolgirls, and other groups have typically been used to start businesses and increase their income. In seventeen of nineteen cash transfer programs in Asia, Africa, and Latin America, the spending of recipients on tobacco and alcohol either remained the same or decreased.[50]

Development experts argue that both CCTs and UCTs have benefits. When parents are required to send their children to school, they often pressure communities to upgrade their educational standards. CCTs are popular with middle-class taxpayers because "the poor are not getting something for nothing." However, UCTs are much easier and cheaper for charities to administer; they can be dispensed to millions, not just tens of thousands.[51]

48. "Pennies from Heaven."

49. Ibid.

50. Blattman, "Let Them Eat Cash." See also "Enterprises for Ultra-poor Women," http://www.poverty-action.org/project/0104; Evans and Popova, "Do the Poor Waste Transfers?"

51. "Pennies from Heaven."

English economist Milford Bateman complains that overemphasis on microloans has led the international development community to ignore more successful means for ending extreme poverty. Throughout history the destitute have attained better jobs and living conditions and greater opportunities principally through public health and social security programs, minimum wage laws, public education, state-funded jobs, and training courses.[52] Other development specialists contend that investment by foreign businesses in low-income nations is essential to reducing poverty.[53] Lord Brian Griffiths and Dato Kim Tan maintain that reducing poverty in low-income nations is best accomplished by creating jobs that pay employees in relation to their productivity, providing more reliable, less expensive energy, and lowering the price of transportation and telecommunications. They urge Western governments to provide tax incentives to stimulate their citizens to invest in business enterprises that have social objectives.[54]

Viewing microfinance as a cure-all for poverty prevents people from simultaneously taking action on many different fronts. Improving life for poor adults and children requires governments passing and enforcing just laws and preserving order, prudent macroeconomic policies, good schools, welfare programs for the most destitute, and inexpensive, reliable health services.[55] Moreover, as Steve Corbett and Brian Fikkert contend in *When Helping Hurts*, including the indigent in selecting, designing, implementing, and evaluating interventions to alleviate poverty greatly increases the likelihood that they will be successful.[56]

How Can Christians Use Microfinance to Best Help the Poor?

Christians can aid indigent children by donating to microfinance organizations that help the poor open savings accounts, buy insurance, or obtain loans at low interest rates and provide them with training in money management. Christians should choose carefully which organizations and

52. Bateman, *Microfinance*, 2, 209, passim.

53. "Hopeful Continent"; Griffiths and Tan, "Fighting Poverty," 186–87, 193

54. Griffiths and Tan, "Fighting Poverty," 180–81, 189, 193–200. See also Schneider, *The Good of Affluence*, 19.

55. Hulme, "Microdebt," 21. See also Karlan and Appel, *More Than Good Intentions* and Banerjee and Duflo, *Poor Economics*.

56. Corbett and Fikkert, *When Helping Hurts*, 142–52.

entrepreneurs to support. We should work through organizations that utilize fair lending practices, prod loan recipients to act responsibly, have competent staff, and are financially sound, accountable to donors, and transparent. Christians should carefully assess the mission, values, experience, and practices of microfinance organizations and donate to ones that are faith-based, treat the poor with respect, and help the indigent become self-sustaining.[57]

In determining which individuals to fund, we should give priority to people who have no access to conventional credit and to loans that will help create or expand businesses and thereby enable families to supply their own needs and enrich their communities. Considering whether a potential borrower has a good reputation, proven business aptitude, and a solid credit history is also important. Especially significant is whether the proposed project will provide jobs in a community. Christians should also take into account the viability of proposed businesses in light of the resources of various areas and the needs of particular communities. Finally, we encourage readers to direct their loans to individuals who plan to reinvest their profit in their businesses and who have children to support and educate.[58]

While engaging in these activities, Christians should remember that poverty often involves a spiritual dimension. Therefore, we should pray for the poor and for organizations (microfinance, missionary, educational, and charitable) that provide both material and spiritual assistance to the destitute.

57. Mech, "Microfinance."

58. Ibid.

12

How Government Can Help Impoverished Children

Speak up for those who cannot speak for themselves;
defend the rights of all those who have nothing. Speak up and judge fairly,
and defend the rights of the poor and needy.

PROVERBS 31:8–9

Government can either support or undermine families as they cope with the moral, social, and economic stresses of caring for children.

UNITED STATES CONFERENCE OF CATHOLIC BISHOPS, *Putting Children and Families First: A Challenge for Our Church, Nation, and World*, 13

If it takes a village to raise a child, the prognosis for American children isn't good: in recent years, villages all over America, rich and poor, have . . . shirked collective responsibility for our kids."

ROBERT PUTNAM, *Our Kids*, 205

After I spoke at a conference at the college where I teach, an audience member berated me for discussing ways that the government could help children. He—and numerous other Christian social conservatives—question whether the government has any legitimate role to play in improving the circumstances of the poor. Some conservatives contend that the government's responsibilities do not involve promoting economic development, funding education, or dispensing welfare. Others protest that the separation of church and state prevents the government from addressing the deeper spiritual needs of the poor. The government requires people who work for it or use its money to supply services to avoid evangelizing or even discussing God and spiritual issues. This limits what Christians can say, do, or accomplish. They cannot focus on people's greatest need—to have an intimate relationship with the God who loves them deeply.

In assessing the government's role in helping the indigent, we must remember that justice is a major theme in Scripture. The Bible teaches that God loves justice (see Ps 89:14; Ps 96:13; and Isa 61:8) and established government to provide it. Numerous Psalms, Old Testament prophets, and the apostle Paul in Romans 13 underscore this point. For example, Ps 72:4 instructs kings to "vindicate the afflicted," "save the children of the needy," and "crush the oppressor." Jeremiah praises a king for acting justly and pleading "the cause of the afflicted and needy" (22:16). God commands the Israelites in Amos 5:24 to "let justice roll on like a river, righteousness like a never-failing stream!" Isaiah exhorts the Israelites to "learn to do right; seek justice. Defend the oppressed. Take up the cause of the fatherless; plead the case of the widow" (1:17). Christians can accomplish some of these tasks through our families, schools, businesses, churches, and community organizations. God, however, assigns the state the principal responsibility to ensure that society's norms and practices are just.[1]

Although many factors contribute, injustice and oppression play a significant role in creating and sustaining individual poverty. Institutional policies and public practices that promote or permit injustice can only be changed through political action. Legislative and judicial remedies are often needed to eradicate discrimination and inequality as ending America's Jim Crow laws and South Africa's apartheid illustrate. Moreover, a nation's criminal justice system, protection of property rights, and tax policies have a great impact on its citizens' opportunities, mobility, and lifestyle. Western governments now furnish extensive social welfare programs in large part

1. Marshall, *Thine Is the Kingdom.*

because voters demanded that they do so and because private organizations were unable to provide essential services and sufficient financial assistance. Those who subscribe to the philosophy that the government has a very limited social responsibility must be willing to supply the material needs of our poorest inhabitants, especially our children, through the activities of churches, parachurch ministries, community organizations, businesses, educational enterprises, and other private sector endeavors.

Given their biblical mandate to provide justice and the role institutions play in causing and perpetuating destitution, federal, state, and local governments should work to help alleviate child poverty throughout the world. As discussed in other chapters, if governments do not ensure that order and justice prevail, protect property rights, and promote economic development, many people will remain mired in poverty. Moreover, their support of education and provision of welfare help many children to avoid destitution and improve their life circumstances. By guaranteeing religious liberty, treating people fairly in the criminal justice system, and abolishing human trafficking, governments can enable their poorest citizens to live more productive, fulfilling lives. International governmental bodies, especially the United Nations, can reduce child poverty by promoting children's rights and working to resolve disputes between and within nations, end armed conflicts, and stop the persecution of religious, racial, and ethnic minorities.

Christians and Government Policies Affecting Children

Christians should support these efforts by actively participating in government at all levels and in various capacities. Because most of the world's governments today are democracies, Christians have an obligation and opportunity to shape their policies. We can do this by carefully studying political issues, praying for elected officials, voting prudently, lobbying effectively, campaigning for candidates, and serving in political positions. Christians should seek to be well educated about major political topics, especially the one or two policy areas on which they feel called to focus. Those who want to advance the welfare of low-income children should read extensively about their problems to determine which policies are most likely to help them. Scripture exhorts us to pray for those who govern us (1 Tim 2:2). We should vote for candidates whose character, experiences, and political agendas make them likely to promote public justice and advance the well-being of children. Christians should also work to help such candidates get elected. In addition, we should seek to persuade elected officials to pass policies that aid the indigent. Finally, Christians who feel called and have the requisite gifts should run for public office at the national, state, or local level. While campaigning they can accentuate social justice and the welfare of children, and, if elected, they can promote these causes in the halls of government.

A Contemporary Daniel

Many committed Christians are working diligently at all levels of government to improve the lives of children. Former Congressman Frank Wolf illustrates their efforts. While representing a district in northern Virginia from 1980 to 2014, Wolf zealously defended religious liberty and worked vigorously to aid indigent children. Wolf's visit to famine-stricken Ethiopia in 1984 transformed his life. Shocked by the withered crops, starvation, and social chaos that killed one million people in two years, Wolf vowed to fight hunger, poverty, and persecution. During the next three decades, he traveled to numerous places where drought, war, or political oppression robbed people of their rights, economic opportunities, and dignity, including Romania, Tibet, communist China, and war-torn Darfur and Iraq. He protested against "political prisoners languishing in the Soviet gulags," "Tibetans suffering under the brutal control of the Chinese government," China's one-child policy, and Christians living in Muslim countries who were being persecuted for their faith.[2] Wherever "bullets fly, babies starve, and thousands of people suffer in obscurity," a *Washington Post* reporter observed, Wolf was likely to be.[3]

More than any other Congressman during these years, Wolf championed the cause of religious liberty. In 1988 he introduced legislation to establish the US Commission on International Religious Freedom and the International Religious Freedom Office at the State Department. He also founded and co-chaired an organization consisting of almost 200 Congressmen who promote various international human rights issues. Wolf fought to end discrimination against oppressed religious minorities, particularly Christians in Egypt, Syria, and Pakistan.[4] His 2013 book *Prisoner*

2. Wolf, *Prisoner of Conscience*, 27.
3. Dean, "Light of the Sun."
4. Hess, "Former Rep. Frank Wolf."

of Conscience: One Man's Crusade for Global Human and Religious Rights details his efforts. Wolf was widely hailed as the conscience of Congress and was honored for his human rights advocacy by the Christian Legal Society and the National Endowment for Democracy. *World* magazine gave him its 2014 Daniel of the Year award.[5] Human rights advocate John Prendergast called Wolf "a champion with few equals for human rights issues." Although it brought him few political benefits, he "worked tirelessly" to assist people suffering from conflict and repression around the world.[6] Fellow Republican Congressman Chris Smith praised Wolf's "remarkable thirty-four-year career of altruistic deeds, selfless service, bold humanitarian initiatives, and durable achievement."[7] Since retiring from Congress, Wolf has served as Baylor University's advocate on Capitol Hill to exhort Christians to combat human trafficking, defend the rights of women and refugees, and alleviate suffering around the world.[8]

Wolf has long labored to reduce hunger abroad and at home and abolish human trafficking. He has called attention to the plight of millions of hungry children around the world and has sought to "reenergize the global community" to combat this tragedy.[9] In 2013 he pointed out that a record number of Americans were "struggling to put food on their tables." Across the country 49 million people, including 17 million children, were going hungry. Local food banks could not meet the demand caused by high rates of unemployment and underemployment. "It's simply unacceptable that people are going hungry in America, the land of plenty and the world's wealthiest nation," Wolf declared.[10]

As a congressman, Wolf proposed several remedies for hunger problems. In 2008 he launched the Office of Personnel Management's "Feds Feed Families" food drive; in the next six years federal employees donated 24 million pounds of groceries to food pantries across the nation.[11] Wolf introduced legislation to create a National Commission on Hunger in 2014 to help empower civic groups, faith-based organizations, and the private sector to fight hunger. He also commended Virginia's governor for es-

5. Morgan and Moon, "Frank Wolf."
6. Pershing, "Frank Wolf to Retire."
7. "Wilberforce," http://www.21wilberforce.org/news.html.
8. Hess, "Former Rep. Frank Wolf."
9. Wolf, *Prisoner of Conscience*, 26.
10. Wolf, "Virginia Can Do More."
11. "Congressman Frank Wolf."

tablishing a "Hunger Action Month" to encourage residents to volunteer with food drives and support Feeding America's network of more than 200 food banks and partner agencies. Wolf exhorted the governor to devise a statewide hunger initiative to challenge all state agencies, schools, businesses, churches, and civic organizations to re-stock the shelves of local food pantries year-round. In addition, Wolf recommended that Virginia create a central "one-stop" website that all food banks and pantries could use to provide information for donors, volunteers, and clients to replace the current disjointed, haphazard system. This would enable donors and volunteers to easily determine the food pantry closest to them and learn how they could get involved. Wolf also proposed requiring states to donate their unused food to food banks and passing an act to protect schools that gave their unneeded food to local pantries from liability issues.[12] Wolf sent a letter to the rest of the nation's governors urging them to make ending hunger a priority in their states. He urged them to designate someone to coordinate state efforts to alleviate hunger and create a website to supply information about organizations that provide food assistance.[13] Wolf also implored every American farmer to donate one acre of land to a church so that members could grow food to feed the indigent and exhorted every church, school, business, and community club to regularly hold a food drive.[14]

In addition, Wolf fought long and hard to reduce human trafficking, which he pointed out was occurring not only in Thailand but in Tysons Corner, not only in Albania but in Arlington. He publicized the issue, challenged churches to create safe houses for victims, and beseeched the federal government to prosecute pimps and shut down trafficking websites.[15] He held Congressional Appropriations subcommittee meetings to discuss this scourge, increase funding to abolish it, and make the targeting of traffickers a higher federal government priority. In 2014 the committee appropriated $45.3 million for Victims of Trafficking grants—quadruple what President Barack Obama requested—and directed the US Attorney General to sponsor a national conference on sex trafficking. The bill also mandated that the attorney general lead a task force to investigate and curtail trafficking,

12. Wolf, "Virginia Can Do More."

13. "Ending Domestic Hunger."

14. Interview with Frank Wolf at Grove City College, May 15, 2015.

15. Lippard, "Interview with Frank Wolf."

especially by closing websites that facilitate it.[16] Wolf complained that Congress had refused to shut down these websites because of the high tech industry's bogus argument that doing so would violate First Amendment freedom of speech rights and because many senators and representatives received major financial support from the industry.[17]

Wolf exhorts Christians to "choose righteousness, both personally and as a society," encourage youth "to bring their faith into the public square," and attempt "to persuade their fellow citizens of the rightness of their cause." He urges those on the political right and left to join forces through both governmental action and volunteer efforts to combat human trafficking, genocide, world hunger, health problems in developing nations, and religious persecution.[18] Although Wolf prodded Congress to send emergency aid to famine-stricken regions of Africa, he insists that the best way to help these countries is by promoting their economic development. They need to devise "long-term strategies to tackle the root causes of food shortages," including "improving irrigation, drilling wells, developing drought-resistant crops," teaching farmers about "sustainable agricultural practices," striving to diversify their economies, and increasing private ownership of property. Moreover, he contends that while governments should work to alleviate poverty, private organizations and individuals have an even greater role to play.[19] Because Americans have little confidence in Congress and we lack the exceptional political leaders of earlier eras, Wolf asserts, we must pray for religious revival and work more vigorously through churches to eradicate social ills.[20]

Biblical teachings and his strong faith inspire Wolf's efforts to aid the poor and persecuted. "As a follower of Jesus," he declares, "I am called to work for justice and reconciliation" and to "advocate for those who cannot speak for themselves." Jesus' statement—"To whom much is given, much is required"—Wolf argues, applies not only to individuals but also to countries that God has blessed with great power and resources. God will hold individuals and their nations accountable for how they use their gifts and opportunities to meet the world's needs. Wolf is also motivated by Jesus' declaration in Luke 4:18–19 that his mission was to proclaim liberty to the

16. "FBI: 168 Kids Rescued."

17. Interview with Wolf.

18. Wolf, *Prisoner of Conscience*, 263 (quotation), 264.

19. Ibid., 24–26; quotation from 24.

20. Interview with Wolf.

captives, set the oppressed free, and give sight to the blind. When asked what he wants his gravestone to read, Wolf replied, "Well done, good and faithful servant."[21]

Christians and Political Advocacy

Despite biblical injunctions to advocate on behalf of the poor, the example of Wolf and other Christian politicians, and the potential benefits of activism, most Christians, for a variety of reasons, do little to try to influence public policy. As previously noted, some protest that the government has greatly overstepped its biblical mandate by taking on numerous social and economic responsibilities. Other Christians are reluctant to participate in advocacy because they view the political process as bewildering or even sinful. Some concentrate on meeting immediate material needs through private organizations rather than correcting deeper structural problems through political action. Many Christians contend that they lack the knowledge, experience, resources, or time to get involved in advocacy. Others insist that individuals can have little effect on political outcomes.[22]

Granted, political issues are often complex and confusing. Nevertheless, Christians should try to direct governmental decisions because the Bible calls us to be advocates for the poor and governments today often have a huge impact on their lives. Proverbs 31:8 commands us to "Speak up for those who cannot speak for themselves; defend the rights of all those who have nothing." Christians are called to plead the cause of the destitute, to side with and help vindicate them. While we can do this in a variety of settings, government chambers are an important venue for defending their rights and advancing their welfare. Isaiah 10:1–2 declares, "How terrible it will be for those who make unfair laws, and those who write laws that make life hard for people. They are not fair to the poor, and they rob my people of their rights" (New Century Version).[23] These passages require us to devise equitable laws and aid the impoverished.

World Relief and many other Christian aid organizations argue that their political advocacy on behalf of the poor and oppressed is based on the biblical principles of compassion, justice, and mercy and on Christ's example. As Jesus' representatives on earth, Christians must defend the

21. Smith, "Frank Wolf Reflects."

22. Fulgham, *Educating All God's Children*, 186–89.

23. See also Deut 15:11, Prov 22:22–23, Ps 82:2–4, and Isa 58:9.

vulnerable, voiceless, and victimized. Doing this requires Christians not simply to meet individuals' material needs but to change "policies and structures that create poverty and oppress God's children."[24]

Moreover, numerous individuals advocated before a foreign ruler or an Israelite king to aid the Jewish people. Joseph intervened with pharaoh (Genesis 41–45). Moses pleaded with a later pharaoh to let the Jews leave Egypt (Exodus 5–12). Nehemiah asked Persian King Artaxerxes for a leave of absence to return to Jerusalem to rebuild its walls (Nehemiah 1–2). Esther, Isaiah, Jeremiah, Amos, John the Baptist, and Paul all made pleas before governing authorities on behalf of Jews or Christians.[25]

Promoting social justice through the political process is essential for several reasons. Social conditions and public policies strongly affect how Christians minister to individuals. Because sin is structural as well as individual, it can be codified in laws and promote or preserve injustice. We must work to change laws that perpetuate injustice and to adopt policies and pass laws that ensure equality and aid the poor. The actions of Moses, Joshua, Esther, Daniel, Nehemiah, and others show that furthering social justice is part of the biblical mandate. God is building his kingdom on earth and Jesus is Lord over all life—the ballot box as much as the boardroom and the bedroom. Efforts to create institutions that embody God's concern for justice and fairness call attention to his character and biblical values.[26] Conversely, when Christians do not participate in the political process to end injustices or advance the common good, we appear to be callous, indifferent, self-serving, and irrelevant.[27]

Political Advocacy for Poor Children

So how can Christians work effectively in the political arena to help low-income children? To have influence, we must study, comprehend, and be able to cogently discuss the key issues and policies that affect them. We can read books, articles, and op-eds, join church groups or organizations that work to aid indigent children, write letters to newspaper editors, respond to on-line opinion pieces, and pen op-eds. Christians can also call, email, or visit local, state, or federal officials or their staff, sponsor or support reform

24. "World Relief," http://worldrelief.org/advocate.

25. Martin, *The Just Church*, 205.

26. Sider, Olson, and Unruh, *Churches*, 93–96.

27. Ibid., 43.

initiatives, promote referenda, and speak at public meetings or court hearings that discuss policies that affect low-income children. Moreover, we can support financial policies that aid poor children such as increasing EITC, food stamps, or the minimum wage, rezoning neighborhoods to allow the building of affordable housing, and adopting policies that improve education.

Churches can use a variety of means to inspire and equip their parishioners to change social structures and implement public policies that aid poor children. Ministers can preach and teach about the scriptural foundation for political engagement and social justice. Church leaders can help parishioners understand social issues that affect low-income children and are integrally connected to their congregation's ministry. Churches can issue or endorse public statements about policies designed to aid children if members believe they are consistent with biblical presuppositions. Congregations must do this very carefully and cautiously because earnest Christians often disagree about what the Bible teaches on various issues and political pronouncements can be contentious and potentially divisive. However, if a strong consensus exists among its members on an issue, a church can take a political stand and work to shape public policy. Such action, however, is usually best left to parachurch organizations that have been established to accomplish particular social aims. Congregations can also form small groups to enable members to study specific social problems, equip parishioners to participate in political action, and create ministries to remedy particular social ills. In addition, they can organize their members or the larger community to pray, disseminate information, lobby, march, or boycott a product or establishment in order to reform corrupt courts, stop predatory loan practices, or end an immoral, harmful activity.[28]

Life in Christ Cathedral of Faith in Chester, Pennsylvania, undertakes many of these activities. Violence, substance abuse, unemployment, dysfunctional families, and welfare dependency are all prevalent in this community near Philadelphia. To combat these ills and provide a better life for the next generation, church members provide substance abuse and financial counseling, mentor middle and high school students, and sponsor educational programs. Seeking to balance evangelism and social action, the church strives to revitalize Chester's spiritual, political, economic, educational, and social life. To accomplish this, the church created the Political

28. Ibid., 98.

Involvement Ministry to educate its members and mobilize them to respond to local, state, and national issues affecting their community.[29]

Whether Christians should prod the US government to appropriate more funds to alleviate poverty at home and abroad is a very controversial issue. Various campaigns—End Poverty Now, "Make Poverty History," ONE, and the Global Poverty Project—exhort governments to provide more aid to help the indigent around the world.[30] Many object that this assistance does not actually help developing nations (as the historical record purportedly proves). Some maintain that aid makes matters worse by strengthening the position of ruthless dictators or incompetent governments, undercutting local production (how can local farmers or merchants compete with free goods?), or creating a culture of dependency.

In evaluating this argument, consider several facts. First, polls show that many Americans greatly overestimate how much of the federal budget goes to foreign aid. In various surveys, they guess that 25 to 30 percent of the budget is used for this purpose. In reality, only 1 percent is typically devoted to international aid.[31] Second, if all Christians tithed and directed more of their individual giving and the resources of their congregations to help the destitute, much less government assistance would be necessary. Moreover, if all Christians gave 10 percent of our personal income to charities, it would be easier to convince elected officials to allocate more funds to aid the impoverished. Many politicians who want to do more to help the destitute are reluctant to champion social causes because they believe that their constituents do not support this.[32] Third, even if we think that the government has no responsibility to help the indigent at home or abroad, does it not make sense to try to influence how American aid is spent? Through our involvement, we can strive to ensure that money is used primarily for development rather than relief, that aid is given principally to the extremely

29. Ibid., 99–101; "Bishop Dickie Robbins," http://www.urbanministry.org/f/bishop-dickie-robbins-life-christ-cathedral-faith.

30. "End of Poverty?" http://www.theendofpoverty.com/index.html; "Global Poverty Project," https://www.globalcitizen.org/en/gpp/governance/; "ONE," http://www.one.org/us/take-action/.

31. Offenhesier, "Top Myths"; "WorldPublicOpinion," http://www.worldpublicopinion.org/pipa/pdf/nov10/ForeignAid_Nov10_quaire.pdf; "Global Poverty Facts," http://www.one.org/us/2014/10/21/25-most-shocking-global-poverty-facts/; Bearak and Gamio, "U.S. Foreign Assistance Budget."

32. Todd, *Hope Rising*, 127, 133.

poor, and that nations, organizations, groups, and individuals who receive aid are held accountable.

The Nuts and Bolts and Results of Advocacy

The International Justice Mission, Bread for the World, World Vision, and the Children's Defense Fund all offer advocacy training and exhort their constituents to take actions on various issues to aid children. They provide sample messages or scripts people can use in emails or phone calls to members of Congress. Several of these organizations also host "Lobby Days" when supporters can travel to Washington, DC, to receive advocacy training and then discuss issues with their representatives and senators. Founded in 1974, Bread for the World is a major Christian voice (some 74,000 strong) in the fight to end world hunger. BFW has long had a significant impact on US domestic and foreign policies pertaining to food insecurity, poverty alleviation, and economic and social development. For example, in 2014 its members sent thousands of emails and made hundreds of phone calls to congressmen that helped defeat a provision in a bill that would have eliminated food aid to two million Americans. Their advocacy also contributed to passing a measure that appropriated $130 million to reduce violence, poverty, and hunger in Central America—factors that drive thousands of children to come to the United States. In addition, in 2014 Congress passed a long-standing BFW priority—Feed the Future—a global hunger and food-security initiative, designed to enhance the livelihood of smallholder farmers, strengthen maternal and child nutrition, and improve agricultural production in developing nations.[33]

Christians who want to engage in advocacy can learn from a secular organization that has crafted a successful strategy to help children. Founded in 1980 by musician Sam Daley-Harris, RESULTS educates Americans about global poverty and trains them how to lobby effectively. The organization backs programs to combat the basic causes of destitution, including lack of education, limited access to medical care, and meager opportunity for advancement. RESULTS seeks to empower ordinary people to play an extraordinary role in the media, halls of government, and community organizations to end poverty. Through chapters in 100 American cities, these grassroots activists help channel millions of dollars into programs and policies that provide low-income individuals with tools to overcome poverty.

33. *2014 Annual Report*, http://files.bread.org/pdf/2014-Annual-Report.pdf.

RESULTS has lobbied politicians to provide vaccinations and oral rehydration therapy to save millions of children's lives around the world, increase funding for Head Start and microfinance, reduce tuberculosis and malaria, and improve education and nutrition for children.[34]

RESULTS helps citizens become persuasive advocates for poverty alleviation. Through websites, webinars, conference calls, and workshops, the organization equips people to work with Congress and the media and within their local communities to effect change. RESULTS educates participants about how to communicate effectively with members of Congress through emails, letters, and phone calls, establish relationships with congressional aides who handle the particular issues about which they have developed expertise, and convince these congressmen to respond to their requests. RESULTS also teaches activists how to ask astute questions at town meetings and candidates' forums. The organization trains its partners how to meet in person with members of Congress, arranges for them to visit poverty-stricken communities, inspires them to write op-eds about a poverty issue, and even take leadership roles in remedying social problems. In addition, RESULTS equips people to work with the media. To influence public opinion, partners write letters to editors, op-eds, and articles, and meet with editors and editorial boards. To improve their communities, RESULTS members write letters about issues, speak to community groups, train members of local organizations about advocacy, arrange visits of residents to low-income neighborhoods, convene community forums, and raise funds.[35]

Faith in Public Life is a Christian organization that provides similar training to equip clergy, lay leaders, and faith-based community organizers to promote "justice, compassion and the common good." Since its creation in 2005, FPL has worked to give these faith leaders "the media savvy that matches their moral authority" by training them in op-ed writing, interview skills, and the best tactics to use with the media. To influence public debates on immigration, livable wages, and other issues, FPL strives to create opportunities for its members to build and support broad coalitions,

34. Kristof and WuDunn, *Path* , 27; "About RESULTS," http://www.results.org/about/about/.

35. "Advocacy How-Tos," http://www.results.org/skills_center/advocacy_how_tos/; Shear, "Sharing the Secret."

design and implement innovative campaigns, and carry out initiatives to help the poor and disadvantaged.[36]

What Christians Can Do to Influence Government Policies Pertaining to Children

Christians can take numerous actions in the political arena to improve the lives of impoverished children. We can support candidates who pledge to help children and have a strong record of doing so. Christians can campaign and vote for them, publicly commend their actions, and privately thank them for their work. Our emails, phone calls, and visits can help shape the attitudes and actions of elected officials. Frank Wolf insists that the two things his constituents did that influenced him the most were personal conversations and inviting him to see the social services they were providing. He was impressed by both advocates' expertise about and passion for their causes.[37] By becoming knowledgeable about the problems poor children face, joining organizations created to improve their lives, and constantly encouraging our representatives to adopt policies that help destitute children, we can make a difference. Because most people are apathetic about the political process, a small number of dedicated advocates can have a huge impact, as the successes of Bread for the World and RESULTS and the petitions of Change.org and other organizations illustrate. Christians can speak at town meetings, write op-eds and letters to editors, call radio talk shows, and participate in other conscience-raising activities to help poor children.

Finally, God calls some of us to run for political office in order to aid children in our local communities or at the state, national, or world level. Perhaps you will be the next Frank Wolf. The son of a policeman, Wolf grew up in a working-class neighborhood in Philadelphia, had poor grades in high school, and had to overcome a stuttering problem, but God used him mightily in Congress to help impoverished children and victims of religious persecution. Wolf stands in a long line of Christian statesmen, including his hero British abolitionist William Wilberforce, British Prime Minister William Gladstone, Dutch Prime Minister Abraham Kuyper, numerous American presidents, and Oregon Senator Mark Hatfield, who

36. "Faith in Public Life," http://www.faithinpubliclife.org/.

37. Interview with Wolf.

have changed the world. While few people can accomplish what they did, small efforts add up and provide a better life for low-income children.

13

How Churches Can Help Impoverished Children

The Lord your God . . . defends the cause of the fatherless and the widow, and loves the foreigner residing among you, giving them food and clothing. And you are to love those who are foreigners, for you yourselves were foreigners in Egypt.

DEUTERONOMY 10:17–19

Suppose a brother or a sister is without clothes and daily food.
If one of you says to them, "Go in peace; keep warm and well fed,"
but does nothing about their physical needs, what good is it?

JAMES 2:15–16

The church has a great capacity to reduce child poverty. Its resources, numbers of adherents, and (hopefully) participants' passion for the task exceed those of all other entities. More than any other NGO, the church has the human, material, and financial resources as well as the moral foundation and credibility to devise and execute initiatives to aid the poor. Its largely volunteer workforce enables the church to undertake various enterprises to reduce poverty in a cost effective way.[1] The church has an impressive track record of providing social services and a generally positive reputation in much of the world, including high poverty areas of sub-Saharan Africa and the Asia-Pacific region.[2] A recent Gallup poll conducted in nineteen African nations found that their residents were more likely to trust the church than any other organization.[3] This is especially important because social trust is a key ingredient in promoting economic prosperity.[4]

To help destitute children, congregations can participate in four types of activities: relief, individual development, community improvement, and structural change. Relief involves aiding children who are suffering because of inadequate food, shelter, clothing, or medicine. Individual development helps children to get a better education through operating preschool, afterschool, summer school, and mentoring programs, to grow spiritually through church programs, to develop physically through recreational opportunities, and to improve their interpersonal skills through relationships with caring adults. Community development focuses on providing better housing, schools, healthcare, and jobs in the neighborhoods where low-income children reside. Structural change concentrates on abolishing unjust economic, political, and social systems and patterns and ending discriminatory lending practices.

The Dream Center

Numerous individual congregations, large and small, in varied geographical settings, with different racial and ethnic compositions and theological traditions, are engaging in these four kinds of endeavors to help low-income children. The Dream Center is a megachurch Tommy Barnett and his son Matthew founded in Los Angeles in 1994. Jointly operated by the Assemblies of God and the Foursquare Church, it provides a wide range of ministries and services that help thousands of poor residents of the area. The Dream Center has seventy-five paid staff, 200 full-time one-year volunteers, and thousands of other volunteers (including about 7,000 Christians a year

1. Lenk, "Global Poverty;" Todd, *Hope Rising*, 147.
2. Green, "AIDS Prevention," 65–80.
3. Tortora, "Africans' Confidence in Institutions."
4. Wydick, "Key to Prosperity."

who come on short-term mission trips).[5] Collectively, they conduct more than 250 different ministries that assist impoverished families, victimized women, and troubled youth living in inner-city Los Angeles. The center's outreach programs provide material aid, job training, and educational assistance. They feed the hungry, furnish medical care, rescue women from human trafficking, and help youth who age out of foster care successfully transition to independent living.[6]

To help address a shortage of affordable housing, the Dream Center bought a fourteen-story former hospital building in 1994. They converted it into housing for about 900 residents, primarily families facing homelessness or adults recovering from addiction.[7] The Dream Center also directly aids the homeless. On an average day, Los Angeles County has an estimated 82,000 homeless people, 15 percent of whom are children. Because of their lack of medical care or medications, the homeless and other impoverished individuals have a much higher rate of chronic illnesses and suffer from untreated infections and injuries that can lead to long-term disability and death. To meet these needs, the Dream Center partners with the City Help Mobile Medical Clinic, which furnishes free health care to indigent and uninsured residents. "Relief of suffering and physical healing," leaders argue, "are critical first steps to sharing hope and the love of Christ."[8]

The Dream Center also sponsors and supports various ministries to help the hungry in the Los Angeles area—where almost 1,000,000 adults and 640,000 children are classified as "food insecure." Through these programs, the center distributes more than $2,000,000 worth of food every month to both the residents and guests of its recovery programs and through its food bank, Food Truck Ministry, and Skid Row Feeding program. Its large food bank processes more than one million pounds of food each month. Each week its Food Distribution trucks deliver bags of food to thirty-one locations. This enables many recipients to retain enough money to pay their rent and utility bills. Every day the center's Under the Bridge team provides hot meals for hundreds of homeless individuals and families. These ministries provide "comfort, relief, hope and evidence of God's love."[9]

5. Crosby, "Dream of a Center."

6. Martinez, "Transitional Home."

7. Vincent, "Dream Center."

8. "Mobile Medical Clinic," http://www.dreamcenter.org/our-outreaches/poverty/mobile-medical-clinic/#sthash.i6tyZADn.dpuf.

9. "Hunger," http://www.dreamcenter.org/our-outreaches/hunger-outreach/.

Participants in the center's Adopt-A-Block program spend Saturday mornings asking area residents is "there anything we can do to serve you?" This outreach program enables members to minister to the material, spiritual, and emotional needs of many poor adults and children. The church also operates an emergency shelter and a sixty-bed human trafficking rescue center, the largest one in the country. Its six-month recovery program provides counseling and classes in effective communication, coping with trauma, managing anger, setting boundaries, budgeting, personal fitness, and Bible study to help individuals recover psychologically, deepen their relationship with God, and prepare to reenter society. In addition, the Dream Center runs a regionally accredited college where students can take classes and gain extensive practical ministry experience.[10]

Financial assistance from a foundation established by Clayton Kershaw, a Los Angeles Dodger pitcher and committed Christian, enables the Dream Center to carry out a Foster Care Intervention program. It helps preserve families who are in danger of having their children removed because of their inadequate finances. Many children in foster care are taken from their homes because their parents cannot supply their basic needs. Since 2006 the program has enabled more than 1,000 sets of parents to keep their children by providing food, clothing, appliances, and other material necessities. In addition, the center provides space where parents whose children are in foster care can hold supervised visits and trains monitors to oversee these visits. These programs help many families to either stay connected or be reunited.[11]

In 2014, the Dream Center opened Freedom House, a sixty-bed facility to assist youth who age out of foster care. Tragically, 40 to 50 percent of these children end up either homeless or in jail soon after they turn eighteen. The home's staff help youth develop a personal relationship with Jesus and make prudent lifestyle choices. They also assist residents to find housing after their one-year stay ends. Mentors and coaches teach residents about making decisions, setting goals, resolving conflicts, managing money, and preparing food. Equally important, residents learn job skills and can receive funding for post-secondary education.[12]

10. "Human Trafficking."

11. "Kershaw's Challenge," http://www.kershawschallenge.com/dream-center-los-angeles/; "Foster Care Intervention," http://www.dreamcenter.org/our-outreaches/poverty/foster-care-intervention/#sthash.CVRLtN31.dpuf.

12. Martinez, "Transitional Home."

Tim and Jeremy's stories are illustrative of the many children the Dream Center has helped. Tim spent most of his childhood in foster care, where he was frequently beaten. In his late teens, he visited the center and realized that he could have a better life. "When I got here," Tim explained, "I started praying for God to give me a family that will love me just like He always has." The staff at the center became the family for which he prayed. "The Dream Center," he rejoices, "has taken away all the pain that was inside my heart."[13] As a young boy, Jeremy saw his father and older brothers repeatedly rape his older sister. After his father was incarcerated, his brothers beat and raped him. Beginning at age ten, he was placed in a series of foster homes where he was frequently punched and raped. At age eighteen, he ended up on the streets with little guidance and no money. He is thriving at Freedom House and wants to help other former foster children who are dealing with similar problems.[14]

Lawndale Community Church

Two thousand miles from the City of Angels, North Lawndale, a community on Chicago's west side, has long struggled with poverty and crime. Concluding in 1966 that it epitomized the plight of blacks living in the inner city, Martin Luther King Jr. occupied a tenement there to publicize the nation's appalling segregation and deplorable urban living conditions. Race riots, inspired by King's assassination in 1968, destroyed many businesses, further devastating North Lawndale's economy. Seven years later, Wayne Gordon, a white teacher and football coach at North Lawndale's Farragut High School, felt called by God to try to transform this community plagued by abandoned storefronts, dilapidated housing, unemployment, crime, and poverty. In 1975 Wayne and his wife Anne moved their family to North Lawndale and founded the Lawndale Community Church, which Gordon still serves as pastor. More than 1,000 families worship each Sunday at this church, whose members have worked since its inception to revitalize the surrounding neighborhood.

Lawndale Church seeks to equip community residents to become disciples of Christ and assist them to obtain jobs, decent housing, affordable

13. "Freedom House Is Open," http://www.dreamcenter.org/uncategorized/freedom-house-is-open/#sthash.UFnucKBK.dpuf.

14. "Against All Odds," http://www.dreamcenter.org/dream-center/against-all-odds/#sthash.pbKLxotn.dpuf.

medical care, and better education for their children. The church has helped build a strip mall, condominiums, and a health clinic. Members have constructed more than 400 affordable apartments in previously abandoned buildings. Their efforts have also helped increase home ownership, high school and college graduation rates, and the job skills and employment opportunities of community residents. By renovating vacated or tax-delinquent buildings and selling them at below market prices, the church has enabled more than 200 low-income families to become homeowners. Church members also teach them how to care for their houses, make repairs, and budget their money. In addition, Lawndale Church assists families experiencing crises and provides temporary housing for homeless families.

Opened in 1984, the Lawndale Christian Health Center treats about 150,000 patients per year, primarily residents of North and South Lawndale. Most North Lawndale patients are single African-American mothers whose predominant problems are diabetes, substance abuse, and HIV/AIDS. South Lawndale, Chicago's largest Mexican-American neighborhood, serves as a gateway to the Midwest for immigrants. Depression and anxiety is common among this community's first generation of women. The health center offers primary medical care, obstetrical services, child immunizations, laboratory services, and aerobics classes.[15]

The center's medical staff seek to meet patients' physical, emotional, and spiritual needs. As patients come to trust doctors, they reveal problems that have contributed to their illnesses. When a mother says, "'I have a headache,' instead of just writing a prescription for Tylenol," Art Jones, the center's director explains, we typically ask, "what's causing the headaches?" The mother often replies, "my kids are being recruited by the gangs." Most medical facilities cannot address this problem, Jones asserts, but our center helps their children participate in church programs and activities that provide an alternative to gangs. In addition, physicians offer to pray with their patients and encourage them to talk with the center's pastoral staff to receive spiritual counseling and emotional support.[16]

In 1995 the church created a residential program to help men who are recovering from addictions or have been recently released from prison. Its participants receive biblical instruction, counseling, and emotional support, and are prepared to find jobs and work conscientiously. After three months in the program, men are assigned jobs with one of the church's

15. Wang, "Faith-Based Clinic."

16. Ibid.

partnering employers. The program also strives to help them improve their marriages and parenting skills. Men who successfully complete nine months in the program can move into another facility where they receive further guidance and are discipled. The program, which currently enrolls fifty men, has aided about 2,500 people since it began. About 90 percent of participants have stopped using drugs or abusing alcohol and have become productive workers and better parents.[17]

One place where these men work is Lou Malnati's pizzeria in Lawndale. The Malnati family, which operates forty-one other eateries in Chicago, has partnered with Lawndale Church since 1996 to provide a full-service family restaurant that uses its profits to fund children's educational and recreational programs in the local community. As the sole sit-down restaurant in Lawndale, it is the only place suitable to have a business lunch or family birthday party and has positively impacted the men who work there.[18]

Lawndale Community Church operates other programs that specifically help children and youth. In 2010 the congregation established the Lawndale Christian Legal Center to aid area youth and young adults who are brought before juvenile and adult criminal courts. By providing competent legal representation, quality social health services, and caring mentors, the center tries to help these individuals overcome the problems that contributed to their criminal acts, change their attitudes and behaviors, and become responsible citizens. Each youth has a case manager who devises an intervention program to help him or her develop short and long-term goals and plan concrete steps to achieve them. The center typically works with youth for three years until their supervision by the criminal justice system ends. The center also sponsors after school and weekend programs that furnish life skills and job training, substance abuse counseling, and academic tutoring to teens who are on probation.[19] Another after school program provides computer instruction, exercise, spiritual nurture, and assistance in completing homework to neighborhood children who are in grades two through six.

The church strives to revitalize North Lawndale by producing a new generation of leaders. It has helped more than 200 community youth graduate from college, more than half of whom have returned to live and

17. "Hope House," http://www.lawndalechurch.org/hope-house.html.

18. "Lawndale Christian Community Church," http://www.lawndalechurch.org/; Konkol, "Lawndale Pizzeria"; Pick, "Pizza on Earth."

19. "Lawndale Christian Legal Center," http://lclc.net/.

work in North Lawndale. Kelly Smith is one of the dozens of young people Lawndale Community Church has groomed to be a neighborhood leader. After graduating from college, he returned to work as a project manager. If church members had not mentored him, Smith declares, he would likely have ended up either incarcerated or dead. Luis Jesus, a pharmacy technician at the Lawndale Christian Health Center, testifies: "Before I got saved, I was on the streets of Chicago gang-banging, selling drugs, [and] dancing." Many other young adult community leaders tell similar stories.[20]

A Jesus Church Family

A third large church whose social ministries greatly benefit children is A Jesus Church Family in Portland, Oregon. Its Hear The Cry ministry strives to "bring compassion and justice" by equipping individuals, communities, and churches to participate in "meaningful, tangible and sustainable efforts that make a difference." Church members focus on three areas in Portland—supporting foster care, aiding refugees, and stopping sex trafficking by partnering with other congregations, government agencies, and community organizations to help every child become "part of a family that accurately reflects the image of God."[21] They engage in social outreach primarily through missional communities—ten to twenty individuals who eat, pray, and volunteer together. About half of the 9,000 members who belong to the three congregations that comprise A Jesus Church Family participate in these groups.[22]

In 2012 A Jesus Church Family and several other Portland congregations decided to mobilize people and resources to help the area's more than 3,000 foster children. Today more than seventy-five churches are working together to transform the city's child welfare system. Cordial relationships have developed between church members and local government officials as they have witnessed each other's deep love for Portland's vulnerable children. Serving as a foster parent is very demanding, and because burnout is common, many foster children move from one placement to another. To support foster parents, these Portland congregations sponsor Foster

20. "Lawndale Community Church." See also Gordon, *Real Hope in Chicago* and Gordon and Perkins, *Making Neighborhoods Whole*.

21. "Hear the Cry" (all quotations except the last phrase), http://www.hearthecry.org/; "A Jesus Church Family," http://ajesuschurch.org/justice/.

22. Phone interview with Mike McDonald, July 20, 2015.

Parents' Night Out. Once a month foster parents can drop off their children at various churches and enjoy a free evening. A Jesus Church Family has also trained about 300 members to provide respite care for foster children so that their parents can have occasional longer breaks.[23]

Hear The Cry has developed other practical ministries that enable participants to assist these vulnerable children. An initiative called Welcome Boxes has supplied more than 10,000 age and gender appropriate boxes to children to help them as they wait for a foster home placement after being removed from their homes. Trained church volunteers also visit with children while they are waiting to receive a new placement. Once children are placed, the church's Foster Closet supplies much needed clothing and other personal items. Having stylish clothes and school supplies can ease their transition to a new school and help children feel better about themselves. Moreover, Hear The Cry sponsors a Royal Family Kids Camp for children who have experienced abuse and neglect. In these and other ways, hundreds of church volunteers are helping bruised and broken children encounter a loving, healing God.[24]

A Jesus Church Family also challenges its members to consider providing foster care for one or more of the hundreds of children who need to be placed every month in the Portland area. While their ultimate goal is for children to be reunited with their biological parents, many church members provide loving, nurturing foster care until this can occur.[25]

In addition, church members have developed close relationships with the county's Department of Human Services' staff. They have listened to their concerns and helped remodel DHS offices to make them more inviting. Trying to be proactive, some members asked DHS if they could meet with parents who were in danger of having their children placed in foster care. DHS supervisors initially said no, but after they got to know these members, they welcomed this preventative approach. Missional group participants have provided financial planning for many such families and repaired their houses, helping these parents, who often feel overburdened and struggle financially, keep their children in their homes.[26]

A Jesus Church Family also ministers to Portland's refugee community. Only seven other American cities take in more refugees per year than

23. "Hear the Cry"; interview with McDonald.

24. Ibid.; interview with McDonald.

25. Ibid.

26. Interview with McDonald.

the 1,000 who arrive there each year. Church leaders emphasize that "most refugees suffer unthinkable tragedy in their homelands and arrive in the US with next to nothing, and knowing no one." Portland's refugees come primarily from Iraq and Somalia. Church members welcome refugees with gift baskets and gift cards, provide transportation, and help them adjust to American life and culture. Numerous missional groups adopt refugee families; they help them set up their apartments, answer their questions, take them grocery shopping, teach them how to use appliances, eat meals with them, help refugees find jobs, and keep in touch with them via phone and social media.[27]

Members of A Jesus Church Family reach out to victims of sex trafficking by participating in three local ministries—Door to Grace (DTG), the Sexual Assault Resource Center (SARC), and Adorned in Grace.[28] Established in 2009 and supported by numerous Portland congregations, DTG helps rescued victims develop the skills they need to live productively. DTG trains married couples and single women to provide short-term and long-term homes for sex trafficking victims. Through these host homes and its REACH (Restore, Educate, Activity, Community, Home) daytime program, DTG supplies instruction, medical assistance, and spiritual nurture.[29]

Created in 1977, SARC works to reduce sexual violence through education, advocacy, and support of victims. Its volunteers staff a 24-hour a day phone line to provide these victims with crisis counseling, resources, and referrals. SARC operates a free clinic that furnishes mental health services and sponsors support groups for victims of sexual assault. SARC also provides classes for both middle school and high school students to teach them how to avoid sexual exploitation.[30]

Adorned in Grace has created two primary enterprises to raise awareness and provide funds "to bring hope and healing to at-risk girls and victims of human trafficking." The Adorned in Grace Bridal and Formalwear Shop redesigns bridal gowns, formal wear, and accessories. The store's profits are used to publicize and prevent sex trafficking or to assist trafficking victims. It partners with the Adorned in Grace Design Studio Outreach to At-Risk Girls where designers, seamstresses, and mentors build personal,

27. "Hear the Cry" (quotation); interview with McDonald.

28 "Hear the Cry"; interview with McDonald.

29. "Door to Grace," http://www.doortograce.org/; "Hear the Cry."

30. "SARC," http://sarcoregon.org/; "Hear the Cry."

loving relationships with vulnerable girls to help them avoid the horrors of the sex trade.[31]

Mid-sized Congregations

Many medium-size congregations engage in similar ministries to these large churches. For example, in 2002 the nondenominational River Church Community relocated from the suburbs to downtown San Jose, California, to enable its parishioners to develop relationships with and minister to and alongside of people who differ from them culturally and socio-economically. Its members strive to express Jesus' concern for compassion and justice in a variety of ways. A significant number of them have moved to the Washington/Tamien neighborhood, a low-income Latino community adjacent to downtown San Jose.[32]

By working with the Heritage Home in downtown San Jose, the church seeks to furnish housing and services for homeless pregnant women. Women live at the home while they are pregnant and for several months after giving birth. They take prenatal classes and receive instruction about the child birth process and parenting, help to break addictions, and assistance to complete their GED. Residents also participate in Bible studies and individual and group counseling and are encouraged to consider adoption.[33]

To enrich the lives of children who live in the Washington/Tamien neighborhood or attend their church, River Church Community opened the Washington Maker Workshop. It uses science, technology, math, and art projects to help children expand their imagination and ingenuity.[34]

In addition, the church's youth group focuses on social justice issues. Group discussions and cross-cultural training teach youth to identify with the poor as Jesus did. In 2015 youth group members participated in the "Walk for Water" to raise money for Water Mission and to simulate the experience of millions of other teens who carry heavy buckets of water for many miles to provide for their families. In conjunction with World Vision's 30 Hour famine, they fasted to raise money to reduce food insecurity,

31. Adorned in Grace," http://www.adornedingrace.org/; "Hear the Cry."

32. "River Church Community," http://www.the-river.org/.

33. Ibid.

34. Ibid.

and they also completed a service project with the Yahama Nation in southern Washington.[35]

The New Heart Community Church, La Mirada, California, is a medium-size church whose members care deeply about indigent children in developing nations. In the first decade of the new millennium, they halted a capital campaign to build a new church to instead fund the construction of an after-care facility in the Philippines for girls and women IJM had liberated from commercial sexual exploitation. They also helped found a facility in Port-au-Prince, Haiti, to protect children from human trafficking and assist victims who have been rescued from sexual slavery.[36]

In 1988 two of San Francisco's houses of worship—Third Baptist Church and Congregation Emanu-El—created a tutoring program called Back on Track. Since then hundreds of volunteers have tutored and mentored more than 3,000 underprivileged students in grades K-12 and helped prepare many of them to attend college. The program focuses on writing, mathematics, science, and reading comprehension across all disciplines. The program also furnishes workshops for parents, a computer lab and library, and cultural enrichment activities. Back on Track seeks to help children grow intellectually and personally, increase their self-confidence, and thrive in college.[37]

Smaller Congregations

Many smaller congregations are also working energetically to improve the lives of low-income children. The New Creation Lutheran Church in Philadelphia, for example, aids a local elementary school by sponsoring special events for students, operating an after-school program, and hosting an annual breakfast to honor teachers and staff. Church members also develop relationships with the leaders of key community organizations and work cooperatively with other houses of worship, the police department, social service agencies, businesses, and health clinics.[38]

35. Ibid.

36. Martin, *The Just Church*; "New Heart Community Church," http://www.newheart.com/.

37. "Third Baptist Church of San Francisco," http://www.thirdbaptist.org/; "Back on Track," http://www.backontracksf.org/.

38. Sider, Olson, and Unruh, *Churches*, 156–59.

First Presbyterian Church of Mt. Holly, New Jersey, helps low-income families primarily by providing better housing conditions. The congregation created Homes of Hope to purchase, renovate, and manage low-cost rental properties in its vicinity. Recognizing that indigent people need instruction about how to live and manage money as well as affordable housing, the church developed a counseling center to provide personal and financial advice. The congregation also helped establish an organization to ensure that the local government and banks follow fair housing policies and reinvest in the community. When families living in Mt. Holly Gardens were forced to sell their homes for less than market value to facilitate gentrification, the church partnered with them and other congregations to help pass a zoning variance. Moreover, this battle eventually led to a Supreme Court decision that other housing advocates have used to provide affordable accommodations for low-income Americans. Before the church founded these social ministries, many parishioners, echoing thousands in other locales, said, "I don't notice any poor people in Mount Holly."[39]

Umbrella Organizations

Countless stories could be told about how churches have significantly improved the lives of children. Consider Billie, a single mother with three children, who lives in Live Oak, Florida. Her children's father, who physically abused her, is in prison. She works two jobs to pay her family's expenses. Her home was dilapidated, and the roof leaked when it rained. Her two teenage daughters shared a shabby futon. At the end of her rope, Billie called Love in the Name of Christ (Love INC), and a church in its network volunteered to help the family. Members found a better home for her to rent. They moved her family into their new home, bought twin beds for the girls, set up their furniture, and supplied food. Because of their loving actions, Billie and her children experienced joy and hope.[40]

Love INC helps churches minister more effectively to their communities. Founded in 1977 by social worker Virgil Gulker, it provides structure, training, and encouragement to congregations whose members want to help the needy in their communities. Its network includes more than 8,600 churches, 9,200 community-based organizations, and 100,000 volunteers who each year meet about two million needs in thirty states. Love INC

39. Ibid., 90–92.

40. "Love INC," www.loveinc.org.

provides congregations with tools to motivate and mobilize parishioners to serve the poor and vulnerable more effectively. It helps pastors and laypeople better understand the problems of the indigent and identify ministries that their communities need. The organization also assists congregations to start these enterprises in response to the biblical mandate to aid the impoverished and powerless. In addition, Love INC teaches churches how to advocate with local governments, agencies, and charities to solve such community problems as lack of medical access, public transportation, and affordable housing.[41]

Another organization that aids churches in ministering to low-income Americans (and poor people around the world) is the Christian Community Development Association. Established by John Perkins and Wayne Gordon in 1989 to help revitalize inner-city neighborhoods, this nationwide network of 1,000 ministries share ideas and best practices through local meetings, regional summits, and national conferences to promote community development.[42] Its mission is "to inspire, train, and connect Christians" to advance "the Kingdom of God by reclaiming and restoring under-resourced communities." Many of its leaders commit to living in a disadvantaged neighborhood for at least ten years to promote its well-being.[43]

What We Can Do

As these examples demonstrate, congregations can do much to help destitute children. Pastors and lay leaders can prod parishioners to pray privately for poor children and sponsor times of corporate prayer for addressing social evils. Ministers can preach sermons about social justice. If your pastor is not doing so, encourage and help equip him or her by providing books and other resources; you can also urge church staff to attend relevant conferences. Sunday school classes and youth groups can study biblical teaching about social justice and explore practical ways to abate them. Congregations can create small groups to analyze and remedy social ills and fill their libraries with books on social justice. Church leaders can assess their members' gifts and skills that can be used to devise and conduct

41. Ibid.

42. "Lawndale Christian Community Church"; "Lawndale Community Church"; Wang, "Faith-Based Clinic."

43. "Christian Community Development Association," http://www.ccda.org/.

social ministries. Members who are law enforcement employees, lawyers, social workers, teachers, medical personnel, counselors, business people, and entrepreneurs especially have expertise and practical experience to contribute. Congregations can also evaluate the resources they possess that they can employ to meet social needs. Church members can investigate the needs of low-income children who live in their local communities and create specific ministries to assist them. They can call attention to social ills that harm children, especially poverty, hunger, domestic violence, human trafficking, and sexual abuse.

If you have a passion for helping children, you can strongly encourage your church to do more. Your church exists to serve as light, salt, and leaven in your community and to advance God's kingdom.[44] Evaluate what your congregation can do most effectively, given its location, resources, and other ministries, to help poor children have a better life. Congregations that are small, have limited resources, or lack expertise or access can work collaboratively with other churches and parachurch and community organizations.[45] Suburban congregations can collaborate with urban ones to provide social and spiritual ministries to low-income families. Churches can also partner with aid organizations in other nations that are working to improve the life circumstances and opportunities of children. Congregations can designate a substantial percentage of their budget to fund social justice enterprises.[46] Congregations should also better equip their volunteers by providing more practical instruction and wise counsel and commend their service."[47] Ideally, congregations whose members feel called to help children should develop ministries that include activities ranging from relief to reform.[48]

44. Rusaw and Swanson, *Externally Focused Church*, 25.

45. Sherman, *Restorers of Hope*, 157–70.

46. Martin, *The Just Church*, 122–30; 153, 162.

47. Mallory, *Equipping Church*; Wilson, *Church Volunteers*.

48. Sider, Olson, and Unruh, *Churches*, 86–88. See also Sider et al., *Linking Arms*.

14

The Moral Equivalent of War

The fact that there are still 1.2 billion people in extreme poverty
is a stain on our collective conscience.

WORLD BANK GROUP PRESIDENT JIM YONG KIM.

If America does not use her vast resources of wealth to end poverty
and make it possible for all of God's children to have the basic necessities of life,
she . . . will go to hell.

MARTIN LUTHER KING JR.

From everyone who has been given much, much will be demanded; and from
the one who has been entrusted with much, much more will be asked.

LUKE 12:48

In his famous 1910 essay, Harvard philosopher William James argued that humanity must fight as vigorously to promote peace as some nations had to wage war. James urged people to adopt "a shared objective" that could "elicit the same willingness to sacrifice, and the same disciplined and purposeful ethos, as military conflict does, yet direct them toward entirely peaceful purposes." "So far," James lamented, "war has been the only force that can discipline a whole community."[1]

Unfortunately, more than a century later, James's observation is still true. Thus far no peaceful humanitarian crusade has elicited the same energy, enthusiasm, and total mobilization of people and resources as has waging war. The Civilian Conservation Corps, the Peace Corps, and other government efforts have sought to transform "military values into non-military virtues." But none of these has been able to "discipline a whole community" or create a powerful national purpose.[2]

The suffering and stunting of human potential that child poverty causes, the world's abundant resources, and biblical directives compel us to make abolishing child poverty that common goal. Its elimination requires a full-scale frontal assault. While Christians debate the best ways to reduce poverty, we can agree that God cares deeply about the indigent, we have an obligation to help them, and destitution is "an affront to human dignity." Their poverty prevents billions of children from fulfilling their full potential as God's image-bearers.[3]

Scriptural Teaching

Almost four hundred biblical passages express God's passionate concern for widows, orphans, aliens, the homeless, hungry, disabled, sick, and vulnerable. In Deut 15:11, for example, God commanded the Israelites to be generous toward the poor and needy. He defends "the fatherless and oppressed" (Ps 10:18). God is the "father of orphans and protector of widows" (Ps 68:5, NRV). God instructed the Israelites to cancel debts every seventh year, restore property to its original owners in the Year of Jubilee, permit the poor to harvest the corners of fields, and establish a food bank to help feed widows, orphans, and aliens (Deut 24:18–22; Exod 23:10–11). These practices were intended to enable families to provide for themselves and the needs of the indigent to be met.[4] The Bible also plainly states that God abhors injustice. Amos proclaims: "Hate evil, love good; maintain justice

1. James, "Moral Equivalent of War," 468 (second quotation); McClay, "Moral Equivalent of War?" (first quotation).

2. McClay, "Moral Equivalent of War?"

3. Griffiths and Tan, "Fighting Poverty," 181–82.

4. Ibid., 183.

in the courts" (5: 15). Jeremiah denounces the rich who do not justly judge "the cause of the fatherless" or "defend the rights of the needy" (5:27–28).

Aiding the indigent is a major biblical theme. Those who are "gracious to the needy" honor God (Prov 14:31). "Suppose a brother or a sister is without clothes and daily food. If one of you says to them, 'Go in peace; keep warm and well fed,' but does nothing about their physical needs, what good is it?" (Jas 2: 15–16). First John 3:17 declares: "If anyone has material possessions and sees a brother or sister in need but has no pity on them, how can the love of God be in that person?" And we will be held accountable. Jesus, in his parable of the sheep and goats, tells his hearers that those who do not take care of the less fortunate will be cursed. Ezekiel 16:49 asserts that Sodom was destroyed because its inhabitants were "arrogant, overfed and unconcerned" and refused to "help the poor and needy."

Abolishing Child Poverty

Numerous actions can help abolish child poverty. We should pray faithfully, study carefully, give generously, live modestly, volunteer enthusiastically, invest and shop prudently, support candidates who strive to eliminate poverty, advocate passionately, and work to reform social structures.

Prayer

As Jim Martin argues, prayer is essential "in the battle for justice."[5] We should pray faithfully and fervently that God will topple tyrants, break the chains of oppression, and provide food for the hungry. We should beseech God to motivate millions to use our resources wisely, to combat injustice, and to work to improve the lives of children. As we deal with roadblocks, resistance, and unfavorable results, we must continually seek God's guidance and assistance. When we pray for poor children, we should listen carefully to God's response to see what he is directing us to do. To effectively assist destitute children, we need the empowering of the Holy Spirit. Some aid organizations help guide their supporters' prayers by regularly sending them emails with specific requests.

5. Martin, *The Just Church*, 194.

Study

To help the world's impoverished children, we need to understand their problems and potential solutions. Hopefully, reading this book has given you deeper insights into both of these matters. Thankfully, many other very helpful books, articles, and websites supply essential information about the plight of poor children and steps we can take to aid them. Many of these resources are cited in our bibliography. In addition, playing the simulations, doing the exercises, watching the videos, and perusing the websites of the organizations listed in our online appendix (http://www.sufferthechildrenbook.org/) can increase your knowledge about indigent children and give you a greater passion to help them. Encourage others to read this book and act on its suggestions. Investigate the conditions of poor children in your own community and organizations that are working to improve them.

Giving

We also need to give more judiciously and generously. As Nicholas Kristof and Sheryl WuDunn argue, "people rarely give money away as intelligently as they make it" and, as a result, "much charitable giving isn't very effective."[6] Christians should carefully distinguish between aid and development, and whenever possible, focus on the latter. When an earthquake, tsunami, drought, or war strikes, we should provide immediate but temporary relief. Development assistance, however, equips people to be self-sustaining by providing them with education, vocational training, loans, or jobs. Rather than dispensing charity, we should help the poor help themselves.[7] In deciding which organizations to support, Ronald Sider, the founder of Evangelicals for Social Action, suggests donating to "truly indigenous," holistic projects that "work through and foster the growth of local churches." We should also support projects that will be self-sustaining after the initial seed capital is exhausted and that benefit the poorest of the poor.[8] Currently, only about a third of all charitable gifts go to help

6. Kristof and Wudunn, *Path*, 10.

7. See Greer, "Stop Helping Us," 322–28; Lupton, *Toxic Charity*; Bolton, *Africa Doesn't Matter*.

8. Sider, *Rich Christians*, 194.

the world's most destitute people.[9] Finally, Christians should donate to organizations that operate efficiently and wisely.

In addition to giving prudently, Christians should also give generously to assist the impoverished. Doing so fulfills biblical exhortations, greatly aids the poor, substantially benefits givers, and strengthens communities. The biblical basis for assisting the destitute has already been described. The essential role that money plays in improving the lives of poor children has been explained in other chapters. So here we focus on the many benefits givers receive.

Rescuing an individual from a burning building or from drowning would undoubtedly be very satisfying. Few of us will ever have that direct opportunity, but we can save (or at least significantly enhance) the lives of poor children through our donations. The "effective altruism" movement, led by Princeton philosopher Peter Singer, challenges people to use their financial contributions to make the optimum difference in the world. What has a greater impact than helping a child avoid a major illness, receive an education, escape poverty, and realize her potential?

Research indicates that those who practice generosity enjoy more happiness, better health, and a greater sense of satisfaction and purpose in life. Numerous studies detail how giving liberally reduces people's stress, enhances their physical health, and boosts their self-image. Charitable giving also strengthens people's social connections, improves relationships, and increases longevity. Moreover, focusing on giving rather than receiving shifts our attention away from ourselves and obeys biblical commandments to serve others.[10]

God has designed the world so that giving provides many blessings. Scripture repeatedly makes this point. Proverbs 11:24–25 declares, "A generous person will prosper; whoever refreshes others will be refreshed." The Psalmist proclaims, "Good will come to those who are generous and lend freely, who conduct their affairs with justice" (112:5). The Apostle Paul asserts, "Whoever sows sparingly will also reap sparingly, and whoever sows generously will also reap generously" (2 Cor 9:6). In Acts 20:35 he quotes the words of Jesus: "It is more blessed to give than to receive."

9. *Household Charitable Giving*, 30

10. Firestone, "Benefits of Generosity"; Brown, "Social Support Hypothesis," 49–57; Post, "Altruism, Happiness, and Health," 66–77; Nauert, "Doing for Others"; Collett and Morrissey, "Generosity"; Szalavitz, "Helping Others."

People around the world report that they feel good when they use their financial resources to help others. One cross-cultural study found that in almost every country people who donated to charity were happier. Remarkably, giving to charity increased an individual's happiness as much as a doubling of her household income.[11]

Sociologists Christian Smith and Hilary Davidson feature many case studies in *The Paradox of Generosity* to illustrate the benefits of generosity. Individuals who give generously and volunteer regularly feel good because they know they are improving others' lives and adhering to high moral standards. Munificence, they argue, also increases people's belief that they are contributing to positive outcomes in the world, prevents them from being self-absorbed, boosts their optimism, strengthens their relationships, and increases their knowledge about the world.[12] Moreover, charitable giving augments people's sense of meaning, enables them to support causes they value, and connects them with others who have the same passions and interests.[13] Strikingly, American Christians who tithe typically have healthier family finances than those who do not.[14] Charity can also help increase a community's trust and social cohesion. In *Bowling Alone: The Collapse and Revival of American Community* Robert Putnam describes how giving and volunteering strengthen social networks and enriches their communities.

To date, 156 of the world's richest individuals or couples have signed a pledge to use most of their wealth to advance philanthropic causes.[15] Bill Gates and Warren Buffet have promised to donate more than 90 percent of their fortunes to help the less fortunate. They explain: "We are inspired by the example set by millions of people who give generously (and often at great personal sacrifice) to make the world a better place." Gates and Buffet hope to stimulate many other people with substantially less financial resources to donate more money to charitable causes of all kinds and to discuss the best ways to help the needy. They argue that "grassroots movements are proving every day how a single individual, regardless of wealth, can make a lasting impact on the lives of others."[16]

11. Aknin et al., "Prosocial Spending," 635–52. See also Dunn, Aknin, and Norton, "Spending Money," 1687–88; Piliavin, "Doing Well by Doing Good," 227–47.

12. Smith and Davidson, *Paradox of Generosity*, 53–85.

13. Brooks, *Who Really Cares*, 143–44.

14. Schapiro, "Christians Who Tithe."

15. "Giving Pledge," http://givingpledge.org/index.html.

16. Ibid.

If all 400 billionaires on the Forbes list of the world's wealthiest individuals signed and fulfilled this pledge, Scott Todd points out, it would make about $600 billion available to charities. If this amount was dispensed over a twenty-year period, philanthropic enterprises would receive $30 billion per year. Strikingly, however, if the 138 million American Christians who attend church at least twice a month tithed, charities would receive a staggering $250 billion per year. If ordinary American Christians gave 10 percent of their post-tax income, Christian Smith and Michael Emerson add, they could accomplish "massive and unprecedented spiritual, social, cultural, and economic change."[17]

Sadly, however, various surveys indicate that only 3 to 8 percent of Americans donate 10 percent or more of their income. Despite the many benefits generosity brings to others and themselves, most Americans are not big-hearted. One survey found that 86 percent of Americans give less than 2 percent of their income to charity. Although regular church attenders tend to be more generous than other Americans, the percentage of tithers is still very low. Moreover, most individuals with higher incomes do not increase the percentage they give to charities.[18]

Volunteering

Volunteering one's time and expertise can also significantly help the world's poor and provide the same emotional benefits as generous giving does. Retired individuals usually have more time to volunteer, but all of us can use our talents and time to help the indigent. Many of the world's 1.5 million nonprofits actively solicit volunteers, and thousands of these organizations work to improve the lives of destitute children. Dozens of them are described in our online appendix. You can also consult volunteermatch.org or idealist.org to find organizations that are best suited to your interests and can use your skills and experience.[19]

In a typical year, one-quarter of Americans volunteer. About 10 percent of Americans volunteer one to ten hours per month; another 10 percent volunteer eleven to thirty-nine hours per month; and less than 4 percent volunteer more than forty hours per month.[20] Christians, especially

17. Todd, *Hope Rising*, 164–65; Smith, Emerson, and Snell, *Passing the Plate*, 11.

18. Smith and Davidson, *Paradox of Generosity*, 100–04, 11.

19. See Kadlec, "Giving Back."

20. Smith and Davidson, *Paradox of Generosity*, 105–06; "Volunteering in the United

those who attend church regularly, are more likely than other Americans to engage in volunteer activities.[21] If more Americans devoted their time and energy to myriads of worthwhile projects, including collecting and distributing food, teaching, and tutoring, the benefits to children would be immense.[22]

Volunteering has many physical, psychological, and spiritual benefits. Numerous studies show that those who help others have a greater sense of purpose, focus less on their own problems, experience more happiness and less depression, feel more self-confident, and enjoy many physical benefits.[23] Volunteering also provides an opportunity for us to give back and to see God working in people's lives.[24] Moreover, it enables us to meet interesting individuals, develop friendships, and have challenging and meaningful experiences.

When you analyze where to volunteer to aid children (or alleviate other social ills), consider three things: the gifts God has given you for ministry, the world's—or your community's—greatest needs, and the issues you care most deeply about. This can help you find an organization or ministry through which you can serve faithfully and fruitfully.

Investing

Christians can also help the poor by investing in socially responsible ways. Most people invest to achieve a variety of purposes—to pay for their children's education, provide funds for retirement, and attain financial security. At the same time, these investments also positively impact the world by providing firms with capital to create valuable products, supply beneficial services, and furnish jobs. Christians can buy stock in companies that do not profit from munitions, gambling, alcohol, tobacco, or pornography and seek to protect the environment, pay livable wages, and aid the indigent. Our investments can also help supply microloans to the impoverished who cannot obtain credit through banks. While the return on these investments

States," http://www.bls.gov/news.release/volun.nro.htm.

21. "Charitable Giving, Volunteerism."

22. "Charitable Giving Statistics," http://www.nptrust.org/philanthropic-resources/charitable-giving-statistics/.

23. See Luks and Payne, *Healing Power*; Pearsall, *Pleasure Prescription*; Schwartz et al., "Altruistic Social Interest Behaviors," 778–85.

24. Hybels, *Volunteer Revolution*, 54–55.

will not be as great as those on high-yield mutual funds, we can help the poor while still preparing adequately to meet our own future needs.

Several organizations are actively working to increase socially responsible investing. The Interfaith Center on Corporate Responsibility evaluates "the social impacts of corporate operations and policies" and challenges "the world's most powerful companies" to assess the impact they have on "the world's most vulnerable communities." This organization uses dialogue, roundtables, and resolutions, and, as a last resort, calls for disinvestment, to prod corporations to increase their efforts to improve global health, increase food security and water stewardship, end human trafficking, and protect the environment.[25] The Center for Sustainable Investment Education provides a variety of resources to help investors, investment advisors, and consultants determine how to allot their funds to companies that are having a positive social impact.[26] Christians who seek guidance in choosing where to invest can also consult Social Funds, which bills itself as "the largest personal financial site devoted to socially responsible investing." It provides descriptions of hundreds of domestic equity funds and global funds that practice socially responsible investing. In addition, it supplies corporate sustainability reports for dozens of firms to help guide potential investors.[27] Books can also help Christians determine how to invest in socially-conscious ways. Especially notable are Tom Nowak's *Low Fee Socially Responsible Investing* and Ann Logue's *Socially Responsible Investing for Dummies*. Currently only about one of every six dollars under professional management is screened for ethical and social factors prior to investment.[28]

Living More Simply

By living below our means, millions of Christians can share more of our financial resources with others and support organizations that empower the indigent to help themselves. By buying smaller, less expensive homes, purchasing cheaper, more fuel efficient cars, taking fewer, less costly vacations, and reducing our spending on entertainment and household furnishings,

25. "Interfaith Center on Corporate Responsibility," http://www.iccr.org/.

26. "Center for Sustainable Investment," http://www.ussif.org/education.

27. "Social Funds," http://www.socialfunds.com/.

28. Reisner, "Socially Responsible Investing." See also Chamberlain, "Socially Responsible Investing."

we can give substantially more to help poor children. Scott Todd points out that if the 138 million American Christians who attend church regularly and say that their faith is very important to them were an independent nation, our collective earnings of $2.5 trillion per year would make us the seventh richest nation on earth. Imagine what American Christians could do to alleviate child poverty if we lived more simply (or sacrificially). Spending less on ourselves would enable us to give more to the indigent. The New Testament exhorts us to make sharing with the destitute a way of life. Recognizing the enormous needs of the poor and the world's finite resources, we can manage our money carefully and spend more frugally so that we can give more generously.

Admittedly, adopting a simpler lifestyle is difficult in a consumer-oriented society that entices us to want more, pressures us to spend, and measures our self-worth by how much stuff we possess.[29] Janet Luhrs argues that simple living is not about leading a Spartan existence but rather about making deliberate, thoughtful choices about limiting our spending. She supplies strategies, resources, and inspiring profiles of people who have done this to create richer lives.[30]

In *Rich Christians in an Age of Hunger*, Ronald Sider challenges Christians to adopt "a personal lifestyle that could be sustained over a long period of time if it were shared by everyone in the world." He urges us to "distinguish between necessities and luxuries." Sider exhorts Christians to avoid spending to enhance our social status, feed our pride, or remain fashionable. He offers many practical suggestions. We can reduce our food budget by planting a garden, joining a food co-op, fasting regularly, and eating less meat. We can lower our energy consumption by keeping our thermostat at 68 degrees or lower, carpooling, and riding bicycles. Christians can decrease our consumption of nonrenewable natural resources by not buying products that are designed to wear out quickly and by sharing appliances, tools, and other items.[31] That American pets eat better and receive better health care than do many children in the developing world, John Alexander argues, is obscene.[32] Jesus said considerably more about possessions than any other topic. He repeatedly warned that many are tempted to worship mammon and that people's stuff can preoccupy and even enslave them.

29. E.g., Shi, *Simple Life*; Schor, *Overspent American*; de Graaf and Wann, *Affluenza*.

30. Luhrs, *Simple Living Guide*, xiv, xviii.

31. Sider, *Rich Christians*, 191–93; quotation from 191.

32. Alexander, *Your Money*, 40.

Christians can also practice ethical shopping by buying from companies that employ the poor to make products, pay livable wages, and use their resources to aid the indigent. Our purchasing decisions can influence the approach and activities of companies, prompting them to avoid certain actions and engage in others. Several sites can assist us in this process. The Ethical Shopping Guide, for example, recommends numerous products, brands, and firms in a wide variety of areas, including clothing and shoes, food and drink, furniture and home goods, and toys, based on their protection of the environment, refusal to use forced labor, and ethical treatment of employees.[33] Shopping for a Better World rates companies based on their corporate social responsibility performance.[34] Helpful books include *The Good Shopping Guide* and Ellis Jones's *The Better World Shopping Guide #5*.

Transforming Social Structures

To improve the lives of indigent children, Christians must also work to transform the social structures that deny people equal justice and opportunities—social arrangements and policies that keep them poorly educated, fail to protect their lives and property, and contribute to their unemployment and imprisonment. As Martin Luther King Jr. argued, emulating the Good Samaritan by personally aiding those who are beaten, robbed, and exploited on life's highway is "only an initial act." We must also work to ensure that travelers on the Jericho Road are not attacked, mugged, or oppressed.[35] We must work to change the circumstances that produce poverty. While operating food pantries, starting prison ministries, and volunteering at medical clinics is valuable and commendable, Christians must also help all children receive a quality education, be equipped to procure a job that pays a livable wage, and have access to preventative health care. We must also denounce law enforcement and judicial sentencing practices that discriminate on the basis of race, sex, or class. In short, Christians must work to change unjust social structures around the world that "favor the

33. "Ethical Shopping Guide," http://theartofsimple.net/shopping/. See also "Shop Ethical!" http://www.ethical.org.au/; "Ethical Shopping," http://www.ethicalshopping.com/.

34. "Shopping for a Better World," http://www.shoppingforabetterworld.com/.

35. King Jr., "Beyond Vietnam."

powerful at the expense of the powerless, the rich at the expense of the poor, and the greedy at the expense of the needy."[36]

Federal prosecutor John Richmond argues that changing many of the practices that harm poor children in today's world requires confrontation and conflict, an approach that most Christians avoid as acrimonious, anxiety-engendering, unproductive, and unbiblical. However, Jesus often directly challenged the systemic religious and social evils of his day.[37] As King contended, "true peace is not merely the absence of tension: it is the presence of justice." Few people readily surrender their prerogatives, relinquish their power, or renounce their vested interests. Racial and gender justice has been attained only by vociferously and repeatedly denouncing discrimination and enacting laws to provide it. Similarly, ending child poverty requires explicitly attacking the social institutions and practices that cause and sustain it.

Conclusion

To abolish poverty, we must change not only the moral landscape and institutional structures, but individual attitudes. Several factors inhibit us from acting: a "blaming the victim" mentality; the desire to avoid conflict; recognition that efforts to alleviate destitution require substantial time, energy, or sacrifice; belief that our resources are inadequate and that the impediments are too great; uncertainty about how best to proceed; and our sinfulness. We must repudiate perspectives that portray the destitute as obstacles, burdens, embarrassments, or objects of reform. We must avoid stereotyping the poor and assuming that they cannot make good decisions. Many Christians do little to aid the indigent because they lack information, believe more can be accomplished if they wait until they have more time and resources, or consider poverty to be immutable. This perspective produces paralysis. If we rely on our abilities and resources, we will feel powerless and too intimidated to act to end global poverty. If, however, we depend on God's wisdom, strength, and resources, we can substantially reduce it.[38]

36. Edelman, "Charity." See also Offutt, et al., *Advocating for Justice*.

37. Interview with John Richmond at Grove City College on February 24, 2015; Richmond, Chapel Lecture, Grove City College, February 24, 2015; King, *Stride Toward Freedom*, 40.

38. Richmond, Chapel Lecture.

During the eighth century BCE, wealthy Israelites enjoyed a period of unparalleled prosperity. They reclined on ivory couches, drank expensive wines, imported costly wares, and owned vacation homes. Because they were affluent, comfortable, and secure, they assumed they were righteous. However, they failed to help the poor, hungry, and widows. The prophet Amos denounced them, proclaiming, "Woe to those who are at ease in Zion" (Amos 6:1, ESV).[39] Sadly, many Christians are similarly living comfortably in America (and other post-industrial nations) while the impoverished in our midst and in developing countries languish. Millions of poor children and adults do not have enough to eat or clean water to drink, do not receive an education, suffer from preventable diseases, have no jobs, and cannot realize their potential.

Most affluent people are not hard-hearted. Rather, few of us have much direct contact with the poor or know how to help the indigent effectively.[40] This book has introduced you to the poor and their problems. It has discussed dozens of ways to assist the destitute. The massiveness of the problem leads many to think that despite their awareness of global poverty and desire to help, they cannot effectively do so. Small actions and modest sums, however, do make a difference. Choose one of the solutions we present for ending child poverty—alleviating hunger, providing clean water, improving parenting, education, or criminal justice systems, reducing violence and gangs, ending human trafficking, promoting economic development, protecting property rights, sponsoring or adopting children, serving as a foster parent, or raising the wages of the poor—and work actively to achieve this objective. As discussed, you can do this through your business, church, the government, or hundreds of aid organizations.

History shows that individuals do make a difference. Our book profiles many who have. Consider one more. As a twelve-year-old, Zach Hunter launched a campaign titled "Loose Change to Loosen Chains" to educate people about and to raise money to abolish contemporary slavery. Today many student groups throughout the world participate in this campaign. At age fifteen, he published *Be the Change*, which profiles people around the planet who are making a difference. Every year he speaks to hundreds of groups about human rights violations and the plight of the poor.[41]

39. See Amos, "At Ease in Zion."

40. Kristof, *Path*, 306.

41. "Zach Hunter," https://growingleaders.com/about/keynote-speakers/zach-hunter/.

Christ calls us to minister to the indigent. He declared, "the Son of Man did not come to be served, but to serve" (Matt 20:28) and gave us a marvelous example. Jesus told his disciples: "Anyone who wants to be first must be the very last, and the servant of all" (Mark 9:35). English essayist John Ruskin declared, if you believe in God's kingdom, "you must do more than pray for it, you must work" to bring it. After interacting with suffering Korean children, Bob Pierce, the founder of both World Vision and Samaritan's Purse, wrote: "Let my heart be broken with the things that break the heart of God." "If our lives do not reflect compassion for the poor," David Platt argues in *Radical*, "there is reason to wonder if Christ is really in us at all."[42] May God set our hearts on fire to build his kingdom by abolishing child poverty.

42. Platt, *Radical*, 111.

Bibliography

n in 1 and 2

Adams, Diane. "The Quest for Quality Childcare." In *Parenthood in America: Underpaid, Undervalued, Under Siege*, edited by Jack Westman, 150–57. Madison: University of Wisconsin Press, 2001.

"Africa's Homeless Widows." *New York Times*, June 16, 2004. Online: http://www.nytimes.com/2004/06/16/opinion/africa-s-homeless-widows.html.

"Africa's Land Reform Policies." *World Bank*, July 22, 2013. Online: http://www.worldbank.org/en/region/afr/publication/securing-africas-land-for-shared-prosperity.

Ahern, Laurie. "Orphanages Are No Place for Children." *Washington Post*, August 9, 2013. Online: http://www.washingtonpost.com/opinions/orphanages-are-no-place-forchildren/2013/08/09/6d502fb0-fadd-11e2-a369-d1954abcb7e3_story.html.

Ahu-Ghaida, Dina, and Stephan Klasen. *The Economic and Human Development Costs of Missing the Millennium Development Goal on Gender Equity*. Washington DC: World Bank, 2004.

Aknin, Lara, et al. "Prosocial Spending and Well-Being: Cross-Cultural Evidence for a Psychological Universal." *Journal of Personality and Social Psychology* 104 (2013) 635–52.

Alexander, John. *Your Money or Your Life: A New Look at Jesus' View of Wealth and Power*. San Francisco: Harper & Row, 1986.

Alexander, Karl, Doris Entwisle, and Linda Steffel Olson. "Lasting Consequences of the Summer Learning Gap." *American Sociological Review* 72 (2007) 167–80.

———. *The Long Shadow: Family Background, Disadvantaged Urban Youth, and the Transition to Adulthood*. New York: Russell Sage, 2014.

———. "Urban Poverty, in Black and White." *CNN*, July 11, 2014. Online: http://www.cnn.com/2014/07/11/opinion/alexander-olson-poor-urban-whites/index.html?hpt=hp_bn7.

Allegretto, Sylvia. "Credible Research Designs for Minimum Wage Studies." Online: http://ftp.iza.org/dp7638.pdf.

Alvarez, Ana Cecilia. "Crushers Club Fights for Chicago." *The Daily Beast*, January 14, 2014. Online: http://www.thedailybeast.com/witw/articles/2014/01/14/crushers-club-fights-for-chicago-youth.html.

Amato, Paul. "The Impact of Family Formation Change on the Well-Being of the Next Generation." *Future of Children* 15 (2005) 75–96.

"America after 3 PM." *After School Alliance*, October 2014. Online: http://www.afterschoolalliance.org/documents/AA3PM-2014/AA3PM_Key_Findings.pdf.

Amos, Lynn Tatum. "At Ease in Zion: What It Means to Be God's People." *Seeds Publisher*. Online: http://www.seedspublishers.org/worship/speaking-of-hunger-sermons-of-challenge-and-hope/at-ease-in-zion-what-it-means-to-be-gods-people.

Angrist, Joshua, et al. "Who Benefits from KIPP?" *Journal of Policy Analysis and Management* 31 (2012) 837–60.

Ashe, Jeffrey, and Candace Nelson. "Introduction." In *Savings Groups at the Frontier*, edited by Candace Nelson, 1–12. Rugby, UK: Practical Action, 2013.

Ashe, John. "Remarks: Special High-Level Event on 'Improving the Coordination of Efforts against Trafficking in Persons.'" *United Nations*, July 14, 2014. Online: http://www.un.org/en/ga/president/68/pdf/statements/7142014Special%20highlevel%20event%20on%20World%20Day%20against%20Trafficking%20in%20Persons_final.pdf.

Baklimah, Satyam, and Mfoniso Umoh. "A Sustainable Access to Financial Services for Investment (SAFI) Project." http://savings-revolution.org/doclib/.

Bales, Kevin. *Disposable People: New Slavery in the Global Economy*. Berkeley: University of California Press, 2012.

———. "How to Combat Modern Slavery." *TedTalks*, March 2010. Online: https://www.ted.com/talks/kevin_bales_how_to_combat_modern_slavery/transcript?language=en.

Banerjee, Abhijit, et al. "The Miracle of Microfinance? Evidence from a Randomized Evaluation." *MIT*, March 2014. Online: http://economics.mit.edu/files/5993.

Banerjee, Abhijit, and Esther Duflo. *Poor Economics: A Radical Rethinking of the Way to Fight Global Poverty*. New York: PublicAffairs, 2011.

Bare, John. "Millennials Will Reinvent Charity." *CNN*, June 9, 2013. Online: http://www.cnn.com/2013/06/09/opinion/bare-millennials-charity/.

Barnes, Isaac. "Why I Cheated Families in Poverty." *Hope International*, January 5, 2015. Online: http://blog.hopeinternational.org/2015/01/05/why-i-cheated-families-in-poverty/.

Barnes, Sandra. *The Cost of Being Poor: A Comparative Study of Life in Poor Urban Neighborhoods in Gary, Indiana*. Albany: State University of New York Press, 2005.

Barone, Diane. *Narrowing the Literacy Gap: What Works in High-Poverty Schools*. New York: Guilford, 2006.

Bartle, Phil. "Factors of Poverty: The Big Five." *Community Empowerment Collective*, June 16, 2013. Online: http://cec.vcn.bc.ca/cmp/modules/emp-pov.htm.

Bateman, Milford. *Why Doesn't Microfinance Work? The Destructive Rise of Local Neoliberalism*. London: Zed, 2010.

Bearak, Max, and Lau Gamio, "Everything You Ever Wanted to Know about the U.S. Foreign Assistance Budget." *Washington Post*, October 18, 2016. Online: https://www.washingtonpost.com/graphics/world/which-countries-get-the-most-foreign-aid/.

Bearden, Allison. "When Microfinance Shakes Hands with Education." *Credit Suisse*, January 2015. Online: https://www.credit-suisse.com/us/en/about-us/responsibility/news-stories/articles/news-and-expertise/2015/01/en/when-microfinance-shakes-hands-with-education- main.html.

Becker, Amy Julia. "School Choice of a Different Kind." *Christianity Today* 56 (2012) 22–26.

Befus, David. "Discovering a Role in God's Provision: Sustainable Economic Development for the Church and the Poor." In *Working with the Poor: New Insights and Learnings from Development Practitioners*, edited by Bryant Myers, 81–93. Colorado Springs: Authentic, 2008.

Bellefeuille, Neil. "Stoves, Carbon Credits, Profits and the Poor." Marc Gunther Personal Blog, June 19, 2011. Online: http://www.marcgunther.com/stoves-carbon-credits-profits-and-the-poor/.

Bellew, Rosemary, and Elizabeth King. "Educating Women: Lessons from Experience." In *Women's Education in Developing Countries: Barriers, Benefits, and Policies*, edited by Elizabeth King and M. Anne Hill, 285–326. Baltimore: John Hopkins University Press, 1998.

Besley, Timothy, and Robin Burgess. "Halving Global Poverty." *Journal of Economic Perspectives* 17 (2003) 3–22.

"A Better Mattress: Microfinance Focuses on Lending. Now the Industry is Turning to Deposits." *The Economist,* March 11, 2010. Online: http://www.economist.com/node/15663834.

Bidwell, Allie. "Vocation High Schools: Career Path or Kiss of Death?" *US News,* May 2, 2014. Online: http://www.usnews.com/news/articles/2014/05/02/the-return-of-vocational-high-schools-more-options-or-the-kiss-of-death.

Bishop, Matthew, and Michael Green. *Philanthrocapitalism*. London: Bloomsbury, 2008.

Bittman, Mark. "How to Feed the World." *New York Times,* October 15, 2013. Online: http://www.nytimes.com/2013/10/15/opinion/how-to-feed-the-world.html?pagewanted=all&_r=0&pagewanted=print.

———. "Let's Address the State of Food." *New York Times,* January 20, 2015. Online: http://www.nytimes.com/2015/01/20/opinion/lets-address-the-state-of-food.html?hp&action.

Blair, Clancy, and C. Cybele Raver. "Child Development in the Context of Adversity: Experiential Canalization of Brain and Behavior." *American Psychologist* 67 (2012) 309–18.

Blattman, Christopher. "Let Them Eat Cash." *New York Times,* June 30, 2014. Online: http://www.nytimes.com/2014/06/30/opinion/let-them-eat-cash.html?emc=eta1&_r=2.

Blow, Charles. "How Expensive It Is to Be Poor." *New York Times,* January 19, 2015. Online: http://www.nytimes.com/2015/01/19/opinion/charles-blow-how-expensive-it-is-to-be-poor.html.

Bobonis, Gustavo, Edward Miguel, and Charu Puri-Sharma. "Iron Deficiency Anemia and School Participation." *Journal of Human Resources* 41 (2006) 692–721.

Bolton, Giles. *Africa Doesn't Matter.* New York: Arcade, 2008.

Books, Sue. *Poverty and Schooling in the U.S.: Contexts and Consequences.* Mahwah, NJ: Lawrence Erlbaum, 2004.

Borlaug, Norman. "The Green Revolution, Peace, and Humanity." *Nobel Prize,* December 11, 1970. Online: http://www.nobelprize.org/nobel_prizes/peace/laureates/1970/borlaug-lecture.html.

Bornstein, David. "Energizing the Green Revolution in Africa." *New York Times,* June 6, 2015. Online: http://opinionator.blogs.nytimes.com/2015/06/26/energizing-the-green-revolution-in-africa/?_r=0.

Boyd, Donald, et al. "Explaining the Short Careers of High-Achieving Teachers in Schools with Low-Performing Students." *American Economic Review* 95 (2005) 166–71.

Boyd, Terry. "Tilapia Fish Tacos." *Christian Science Monitor*, June 23, 2011. Online: http://www.csmonitor.com/The-Culture/Food/Stir-It-Up/2011/0623/Tilapia-fish-tacos.

Briggs, Xavier de Souza, Susan Popkin, and John Goering. *Moving to Opportunity: The Story of an American Experiment to Fight Ghetto Poverty*. New York: Oxford University Press, 2010.

Brooks, Arthur. *Who Really Cares: The Surprising Truth about Compassionate Conservatism: America's Charity Divide—Who Gives, Who Doesn't, and Why It Matters*. New York: Basic, 2006.

Brooks, David. "The Inequality Problem." *New York Times*, January 17, 2014. Online: http://www.nytimes.com/2014/01/17/opinion/brooks-the-inequality-problem.html?hp&rref=opinion.

———. "Support Our Students." *New York Times*, January 20, 2015. Online: http://www.nytimes.com/2015/01/20/opinion/david-brooks-support-our-students.html.

Brooks-Gunn, Jeanne, and Greg J. Duncan. "The Effects of Poverty on Children." *Children and Poverty* 7 (1997) 55–71.

Brown, Stephanie. "An Altruistic Reanalysis of the Social Support Hypothesis: The Health Benefits of Giving." *New Directions for Philanthropic Fundraising* 42 (2003) 49–57.

Bruni, Frank. "Can We Interest You in Teaching?" *New York Times*, August 8, 2015. Online: http://www.nytimes.com/2015/08/12/opinion/frank-bruni-can-we-interest-you-in-teaching.html.

———. "Toward Better Teachers." *New York Times*, October 29, 2014. Online: http://www.nytimes.com/2014/10/29/opinion/frank-bruni-toward-better-teachers.html.

Bruns, Barbara, Alain Mingat, and Romahatra Rakotomalala. *Achieving Universal Primary Education by 2015: A Chance for Every Child*. Washington, DC: World Bank, 2003.

"Building a High-Quality Teaching Profession: Lessons from Around the World." Online: https://www2.ed.gov/about/inits/ed/internationaled/background.pdf.

Buntin, John. "What Does It Take to Stop Crips and Bloods from Killing Each Other?" *New York Times*, July 14, 2013. Online: http://www.nytimes.com/2013/07/14/magazine/what-does-it-take-to-stop-crips-and-bloods-from-killing-each-other.html?pagewanted=all&_r=0.

Butterly, John, and Jack Shepherd. *Hunger: The Biology and Politics of Starvation*. Hanover, NH: University Press of New England, 2010.

Byun, Eddie. *Justice Awakening: How You and Your Church Can Help End Human Trafficking*. Downers Grove, IL: InterVarsity, 2014.

Carter, Samuel. *No Excuses: Lessons from 21 High-Performing, High-Poverty Schools*. Washington, DC: Heritage Foundation, 2000.

"The Case for a Higher Minimum Wage." *New York Times*, February 9, 2014. Online: http://www.nytimes.com/2014/02/09/opinion/sunday/the-case-for-a-higher-minimum-wage.html?hp&rref=opinion.

Chamberlain, Michael. "Socially Responsible Investing: What You Need to Know." *Forbes*, April 24, 2013. Online: http://www.forbes.com/sites/feeonlyplanner/2013/04/24/socially-responsible-investing-what-you-need-to-know/.

Chapman, Claudia. "Adoption 101." Personal Blog. Online: http://my—fascinating—life.blogspot.com/p/links.html.

Cheng-Tozun, Dorcas. "The Food Supplier: Christine Moseley." *Christianity Today*, June 23, 2016. Online: http://www.christianitytoday.com/ct/2016/julaug/christine-moseley.html.

Chenoweth, Karin, and Christina Theokas. "How High-Poverty Schools Are Getting It Done." *Educational Leadership* 70 (2013) 56–59.

———. "It Can Be Done, It's Being Done, and Here's How." *Phi Delta Kappan* 91 (2009) 38–43.

Cherlin, Andrew. *Labor's Love Lost: The Rise and Fall of the Working-Class Family in America.* New York: Russell Sage, 2014.

Chester, Tim. *Good News to the Poor: Social Involvement and the Gospel.* Wheaton, IL: Crossway, 2013.

Cohen, Joel, et al. "Introduction." In *Educating All Children: A Global Agenda*, edited by Joel Cohen, David Bloom, and Martin Malin, 1–30. Cambridge, MA: MIT Press, 2006.

Cohen, M. A., and A. R. Piquero. "New Evidence on the Monetary Value of Saving a High Risk Youth." *Journal of Quantitative Criminology* 25 (2009) 25–49.

———, et al. "Estimating the Costs of Bad Outcomes for At-Risk Youth and the Benefits of Early Childhood Interventions to Reduce Them." *Criminal Justice Policy Review* 21 (2010) 391–434.

Cohen, Patricia. "As Demand for Welders Resurges, Community Colleges Offer Classes." *New York Times,* March 11, 2015. Online: http://www.nytimes.com/2015/03/11/business/economy/as-demand-for-welders-resurges-community-colleges-offer-classes.html.

———. "A Company Copes with Backlash against the Raise That Roared." *New York Times,* August 2, 2015. Online: http://www.nytimes.com/2015/08/02/business/a-company-copes-with-backlash-against-the-raise-that-roared.html.

———. "One Company's New Minimum Wage: $70,000 a Year." *New York Times,* April 14, 2015. Online: http://www.nytimes.com/2015/04/14/business/owner-of-gravity-payments-a-credit-card-processor-is-setting-a-new-minimum-wage-70000-a-year.html.

———. "Praise and Skepticism as One Executive Sets Minimum Wage to $70,000 a Year." *New York Times,* April 20, 2015. Online: http://www.nytimes.com/2015/04/20/business/praise-and-skepticism-as-one-executive-sets-minimum-wage-to-70000-a-year.html.

———. "Public-Sector Jobs Vanish, Hitting Blacks Hard." *New York Times,* May 25, 2015. Online: http://www.nytimes.com/2015/05/25/business/public-sector-jobs-vanish-and-blacks-take-blow.html?emc=edit_th_20150525&nl=todaysheadlines&nlid=22350591.

———. "Study Finds Local Taxes Hit Lower Wage Earners Harder." *New York Times,* January 14, 2015. Online: http://www.nytimes.com/2015/01/14/business/local-taxes-hit-lower-wage-earners-harder-study-finds.html.

Cohen, Steve. "How to Make College Cheaper." *New York Times,* February 2, 2015. Online: http://www.nytimes.com/2015/02/25/opinion/how-to-make-college-cheaper.html?action.

Collett, Jessica, and Christopher Morrissey. "The Social Psychology of Generosity: The State of Current Interdisciplinary Research." University of Notre Dame, October 2007. Online: https://generosityresearch.nd.edu/assets/17634/social_psychology_of_generosity_final.pdf.

Collins, Daryl, et al. *Portfolios of the Poor: How the World's Poor Live on $2 a Day.* Princeton, NJ: Princeton University Press, 2009.

Conte, Jon. "Introduction." In *Child Abuse and Neglect Worldwide,* edited by Jon Conte, 1:1–8. Santa Barbara, CA: Praeger, 2014.

———, ed. *Child Abuse and Neglect Worldwide. Volume 3: Interventions and Treatments.* Santa Barbara, CA: Praeger, 2014.

Conway, Gordon. *One Billion Hungry: Can We Feed the World?* Ithaca, NY: Cornell University Press, 2012.

Corbett, Steve, and Brian Fikkert. *When Helping Hurts: How to Alleviate Poverty without Hurting the Poor and Yourself.* Chicago: Moody, 2009.

"Create Savings Accounts and Bring Financial Security to the World's Poorest." *Bill and Melinda Gates Foundation,* November 16, 2010. Online: http://www.gatesfoundation.org/Media-Center/Press-Releases/2010/11/Create-Savings-Accounts-and-Bring-Financial-Security-to-the-Worlds-Poorest.

Crosby, Robert. "A Dream of a Center: 'A Model for Faith-based Organizations.'" *Christianity Today,* August 15, 2011. Online: http://www.christianitytoday.com/ct/2011/august/dreamcenter.html?start=1.

Crosnoe, Robert. *Fitting In, Standing Out: Navigating the Social Challenges of High School to Get an Education.* New York: Cambridge University Press, 2011.

Cuomo, Andrew. "Fast-Food Workers Deserve a Raise." *New York Times,* May 7, 2015. Online: http://www.nytimes.com/2015/05/07/opinion/andrew-m-cuomo-fast-food-workers-deserve-a-raise.html.

Daigle, Katy. "Report: Economic Growth Failing to Help World's Poorest Kids." *Yahoo News,* June 23, 2015. Online: http://news.yahoo.com/unicef-economic-growth-failing-help-worlds-poorest-kids-100037588.html.

Damon, Matt, and Gary White. "A Journey to Sundance to Help Save Lives." *Huffington Post,* January 22, 2015. Online: http://www.huffingtonpost.com/matt-damon/a-journey-to-sundance-to-_b_6518396.html.

Darrah, Jennifer, and Stefanie DeLuca. "'Living Here Has Changed My Whole Perspective': How Escaping Inner-City Poverty Shapes Neighborhood and Housing Choice." *Journal of Policy Analysis and Management* 33 (2014) 350–84.

Davenport, Dawn. *The Complete Book of International Adoption: A Step-By-Step Guide to Finding Your Child.* New York: Harmony, 2006.

David, Ben. "The Benefits of Teen Court." *Business Life* (1997) 30, 63.

———. "Community-Based Prosecution in North Carolina: An Inside-Out Approach to Public Service at the Courthouse, on the Street, and in the Classroom." *Wake Forest Law Review* 47 (2012) 373–411.

Davis, Alyssa, and Lawrence Mishel. "CEO Pay Continues to Rise as Typical Workers Are Paid Less." *Economic Policy Institute,* June 12, 2014. Online: http://www.epi.org/publication/ceo-pay-continues-to-rise/.

Davis, Daniel. "Microsavings: Opening the Door for Individuals to Invest in Themselves." *Federal Reserve Bank of St. Louis.* Online: https://www.stlouisfed.org/publications/bridges/summer-2012/microsavings-opening-the-door-for-individuals-to-invest-in-themselves.

Davis, Julie Hirschfeld, and Tamar Lewin. "Obama Plan Would Help Many Go to Community College Free." *New York Times,* January 9, 2015. Online: http://www.nytimes.com/2015/01/09/us/politics/obama-proposes-free-community-college-education-for-some-students.html.

Davis, Sampson. *Living & Dying in Brick City: Stories from the Front Lines of an Inner-City E.R.* New York: Spiegel & Grau, 2014.

Dawson, Geraldine, Sharon Ashman, and Leslie Carver. "The Role of Early Experience in Shaping Behavioral and Brain Development and Its Implications for Social Policy." *Development and Psychopathology* 12.4 (2000) 695–712.

Dean, Ceri, et al. *Classroom Instruction That Works: Research-Based Strategies for Increasing Student Achievement*. Alexandria, VA: Association for Supervision & Curriculum Development, 2012.

Dean, Jamie. "The Light of the Sun in a Dark Basement." *World*, December 13, 2014. Online: https://world.wng.org/2014/11/the_light_of_the_sun_in_a_dark_basement.

De Graaf, John, and David Wann. *Affluenza: How Overconsumption Is Killing Us—and How to Fight Back*. San Francisco: Berrett-Koehler, 2014.

de Hoop, Jacobus, and Furio Rosati. "Cash Transfers and Child Labor." *World Bank*, March 31, 2014. Online: http://www-wds.worldbank.org/external/default/WDSContentServer/IW3P/IB/2014/03/31/000158349_20140331135854/Rendered/PDF/WPS6826.pdf.

De Soto, Hernando. *The Mystery of Capital: Why Capitalism Triumphs in the West and Fails Everywhere Else*. New York: Basic, 2000.

DeYoung, Kevin, and Greg Gilbert. *What Is the Mission of the Church? Making Sense of Social Justice, Shalom, and the Great Commission*. Wheaton, IL: Crossway, 2011.

Dichter, Thomas. "Introduction." In *What's Wrong with Microfinance?*, edited by Thomas Dichter and Malcolm Harper, 1–8. Rugby, UK: Practical Action, 2007.

Dimon, Jamie "Why We're Giving Our Employees a Raise." *New York Times*, July 12, 2016. Online: http://www.nytimes.com/2016/07/12/opinion/jamie-dimon-why-were-giving-our-employees-a-raise.html?_r=0

Dowla, Asif, and Dipal Barua. *The Poor Always Pay Back: The Grameen II Story*. Bloomfield, CT: Kumarian, 2006.

Dube, Arindrajit. "Minimum Wages and the Distribution of Family Incomes." University of Massachusetts Amherst, December 13, 2013. Online: https://dl.dropboxusercontent.com/u/15038936/Dube_MinimumWagesFamilyIncomes.pdf.

Dube, Arindrajit, T. William Lester, and Michael Reich. "Minimum Wage Effects across State Borders: Estimates Using Contiguous Counties." Online: http://irle.berkeley.edu/workingpapers/157-07.pdf.

Duffy, Maureen. "Introduction: A Global Overview of the Issues of and Responses to Teen Gangs." In *Teen Gangs: A Global View*, edited by Maureen Duffy and Scott Gillig, 1–12. Westport, CT: Greenwood, 2004.

Dugan, Andrew. "Most Americans for Raising Minimum Wage." *Gallup*, November 11, 2013. Online: http://www.gallup.com/poll/165794/americans-raising-minimum-wage.aspx.

Duncan, Greg, and Richard Murnane. *Restoring Opportunity: The Crisis of Inequality and the Challenge for American Education*. New York: Russell Sage, 2014.

Duncan, Natricia. "Crowdfunding Development: 'Kiva's Aim Is to Make Microfinance Easy.'" *The Guardian*, June 10, 2014. Online: http://www.theguardian.com/global-development-professionals-network/2014/jun/10/crowdfunding-for-development.

Dunkelberg, William. "Why Raising the Minimum Wage Kills Jobs." *Forbes*, December 31, 2012. Online: http://www.forbes.com/sites/williamdunkelberg/2012/12/31/why-raising-the-minimum-wage-kills-jobs/.

Dunn, Elizabeth, et al. "Spending Money on Others Promotes Happiness." *Science* 21 (2008) 1687–88.

Easterly, William. *The White Man's Burden: Why the West Efforts to Aid the Rest Have Done So Much Ill and So Little Good*. New York: Penguin, 2006.

Edelman, Marian Wright. "A Call to End Child Poverty Now." *Children's Defense*. Online: http://www.childrensdefense.org/library/PovertyReport/EndingChildPovertyNow.html.

———. "Charity Is Not a Substitute for Justice." *Children's Defense*, June 5, 2015. Online: http://www.childrensdefense.org/newsroom/child-watch-columns/child-watch-documents/charityisnotasubstituteforjustice.html?referrer=https://www.google.com/.

———. "Who Are We? What Do We Americans Truly Value?" *Huffington Post*, March 6, 2015. Online: http://www.huffingtonpost.com/marian-wright-edelman/who-are-we-what-do-we-ame_b_6820880.html.

Editorial Board. "The Cost of Letting Young People Drift." *New York Times*, June 21, 2015. Online: http://www.nytimes.com/2015/06/21/opinion/the-cost-of-letting-young-people-drift.html?_r=0.

———. "A $15 Minimum Wage Bombshell in Los Angeles." *New York Times*, May 21, 2015. Online: http://www.nytimes.com/2015/05/21/opinion/a-15-minimum-wage-bombshell-in-los-angeles.html?emc=edit_th_20150521&nl=todaysheadlines&nlid=22350591.

———. "The Race to Improve Global Health." *New York Times*, September 11, 2015. Online: http://www.nytimes.com/2013/09/11/opinion/the-race-to-improve-global-health.html.

Edsall, Thomas. "What Makes People Poor?" *New York Times*, September 9, 2014. Online: http://www.nytimes.com/2014/09/03/opinion/what-makes-people-poor.html?_r=0.

Egley Jr., Arlen, and James Howell. *Highlights of the 2010 National Youth Gang Survey*. Washington, DC: U.S. Department of Justice, 2012.

Ehrenreich, Barbara. "Nickel and Dimed." *Harper's Magazine* 298 (1999) 37–52.

———. *Nickel and Dimed: On (Not) Getting By in America*. New York: Metropolitan Books, 2001.

Ehrle, Jennifer, Kathryn Tout, and Gina Adams. *Who's Caring for Our Youngest Children? Child Care Patterns of Infants and Toddlers*. Washington, DC: Urban Institute, 2001.

Epstein, Mark and Kristi Yuthas. "Redefining Education in the Developing World." *Stanford Social Innovation Review* 19 (2012). Online: http://ssir.org/articles/entry/redefining_education_in_the_developing_world.

Erickson, Lance, Steve McDonald, and Glen Elder. "Informal Mentors and Education: Complementary or Compensatory Resources?" *Sociology of Education* 82 (2009) 344–67.

Esaki, Nina, Haksoon Ahn, and Gillian Gregory. "Factors Associated with Foster Parents' Perceptions of Agency Effectiveness in Preparing Them for Their Role." *Journal of Public Child Welfare* 6 (2012) 678–95.

Evans, David, and Anna Popova. "Do the Poor Waste Transfers on Booze and Cigarettes? No." *World Bank*, May 27, 2014. Online: http://blogs.worldbank.org/impactevaluations/do-poor-waste-transfers-booze-and-cigarettes-no.

Evans, Gary. "The Environment of Childhood Poverty." *American Psychologist* 59 (2004) 77–92.

Evans, Jon. "A Closer Look: District Attorney Ben David on Violent Crime, Tougher Laws and Re-election." *World Now*, September 27, 2013. Online: http://raycomnbc.

worldnow.com/story/23553368/a-closer-look-district-attorney-ben-david-on-violent-crime-tougher-laws-and-re-election.

Fallon, Nicole. "What Is Corporate Social Responsibility?" *Business News Daily*, June 27, 2016. Online: http://www.businessnewsdaily.com/4679-corporate-social-responsibility.html.

Farb, Amy Feldman, and Jennifer Matjasko. "Recent Advances in Research on School-Based Extracurricular Activities and Adolescent Development." *Developmental Review* 32 (2012) 1–48.

Ferrari, Pierre. "How to End World Hunger." *CNN*, October 22, 2013. Online: http://www.cnn.com/2013/10/22/world/iyw-heifer-international-pierre-ferrari/.

Firestone, David. "Is American Culture to Blame for Failing Schools?" *New York Times*, December 18, 2013. Online: http://takingnote.blogs.nytimes.com/2013/12/18/is-american-culture-to-blame-for-failing-schools/?hp&rref=opinion&_r=0.

Firestone, Lisa. "The Benefits of Generosity." *Huffington Post*, June 13, 2014. Online: http://www.huffingtonpost.com/lisa-firestone/the-benefits-of-generosit_b_5448218.html.

Fishman, Charles. *The Big Thirst: The Secret Life and Turbulent Future of Water*. New York: Free, 2011.

Folson, Rose. "Economic Restructuring and Education in Ghana." In *African Education and Globalization: Critical Perspectives*, edited by Ali Abdi, Korbla Puplampu, and George Sefa Dei, 135–50. Lanham, MD: Lexington, 2006.

Fulgham, Nicole Baker. *Educating All God's Children: What Christians Can—and Should—Do to Improve Public Education for Low-Income Children*. Grand Rapids: Brazos, 2013.

Gash, Megan. "Pathways to Change: The Impact of Group Participation." In *Saving Groups at the Frontier*, edited by Candace Nelson, 101–25. Rugby, UK: Practical Action, 2013

Gebo, Erika, and Brenda Bond. "Introduction to Gang Reduction Responses." In *Looking Beyond Suppression: Community Strategies to Reduce Gang Violence*, edited by Erika Gebo and Brenda Bond, 1–16. Lanham, MD: Lexington, 2012.

Gertler, Paul. "Do Conditional Cash Transfers Improve Child Health? Evidence from Progresa's Control Randomized Experiment." *American Economic Review* 94 (2004) 336–41.

Gertler, Paul, and Simone Boyce. "The Impact of Progresa on Health in Mexico." Online: http://www.povertyactionlab.org/evaluation/impact-progresa-health-mexico.

Gillard, Julia. "Good Education Helps Girls Grow into Strong Women." *Huffington Post*, March 6, 2015. Online: http://www.huffingtonpost.com/australian-prime-minister-julia-gillard/good-education-helps-girl_b_6811314.html.

Gillham, Jane, and Karen Reivich. "Cultivating Optimism in Childhood and Adolescent." *The Annals of the American Academy of Political and Social Science* 591 (2004) 146–63.

"Give the Poor Money." *The Economist*, July 29, 2010. Online: http://www.economist.com/node/16693323.

Gladwell, Malcolm. *Outliers: The Story of Success*. New York: Little, Brown, 2008.

Glazerman, Steven, et al. "Transfer Incentives for High-Performing Teachers: Final Results from a Multisite Experiment." US Department of Education, November 2013. Online: http://ies.ed.gov/ncee/pubs/20144003/pdf/20144004.pdf.

Godfray, H. Charles. "How Can 9–10 Billion People Be Fed Sustainably and Equitably by 2050?" In *Is the Planet Full*, edited by Ian Goldin, 104–21. Oxford: Oxford University Press, 2014.

Goldin, Claudia Dale, and Lawrence Katz. *The Race between Education and Technology*. Cambridge, MA: Harvard University Press, 2008.

Gordon, Wayne. *Real Hope in Chicago: The Incredible Story of How the Gospel Is Transforming a Chicago Neighborhood*. Grand Rapids: Zondervan, 1995.

Gordon, Wayne, and John Perkins. *Making Neighborhoods Whole: A Handbook for Christian Community Development*. Downers Grove, IL: InterVarsity, 2013.

Graham, Efrem. "'Life of a King' Shows the Saving Power of Chess." *CBN News*, September 7, 2014. Online: http://www.cbn.com/cbnnews/us/2014/January/Life-of-a-King-Shows-the-Saving-Power-of-Chess/.

Green, Amanda. "Superintendent Recommends Virgo Middle School Be Shuttered." *Star Online News*, February 16, 2011. Online: http://www.starnewsonline.com/article/20110216/ARTICLES/110219727;

———. "Virgo Middle to Close, Reopen as Charter or Magnet School." *Star Online News*, May 17, 2011. Online: http://www.starnewsonline.com/article/20110517/ARTICLES/110519640.

Green, Duncan. "Ending World Hunger Is Possible—So Why Hasn't It Been Done?" *The Guardian*, February 15, 2012. Online: http://www.theguardian.com/commentisfree/2012/feb/15/ending-world-hunger.

Green, Edward. "How Faith-based Organizations Have Contributed to AIDS Prevention." In *The Hope Factor: Engaging the Church and the HIV/AIDS Crisis*, edited by Tetsunao Yamamori, David Dageforde, and Tina Bruner, 65–80. Monrovia, CA: MARC, 2004.

Green, Elizabeth. *Building a Better Teacher: How Teaching Works (and How to Teach It to Everyone)*. New York: Norton, 2014.

Greene, Melissa Fay. *There Is No Me without You*. New York: Bloomsbury, 2006.

Greenhouse, Steven. "Low-Wage Workers Finding It's Easier to Fall into Poverty, and Harder to Get Out." *New York Times*, March 17, 2014. Online: http://www.nytimes.com/2014/03/17/business/economy/low-wage-workers-finding-its-easier-to-fall-into-poverty-and-harder-to-get-out.html?hp.

Greer, Peter. "'Stop Helping Us': A Call to Compassionately Move Beyond Charity." In *For the Least of These: A Biblical Answer to Poverty*, edited by Anne Bradley and Art Lindsley, 319–39. Bloomington, IN: WestBow, 2014.

Greer, Peter, and Phil Smith, *The Poor Will Be Glad: Joining the Revolution to Lift the World Out of Poverty*. Grand Rapids: Zondervan, 2009.

Griffiths, Lord Brian, and Dato Kim Tan. "Fighting Poverty through Enterprise." In *For the Least of These: A Biblical Answer to Poverty*, edited by Anne Bradley and Art Lindsley, 139–52. Bloomington, IN: WestBow, 2014.

Gruden, Wayne, and Barry Asmus. *The Poverty of Nations: A Sustainable Solution*. Wheaton, IL: Crossway, 2013.

Grytsenko, Oksana. "A Troubled Young Life Led Pittsburgh Girl into the Hands of a Trafficker." *Post Gazette*, August 23, 2015. Online: http://www.post-gazette.com/local/city/2015/08/23/A-troubled-young-life-that-led-Pittsburgh-girl-into-the-hands-of-a-trafficker/stories/201508230037.

Gundersen, Craig, and James Ziliak. "Childhood Food Insecurity in the U.S.: Trends, Causes, and Policy Options." *Future of Children*, Fall 2014. Online: http://www.princeton.edu/futureofchildren/publications/journals/article/index.xml?journalid=82&articleid=606.

Haberman, Martin. *Star Teachers: The Ideology and Best Practice of Effective Teachers of Diverse Children and Youth in Poverty*. Houston: Haberman Educational Foundation, 2005.

Halle, Tamara, et al. "Disparities in Early Learning and Development: Lessons from the Early Childhood Longitudinal Study—Birth Cohort (ECLS-B)." *Child Trends*, May 2013. Online: http://www.childtrends.org/wp-content/uploads/2013/05/2009-52DisparitiesELExecSumm.pdf.

Halpern, Robert. *Making Play Work: The Promise of After-School Programs for Low-Income Children*. New York: Teachers College Press, 2003.

Hanushek, Eric, Paul Peterson, and Ludger Woessmann, *Endangering Prosperity: A Global View of the American School*. Washington, DC: Brookings, 2013.

———. "An Evaluation System Linked to Retention and Reward Is Vital." *New York Times*, March 3, 2015. Online: http://www.nytimes.com/roomfordebate/2015/03/03/how-to-ensure-and-improve-teacher-quality/an-evaluation-system-linked-to-retention-and-reward-is-vital.

Hart, Betty, and Todd Risley. *Meaningful Differences in the Everyday Experiences of Young American Children*. Baltimore: Brooks, 1995.

Jen Hatmaker. "Examining Adoption Ethics: Part One." Personal Blog. http://jenhatmaker.com/blog/2013/05/14/examining-adoption-ethics-part-one.

———. "Examining Adoption Ethics: Part Two." Personal Blog. http://jenhatmaker.com/blog/2013/05/20/examining-adoption-ethics-part-two.

———. "Examining Adoption Ethics, Part Three." Personal Blog. http://jenhatmaker.com/blog/2013/05/29/examining-adoption-ethics-part-three.

Haugen, Gary and Victor Boutros. "The Hidden Reason for Poverty the World Needs to Address Now." *Ted Talks*, March 2015. Online: https://www.ted.com/talks/gary_haugen_the_hidden_reason_for_poverty_the_world_needs_to_address_now?nolanguage=en.

———. Interview with Brian Patrick, *EWTN News Nightly*, December 2, 2014. Online: https://www.youtube.com/watch?v=IBlmIbVTphc.

———. *The Locust Effect: Why the End of Poverty Requires the End of Violence*. New York: Oxford University Press, 2013.

———. "The Poor Deserve Equal Protection by the Law." *Washington Post*, January 26, 2014. Online: http://www.washingtonpost.com/opinions/the-poor-deserve-equal-protection-by-the-law/2014/01/26/e2f40a8a-8556-11e3-bbe5-6a2a3141e3a9_story.html.

Haugen, Gary, Victor Boutros, and Gregg Hunter. *Terrify No More*. Nashville: W, 2005.

Havens, Esther, and Taylor Walling. "Meet Jean Bosco." Online: http://www.charitywater.org/projects/stories/meet-jean-bosco/.

Hawkins, J. David, et al. "Predictors of Youth Violence." *Juvenile Justice Bulletin* (2000) 1–11. Online: http://www.crim.cam.ac.uk/people/academic_research/david_farrington/predviol.pdf.

Hayes, Susan. "Characteristics of Successful High Poverty Schools: What the Research Tells Us." *Roots of Success*, September 2009. Online: https://rootsofsuccess.files.wordpress.com/2009/09/successful_schools_lit_review1.pdf.

Hazelgrove, Sally. "Street Gangs Have a Great Solution for Reducing Violent Crime." *Vice News*, November 5, 2014. Online: https://news.vice.com/article/street-gangs-have-a-great-solution-for-reducing-violent-crime.

Hazen, Jennifer, and Dennis Rodger, eds. *Global Gangs; Street Violence across the World.* Minneapolis: University of Minnesota Press, 2014.

Heckman, James. "Skill Formation and the Economics of Investing in Disadvantaged Children." *Science* 312 (2006) 1900–2.

Helburn, Suzanne, and Barbara Bergmann. *America's Child Care Problem: The Way Out.* New York: Palgrave, 2002.

Henderson, Kaya. "Real Respect Is the Path to Great Teaching." *New York Times,* March 3, 2015. Online: http://www.nytimes.com/roomfordebate/2015/03/03/how-to-ensure-and-improve-teacher-quality/real-respect-is-the-path-to-great-teaching.

Herz Barbara, and Gene Sperling. *What Works in Girls' Education: Evidence and Policies from the Developing World.* New York: Council on Foreign Relations, 2004.

Hess, Hannah. "Former Rep. Frank Wolf Will Lead Baylor University's Efforts on Capitol Hill." *Roll Call,* January 19, 2015. Online: http://blogs.rollcall.com/218/former-rep-frank-wolf-will-lead-baylor-universitys-efforts-on-capitol-hill/.

Hicks, Roderick. "Education and Poverty Alleviation in Eastern Africa—the Causal Links." In *Education, Poverty, Malnutrition and Famine,* edited by Lorraine Pe Symaco, 15–38. New York: Bloomsbury Academic, 2014.

Hill, K. G., et al. "Childhood Risk Factors for Adolescent Gang Membership: Results from the Seattle Social Development Project." *Journal of Research in Crime Delinquency* 36 (1999) 300–22.

Hjelmgaard, Kim. "Oxfam: Richest 1% Own Nearly Half of World's Wealth." *USA Today,* January 20, 2014. Online: http://www.usatoday.com/story/news/world/2014/01/20/davos-2014-oxfam-85-richest-people-half-world/4655337/.

———. "Q&A: Matt Damon on Bringing Water to the Masses." *USA Today*, January 20, 2015. Online: http://www.usatoday.com/story/money/business/2015/01/20/water-qa-matt-damon-gary-white-davos-world-economic-forum/21986151/?utm_source=pulsenews&utm_medium=referral.

Hoddinott, John, and Emmanuel Skoufias. "The Impact of Progresa on Food Consumption." *Economic Development and Cultural Change* 53 (2004) 37–61.

Holzer, Harry, et al. "The Economic Costs of Childhood Poverty in the United States." *Journal of Children and Poverty* 14 (2008) 41–61.

"The Hopeful Continent: Africa Rising." *The Economist*, December 1, 2011. Online: http://www.economist.com/node/21541015.

Hulme, David. "Is Microdebt Good for Poor People?" In *What's Wrong with Microfinance?*, edited by Thomas Dichter and Malcolm Harper, 19–22. Rugby, UK: Practical Action, 2007.

Human Development Report, 2006: Beyond Scarcity: Power, Poverty and the Global Water Crisis. Online: http://www.undp.org/content/undp/en/home/librarypage/hdr/human-development-report-2006.html.

"Hunger Notes." *World Hunger.* Online: http://www.worldhunger.org/2015-world-hunger-and-poverty-facts-and-statistics/#Children_and_hunger.

"Hunger and Poverty Facts and Statistics." *Feeding America.* Online: http://www.feedingamerica.org/hunger-in-america/impact-of-hunger/hunger-and-poverty/hunger-and-poverty-fact-sheet.html.

Huntington, Clare. "Help Families from Day 1." *New York Times,* September 3, 2014. Online: http://www.nytimes.com/2014/09/03/opinion/help-families-from-day-1.html.

Hybels, Bill. *The Volunteer Revolution: Unleashing the Power of Everybody*. Grand Rapids: Zondervan, 2004.

Hymowitz, Kay. "How Single Motherhood Hurts Kids." *New York Times,* February 8, 2014. Online: http://opinionator.blogs.nytimes.com/2014/02/08/how-single-motherhood-hurts-kids/?_php=true&_type=blogs&hp&rref=opinion&_r=0.

———. *Marriage and Caste in America: Separate and Unequal Families in a Post-Marital Age*. Chicago: Dee, 2006.

"I Am Woman, Hear Me Shop." *Bloomberg Businessweek*, February 13, 2005. Online: http://www.bloomberg.com/bw/stories/2005-02-13/i-am-woman-hear-me-shop.

"ILO 2012 Global Estimate of Forced Labour." Online: http://www.ilo.org/wcmsp5/groups/public/—-ed_norm/—-declaration/documents/publication/wcms_181921.pdf.

In Our Own Backyard: Child Prostitution and Sex Trafficking in the United States. 111 Cong., 2nd sess., 2010. Online: https://www.gpo.gov/fdsys/pkg/CHRG-111shrg58003/pdf/CHRG-111shrg58003.pdf.

"IJM: Zambia." *IJM*, February 27, 2014. Online: https://www.ijm.org/articles/ijm-zambia-irene-shares-tearful-thanks-after-8-year-legal-battle-her-land.

"Innovative Social Enterprise Leverages Carbon Offsets with Clean Cooking Stoves." *Ecopreneurist*, April 9, 2012. Online: http://ecopreneurist.com/2012/04/09/social-enterprise-leverages-carbon-offsets-clean-stoves/.

"Interrupting Violence with the Message 'Don't Shoot.'" *NPR*, November 1, 2011. Online: http://www.npr.org/2011/11/01/141803766/interrupting-violence-with-the-message-dont-shoot.

Jacobs, Louis. "Does a $10.10 Minimum Wage Get You Out of Poverty?" *Politifact,* May 8, 2014. Online: http://www.politifact.com/truth-o-meter/statements/2014/may/08/charles-schumer/does-1010-minimum-wage-get-you-out-poverty/.

James, William. "The Moral Equivalent of War." *McClure's Magazine* (1910) 463–68.

Jamieson, Dave. "The Life and Death of an Amazon Warehouse Temp." *Huffington Post,* October 15, 2015. Online: http://highline.huffingtonpost.com/articles/en/life-and-death-amazon-temp/.

Jejeebhoy, Shireen, and Sarah Bott. *Non-consensual Sexual Experiences of Young People: A Review of the Evidence from Developing Countries*. Online: www.popcouncil.org/uploads/pdfs/wp/seasia/seawp16.pd.

Jensen, Eric. *Engaging Students with Poverty in Mind: Practical Strategies for Raising Achievement*. Alexandria, VA: Association for Supervision and Curriculum Development, 2013.

———. *Teaching with Poverty in Mind: What Being Poor Does to Kids' Brains and What Schools Can Do about It*. Alexandria, VA: Association for Supervision and Curriculum Development, 2009.

Jeynes, Wayne. "The Relationship between Parental Involvement and Urban Secondary School Academic Achievement: A Meta-Analysis." *Urban Education* 42 (2007) 82–110.

Jeynes, William. *School Choice: A Balanced Approach*. Santa Barbara, CA: Praeger, 2014.

Johnson, Dave. "Six Myths about Food Stamps." *Bill Moyers*, October 8, 2013. Online: http://billmoyers.com/2013/10/08/six-myths-about-food-stamps/.

Johnson, Susan, and Silvia Storchi. "Savings Group Outreach and Membership." In *Savings Groups at the Frontier*, edited by Candace Nelson, 37–64. Rugby, UK: Practical Action, 2013.

Jones, Mondella. "The Pact: Three Young Men Make a Promise and Fulfill a Dream." Online: http://connection.ebscohost.com/c/book-reviews/7002780/pact-three-young-men-make-promise-fulfill-dream.

Joustra, Robert. "Gary Haugen Gets His Kuyper On: Why Development without Public Justice Is Bound to Fail." *Books and Culture*, February 2014. Online: http://www.booksandculture.com/articles/webexclusives/2014/february/gary-haugen-gets-his-kuyper-on.html?paging=off.

Kadlec, Dan. "Giving Back: How Retiring Boomers Get the Rush They Crave." *Time Business*, September 19, 2013. Online: http://business.time.com/2013/09/19/giving-back-how-retiring-boomers-get-the-rush-they-crave/#ixzz2fO8avsoo.

Karlan, Dean, and Jacob Appel. *More Than Good Intentions: How a New Economics Is Helping to Solve Global Poverty*. New York: Dutton, 2011.

Katz, Michael. *The Undeserving Poor: America's Enduring Confrontation with Poverty*. New York: Oxford University Press, 2013.

Kavilanz, Parija. "Nine Months in Trade School. Job Guaranteed." *CNN Money*, March 14, 2012. Online: http://money.cnn.com/2012/03/14/smallbusiness/trade-schools/.

Kearney, G. R. *More Than a Dream: The Cristo Rey Story: How One School's Vision Is Changing the World*. Chicago: Loyola, 2008.

Keller, Timothy. *Generous Justice: How God's Grace Makes Us Just*. New York: Dutton, 2010.

Kemple, James. "Career Academies: Long-Term Impacts on Work, Education, and Transitions to Adulthood." MDRC Report (June 2008).

Kendall, Diana. *Sociology in Our Times*. Belmont, CA: Wadsworth, 2013.

Kennedy, David. "The Story Behind the Nation's Falling Body Count." *Huffington Post*, January 21, 2014. Online: http://www.huffingtonpost.com/david-m-kennedy/the-story-behind-the-nati_b_4634755.html.

———. *Deterrence and Crime Prevention: Reconsidering the Prospect of Sanction*. New York: Routledge, 2009.

———. *Don't Shoot: One Man, A Street Fellowship, and the End of Violence in Inner-City America*. New York: Bloomsbury USA, 2011.

Kenny, Maureen, et al. "Achievement Motivation among Urban Adolescents: Work, Hope, Autonomy, Support, and Achievement-Related Beliefs." *Journal of Vocational Behavior* 77 (2010) 205–12.

"Kenya: After a Shocking Arrest and a Stroke—Evans Is Now Free." *IJM*, December 8, 2013. Online: https://www.ijm.org/news/ijm-kenya-after-shocking-arrest-and-stroke-evans-now-free.

Kerry, John. "Remarks at the 2015 Trafficking in Persons Ceremony." Online: http://www.state.gov/secretary/remarks/2015/07/245298.htm.

King Jr., Martin Luther. "Beyond Vietnam—A Time to Break Silence." Online: http://www.americanrhetoric.com/speeches/mlkatimetobreaksilence.htm.

———. *Stride toward Freedom: The Montgomery Story*. New York: Harper, 1958.

Kinsman, Kat. "Survey Shows Ongoing Struggle against Hunger." *CNN*, August 18, 2014. Online: http://www.cnn.com/2014/08/18/living/hunger-survey-eatocracy/.

Kirp, David. "The Benefits of Mixing Rich and Poor." *New York Times*, May 10, 2014. Online: http://opinionator.blogs.nytimes.com/2014/05/10/the-benefits-of-mixing-rich-and-poor/?_php=true&_type=blogs&hp&rref=opinion&_r=0.

Klein, Joel. *Lessons of Hope: How to Fix Our Schools*. New York: Harper, 2014.

Konniokva, Maria. "No Money, No Time." *New York Times,* June 13, 2014. Online: http://opinionator.blogs.nytimes.com/2014/06/13/no-clocking-out/.

Konkol, Mark. "Financial Failure Is Success Story: Lawndale Pizzeria Employs Ex-cons." Online: http://www.highbeam.com/doc/1P2-3698963.html.

Kotler, Philip, and Nancy Lee. *Corporate Social Responsibility: Doing the Most Good for Your Company and Your Cause.* Hoboken, NJ: Wiley, 2005.

———, David Hessekiel, and Nancy Lee. *Good Works!: Marketing and Corporate Initiatives that Build a Better World—and the Bottom Line.* Hoboken, NJ: Wiley, 2005.

Kozol, Jonathan. *Savage Inequalities: Children in America's Schools.* New York: Crown, 1991.

Kristof, Nicholas. "Do We Invest in Preschools or Prisons?" *New York Times,* October 27, 2013. Online: http://www.nytimes.com/2013/10/27/opinion/sunday/kristof-do-we-invest-in-preschools-or-prisons.html.

———. "It's Now the Canadian Dream." *New York Times,* May 5, 2014. Online: http://www.nytimes.com/2014/05/15/opinion/kristof-its-now-the-canadian-dream.html?hp&rref=opinion&_r=0.

———. "Putting the Microsavings in Microfinance." *New York Times,* May 26, 2009. Online: http://kristof.blogs.nytimes.com/2009/05/26/putting-the-microsavings-in-microfinance/

———. "Scrooges of the World, Begone!" *New York Times,* December 25, 2014. Online: http://www.nytimes.com/2014/12/25/opinion/nicholas-kristof-scrooges-of-the-world-begone.html.

———. "Those Girls Haven't Been Brought Back." *New York Times,* July 13, 2014. Online: http://www.nytimes.com/2014/07/13/opinion/sunday/nicholas-kristof-those-girls-havent-been-brought-back.html.

———. "TV Lowers Birthrate (Seriously)." *New York Times,* March 20, 2014. Online: http://www.nytimes.com/2014/03/20/opinion/kristof-tv-lowers-birthrate-seriously.html.

———. "When Baltimore Burned." *New York Times,* April 30, 2015. Online: http://www.nytimes.com/2015/04/30/opinion/nicholas-kristof-when-baltimore-burned.html.

Kristof, Nicholas, and Sheryl WuDunn. *Half the Sky: Turning Oppression into Opportunity for Women Worldwide.* New York: Alfred A. Knopf, 2009.

———. *A Path Appears: Enriching the Lives of Others—and Ourselves.* New York: Knopf, 2014.

———. "The Women's Crusade." *New York Times,* August 23, 2009. Online: http://www.nytimes.com/2009/08/23/magazine/23Women-t.html?pagewanted=all&_r=0.

Krueger, Alan, and Mikael Lindahl. "Education for Growth: Why and for Whom?" *Journal of Economic Literature* 39 (2001) 1101–36.

Kudler, Adrian Glick. "LAPD's Radical Solution for Reducing Gang Violence in Watts." *Curbed,* July 11, 2013. Online: http://la.curbed.com/2013/7/11/10221308/the-lapds-radical-solution-for-reducing-gang-violence-in-watts.

Kurnia, Julia. "Microfinance: Do the Micro-loans Contribute to the Well-being of the People or Do They Leave Them Even Poorer Due to High Interest Rates?" Online: http://www.quora.com/Microfinance.

Kurnia, Julia, and Miriam Frost. "Spotlight on Ndeye Bineta Sarr, Senegal." *P2P,* March 22, 2014. Online: http://p2p-microlending-blog.zidisha.org/2014/03/22/spotlight-on-ndeye-bineta-sarr-senegal/.

Kwansah-Aidoo, Kwamena, and Joyce Djokoto, "Swaziland: Toward an Effective Education for Global Citizenship." In *African Education and Globalization: Critical Perspectives*, edited by Ali Abdi, Korbla Puplampu, and George Sefa Dei, 165–86. Lanham, MD: Lexington, 2006.

Laes, Christian. *Children in the Roman Empire: Outsiders Within*. Cambridge, UK: Cambridge University Press, 2011.

Lareau, Annette, and Kimberly Goyette, eds. *Choosing Homes, Choosing Schools: Residential Segregation and the Search for a Good School*. New York: Russell Sage, 2014.

Leathers, Howard, and Phillips Foster. *The World Food Problem: Toward Ending Undernutrition in the Third World*. Boulder, CO: Lynne Rienner, 2009.

Lee, Ellen. "Tegu's Magnetic Blocks Help Build a Business." *SF Gate*, August 5, 2013. Online: http://www.sfgate.com/business/article/Tegu-s-magnetic-blocks-help-build-a-business-4708403.php.

Lee, Valerie, and David Burkam. "Inequality at the Starting Gate: Social Background Differences in Achievement as Children Begin School." Online: http://epsl.asu.edu/epru/articles/EPRU-0603-138-OWI.pdf.

Lenda, Mike. "5 Ways We Can Solve the Water Crisis." *Relevant Magazine*, March 22, 2013. Online: http://www.relevantmagazine.com/reject-apathy/poverty/5-ways-we-can-solve-water-crisis.

Lenk, Michelle. "How the Church Could Help End Global Poverty." *Relevant Magazine*, September 1, 2014. Online: http://www.relevantmagazine.com/reject-apathy/poverty/how-church-could-help-end-global-poverty#BuRQvGE3QspOXu2L.99.

Leonhardt, David, Amanda Cox, and Claire Cain Miller. "An Atlas of Upward Mobility Shows Paths Out of Poverty." *New York Times*, May 4, 2015. Online: http://www.nytimes.com/2015/05/04/upshot/an-atlas-of-upward-mobility-shows-paths-out-of-poverty.html.

Leonhardt, David, and Kevin Quealy. "The American Middle Class Is No Longer the World's Richest." *New York Times*, April 23, 2014. Online: http://www.nytimes.com/2014/04/23/upshot/the-american-middle-class-is-no-longer-the-worlds-richest.html?abt=0002&abg=0.

Lewis, Kristen, and Sarah Burd-Sharps. "Zeroing in on Place and Race: Youth Disconnection in America's Cities." Online: http://ssrc-static.s3.amazonaws.com/wp-content/uploads/2015/06/MOA-Zeroing-In-Final.pdf.

Lippard, Joy. "Let the Truth Be Heard: Interview with Frank Wolf." Online: https://www.youtube.com/watch?v=D5-7kneuSHo.

"A Look Back: Building a Human Trafficking Legal Framework." Online: https://www.polarisproject.org/storage/2014SRM-capstone-report.pdf.

Lowrey, Annie. "50 Years Later, War on Poverty Is a Mixed Bag." *New York Times*, January 5, 2014. Online: http://www.nytimes.com/2014/01/05/business/50-years-later-war-on-poverty-is-a-mixed-bag.html?hp.

Lueneburger, Christoph. "A Company's Good Deeds Can Energize Employees." *Harvard Business Review*. December 2014. Online: https://hbr.org/2014/12/a-companys-good-deeds-can-energize-employees.

Luhrs, Janet. *The Simple Living Guide: A Sourcebook for Less Stressful, More Joyful Living*. New York: Broadway, 1997.

Luks, Allan, and Ellen Payne. *The Healing Power of Doing Good: The Health and Spiritual Benefits of Helping Others*. New York: Fawcett Columbine, 1991.

Lupton, Robert. *Toxic Charity: How Churches and Charities Hurt Those They Help (And How to Reverse It)*. New York: HarperCollins, 2011.

Maholmes, Valerie, and Rosalind King. *Fostering Resilience and Well-Being in Children and Families in Poverty: Why Hope Still Matters*. New York: Oxford University Press, 2014.

———. *The Oxford Handbook of Poverty and Child Development*. New York: Oxford University Press, 2012.

Mallory, Sue. *The Equipping Church*. Grand Rapids: Zondervan, 2001.

Maluccio, John, and Rafael Flores. *Impact Evaluation of a Conditional Cash Transfer Program: The Nicaraguan Red de Proteccion Social*. Washington, DC: International Food Policy Research Institute, 2005.

Mandelbaum, Robb. "Trying to Understand the Impact of a Higher Minimum Wage on Small Businesses." *New York Times*, August 11, 2014. Online: http://boss.blogs.nytimes.com/2014/08/11/trying-to-understand-the-impact-of-minimum-wage-hikes-on-small-businesses/?_php=true&_type=blogs&_r=0.

Mann, Lynn. "Michelin Challenge Education." *South Carolina Business* 31 (2010) 10.

Markley, Andrew. "Corporate Social Responsibility: The New Socialism." Online: http://visionandvalues.org/docs/thechallenge/Markley.pdf?5d595d.

Marr, Chuck, et al. "EITC and Child Tax Credit Promote Work, Reduce Poverty, and Support Children's Development, Research Finds." Online: http://www.cbpp.org/cms/index.cfm? fa=view&id=3793.

Marshall, Paul. *Thine Is the Kingdom: A Biblical Perspective on the Nature of Government and Politics Today*. Grand Rapids: Eerdmans, 1986.

Martin, Jim. *The Just Church: Becoming a Risk-taking, Justice-seeking, Disciple-making Congregation*. Carol Stream, IL: Tyndale, 2012.

Martinez, Jessica. "Jentezen Franklin, Los Angeles Dream Center Launch Transitional Home for Young Adults Out of Foster Care." *Christian Post*, August 27, 2014. Online: http://www.christianpost.com/news/jentezen-franklin-los-angeles-dream-center-launch-transitional-home-for-young-adults-out-of-foster-care-125468/.

Massey, Douglas, et al. *Climbing Mount Laurel: The Struggle for Affordable Housing and Social Mobility in an American Suburb*. Princeton, NJ: Princeton University Press, 2013.

McClay, Wilfred. "The Moral Equivalent of War?" *National Affairs* 5 (2010). Online: http://www.nationalaffairs.com/publications/detail/the-moral-equivalent-of-war.

McLanahan, Sara, and Christine Percheski. "Family Structure and the Reproduction of Inequality." *Annual Review of Sociology* 34 (2008) 257–76.

———. "Fragile Families and the Reproduction of Poverty." *Annals of American Academy of Political and Social Science* 62 (2009) 111–31.

Mech, Timothy. "For-Profits and Poverty Alleviation." Grove City College lecture, April 21, 2015.

———. "Microfinance: Key Points." Grove City College lecture, April 21, 2015.

———. "Two Basic Solutions to Poverty." Grove City College lecture, April 21, 2015.

Medina, Jennifer and Noam Scheiber. "Los Angeles Lifts Its Minimum Wage to $15 Per Hour." *New York Times*, May 20, 2015. Online: http://www.nytimes.com/2015/05/20/us/los-angeles-expected-to-raise-minimum-wage-to-15-an-hour.html.

Mehta, Jal. *The Allure of Order: High Hopes, Dashed Expectations, and the Troubled Quest to Remake American Schooling*. New York: Oxford University Press, 2013.

———. "Treat Teacher Education Like a Medical Residency." *New York Times*, March 3, 2015. Online: http://www.nytimes.com/roomfordebate/2015/03/03/how-to-ensure-and-improve-teacher-quality/treat-teacher-education-like-a-medical-residency.

Mehta, Jal, Robert Schwartz, and Frederick Hess, eds. *The Futures of School Reform*. Cambridge, MA: Harvard Education Press, 2012.

Miguel, Edward and Michael Kremer. "Worms: Identifying Impacts on Education and Health in the Presence of Treatment Externalities." *Econometrica* 72 (2004) 159–217.

Militzer, James. "The BoP Needs Drugs: Can the HealthStore Foundation's Model Deliver?" Online: http://nextbillion.net/blogpost.aspx?blogid=3200.

"The Millennial Development Goals Report, 2014." Online: http://www.un.org/millenniumgoals/2014%20MDG%20report/MDG%202014%20English%20web.pdf.

Miller, Judy "The Girls in the Gang: What We've Learned from Two Decades of Research." In *Gangs in America*, edited by C. Ronald Huff, 125–98. Thousand Oaks, CA: Sage, 2002.

Moinzadeh, Atoosa. "Gun-Toting Protestors Held a Rally Against 'Islamization' Outside a Texas Mosque." *Vice News*, November 22, 2015. Online: https://news.vice.com/article/gun-toting-protesters-held-a-rally-against-islamization-outside-a-texas-mosque.

Mok, Kimberley. "Bringing 5 Million Rocket Stoves to Women Worldwide: The Paradigm Project." *Treehugger*, September 28, 2011. Online: http://www.treehugger.com/culture/bringing-5-million-rocket-stoves-to-women-worldwide-the-paradigm-project.html.

Montgomery, Toni. "Grace in the Streets." *PCUSA*, July 28, 2009. Online: https://www.pcusa.org/news/2009/7/28/grace-streets/.

"More Than 20 Million Mexican Children and Adolescents Live in Poverty." *Yucatan Times*, May 2014. Online: http://www.theyucatantimes.com/2014/05/.

Morgan, Timothy, and Ruth Moon. "Frank Wolf Calls for Safe Haven for Mideast Christians." *Christianity Today*, February 16, 2015. Online: http://www.christianitytoday.com/gleanings/2015/february/genocidal-onslaught-middle-east-christians-isil-beheading-o.html.

"Most Americans Practice Charitable Giving, Volunteerism." Online: http://www.gallup.com/poll/166250/americans-practice-charitable-giving-volunteerism.aspx.

"Most See Inequality Growing, But Partisans Differ Over Solutions." Online: http://www.people-press.org/files/legacy-pdf/1-23-14%20Poverty_Inequality%20Release.pdf.

Moyo, Dambisa. *Dead Aid: Why Aid Is Not Working and How There Is a Better Way for Africa*. New York: Farrar, Straus & Giroux, 2009.

Mui, Ylan. "Microsavings Programs Build Wealth, Pennies at a Time." *Washington Post*, March 15, 2013. Online: http://www.washingtonpost.com/business/economy/microsavings-programs-build-wealth-pennies-at-a-time/2013/03/15/4bad70fe-8740-11e2-98a3-b3db6b9ac586_story.html.

Mullainathan, Sendhil, and Eldar Shafir. *Scarcity: Why Having Too Little Means So Much*. New York: Henry Holt, 2013.

Myers, Bryant. *Working with the Poor: Principles and Practices of Transformational Development*. Maryknoll, NY: Orbis, 2011.

Nadkarni, Avani. "The Aquaculture Person of the Year Is." *Intrafish*, September 29, 2014. Online: http://www.intrafish.com/free_news/article1398115.ece.

Narayan, Deepa, et al., eds. *Voices of the Poor: Crying Out for Change*. New York: Oxford University Press, 2000.

Narayan, Deepa, and Patti Petesch, eds. *Voices of the Poor: From Many Lands*. Washington, DC: World Bank, 2002.

National Center for Missing and Exploited Children. "Child Sex Trafficking: Facts and Figures." Online: http://www.missingkids.com/en_US/documents/rotarians-cst-facts.pdf.

National Human Trafficking Resource Center. "An Overview of Child Sex Trafficking." Online: http://www.traffickingresourcecenter.org/resources/overview-child-sex-trafficking.

National Survey of American Attitudes on Substance Abuse XV: Teens and Parents, 2010. Online: http://www.centeronaddiction.org/addiction-research/reports/national-survey-american-attitudes-substance-abuse-teens-parents-2010.

Nauert, Rick. "Doing for Others Also Benefits Health of Altruistic." *Psych Central*, February 6, 2013. Online: http://psychcentral.com/news/2013/02/06/doing-for-others-also-benefits-health-of-altruistic/51274.html.

"No Jobs, No Benefits, and Lousy Pay." *New York Times*, January 11, 2014. Online: http://www.nytimes.com/2014/01/11/opinion/no-jobs-no-benefits-and-lousy-pay.html?hp&rref.

Nordland, Rod. "Despite Education Advances, a Host of Afghan School Woes." *New York Times*, July 21, 2013. Online: http://www.nytimes.com/2013/07/21/world/asia/despite-education-advances-a-host-of-afghan-school-woes.html?hpw&_r=0.

"Not Everyone Can or Should Foster or Adopt, But Everyone Can Do Something." Online: http://www.childbridgemontana.org/Everyone_Can_Do_Something_Trifold.pdf.

O'Donnell, Kevin, and Gail Mulligan. "Parents' Report of the School Readiness of Young Children from the National Household Education Surveys Program of 2007." US Department of Education, August 2007. Online: http://nces.ed.gov/pubs2008/2008051.pdf.

Offenheiser, Raymond C. "The Top Myths about US Foreign Aid." *The Hill*. April 2, 2014. Online: http://thehill.com/blogs/congress-blog/foreign-policy/201974-the-top-myths-about-us-foreign-aid.

Offutt, Stephen, et al. *Advocating for Justice: An Evangelical Vision for Transforming Systems and Structures*. Grand Rapids: Baker Academic, 2016.

O'Leary, Amy, and Lisa Iaboni. "When No One's Looking, Part 2." *New York Times*, October 27, 2009. Online: http://www.nytimes.com/video/us/1247465377685/when-no-one-s-looking-part-2.html.

"The Pact: Three Young Men Make a Promise and Fulfill a Dream." *Publishers Weekly*. Online: http://www.publishersweekly.com/978-1-57322-216-7.

"Partnerships Provide Tools and Training." Online: https://opportunity.org/content/News/Publications/Impact%20Newsletter/Impact-2009-Spring.pdf.

Patel, Raj, et al. "Ending Africa's Hunger." *The Nation*. Online: http://www.thenation.com/print/article/ending-africas-hunger.

———. *Stuffed and Starved: The Hidden Battle for the World Food System*. Brooklyn, NY: Melville, 2012.

Patterns of Household Charitable Giving by Income Group, 2005. Online: https://scholarworks.iupui.edu/handle/1805/5838.

Pavlich, Katie. "Bill O'Reilly: True Poverty Is Being Driven by Personal Behavior." *Town Hall*. January 10, 2014. Online: http://townhall.com/tipsheet/katiepavlich/2014/01/10/bill-oreilly-true-poverty-is-being-driven-by-personal-behavior-n1777105.

Pearsall, Paul. *The Pleasure Prescription: To Love, to Work, to Play—Life in the Balance.* Alameda, CA: Hunter, 1996.

Peck, Don. "Can the Middle Class Be Saved?" *Atlantic* 308 (2011) 60–78.

"Pennies from Heaven." *The Economist*, October 24, 2014. Online: http://www.economist.com/news/international/21588385-giving-money-directly-poor-people-works-surprisingly-well-it-cannot-deal.

Perkins, John. *Geopolitics and the Green Revolution: Wheat, Genes, and the Cold War.* New York: Oxford University Press, 1997.

Perry, David. "Low Cost College Isn't Enough." *CNN*, May 18, 2015. Online: http://www.cnn.com/2015/05/18/opinions/perry-low-cost-college-isnt-enough/index.html.

Pershing, Ben. "Frank Wolf to Retire after 17 Terms in Congress." *Washington Post*, December 17, 2013. Online: http://www.washingtonpost.com/local/virginia-politics/frank-wolf-to-retire-after-17-terms-in-congress-northern-va-seat-to-be-a-battleground-in-2014/2013/12/17/712bb608-6749-11e3-a0b9-249bbb34602c_story.html.

Phumaphi, Joy, and Danny Leipziger. "Forward." In *Girls' Education in the 21st Century: Equality, Empowerment, and Growth*, edited by Lucia Fort and Mercy Tembon, xvii–xix. Washington DC: World Bank, 2008.

Pick, Grant. "Pizza on Earth, Goodwill toward Men: A Restaurant Opens in Lawndale." *Chicago Reader*, June 29, 1995. Online: http://www.chicagoreader.com/chicago/pizza-on-earth-goodwill-toward-men-a-restaurant-opens-in-lawndale/Content?oid=887853.

Piliavin, Jill. "Doing Well by Doing Good: Benefits for the Benefactor." In *Flourishing: Positive Psychology and the Life Well Lived*, edited by Corey Keyes and Jonathan Haidt, 227–48. Washington, DC: American Psychological Association, 2003.

Platt, David. *Radical: Taking Back Your Faith from the American Dream.* Colorado Springs: Multnomah, 2010.

"The Politics of Financial Insecurity." *People Press*, January 8, 2015. Online: http://www.people-press.org/2015/01/08/the-politics-of-financial-insecurity-a-democratic-tilt-undercut-by-low-participation/.

"The Poor Are Still with Us: Peter Edelman, Policy Advocate." *Christian Century* 129 (2012) 26–27, 29.

Post, Stephen. "Altruism, Happiness, and Health: It's Good to Be Good." *International Journal of Behavioral Medicine* 12 (2005) 66–77.

Pota, Vikas. "Companies Are Spending Too Little on Education—and in the Wrong Places." *The Guardian*, January 14, 2015. Online: http://www.theguardian.com/sustainable-business/2015/jan/14/companies-business-education-health-jobs-employees-careers.

Preventing Child Maltreatment: A Guide to Taking Action and Generating Evidence. Online: http://whqlibdoc.who.int/publications/2006/9241594365_eng.pdf.

Priebe, Alexandra, and Cristen Suhr. "Hidden in Plain View: The Commercial Sexual Exploitation of Girls in Atlanta." September 2005. Online: http://www.childtrafficking.com/Docs/atlanta_women_05_girls_0109.pdf.

Pringle, Peter. *A Place at the Table: The Crisis of 49 Million Hungry Americans and How to Solve It.* New York: PublicAffairs, 2013.

Prior, Karen Swallow. "Why Are Christians Such Bad Tippers?" *Christianity Today*, January 2013. Online: http://www.christianitytoday.com/women/2013/january/why-are-christians-such-bad-tippers.html.

"Prioritize Ending Domestic Hunger." November 19, 2013. Personal Post. Online: https://www.facebook.com/RepFrankWolf.

Progress for Children Beyond Averages: Learning from the MDGs (No. 11). Online: http://www.unicef.org/publications/index_82231.html.

"Progress on Drinking Water and Sanitation." Online: http://apps.who.int/iris/bit-stream/10665/112727/1/9789241507240_eng.pdf.

"Protecting Children from Orphan Dealers." *IRIN News*, May 27, 2009. Online: http://www.irinnews.org/report/84582/west-africa-protecting-children-from-or.

Psacharopoulos, George, and Harry Patrinos. "Returns to Investment in Education: A Further Update." *Education Economics* 12 (2004) 111–34.

Putnam, Robert D. *Our Kids: The American Dream in Crisis*. New York: Simon and Schuster, 2015.

"Putting an End to Abusive Car Loans." *New York Times*, June 14, 2015. Online: http://www.nytimes.com/2015/06/14/opinion/sunday/putting-an-end-to-abusive-car-loans.html?_r=0.

Radelet, Steve. *Emerging Africa: How 17 Countries Are Leading the Way*. Baltimore: Center for Global Development, 2010.

Ragland, J. D., et al. "Working Memory for Complex Figures." *Neuropsychology* 16 (2002) 370–79.

Rangan, V. Kasturi, and Katherine Lee. *CFW Clinics in Kenya: To Profit or Not for Profit* Cambridge, MA: Harvard Business Review, 2011.

Rank, Mark, et al. *Chasing the American Dream: Understanding What Shapes our Fortunes*. New York: Oxford University Press, 2014.

———. *One Nation, Underprivileged: Why American Poverty Affects Us All*. New York: Oxford University Press, 2004.

———. "Poverty in America Is Mainstream." *New York Times*, November 2, 2013. Online: http://opinionator.blogs.nytimes.com/2013/11/02/poverty-in-america-is-mainstream/?hp&rref=opinion.

Rashid, Hamid. "Land Rights and the Millennium Development Goals: How the Legal Empowerment Approach Can Make a Difference." *IDLO Legal Empowerment Working Papers No. 15. Namati*, February 25, 2013. Online: https://namati.org/resources/land-rights-and-the-millennium-development-goals-how-the-legal-empowerment-approach-can-make-a-difference-paper-n-15/.

Reardon, Sean. "The Widening Academic Achievement Gap between the Rich and the Poor: New Evidence and Possible Explanations." In *Whither Opportunity? Rising Inequality, Schools, and Children's Life Chances*, edited by Greg Duncan and Richard Murnace, 91–116. New York: Russell Sage, 2011.

Rebell, Michael, and Jessica Wolff. "U.S. Schools Have a Poverty Crisis, Not an Education Crisis." *Huffington Post*, February 2, 2012. Online: http://www.huffingtonpost.com/michael-rebell/us-schools-have-a-poverty_b_1247635.html.

"'Recycled Orchestra' Turns Trash into Music." *CBN*, April 16, 2015. Online: http://www1.cbn.com/cbnnews/world/2015/April/Recycled-Orchestra-Turns-Trash-in-Music.

Reisner, Rebecca. "4 Ways You Can Give (And Get) Through Socially Responsible Investing." *Forbes*, December 3, 2014. Online: http://www.forbes.com/sites/learnvest/2014/12/03/4-ways-you-can-give-and-get-through-socially-responsible-investing//.

"Remarkable Declines in Global Poverty, But Major Challenges Remain." *World Bank*, April 17, 2013. Online: https://www.worldbank.org/en/news/press-release/2013/04/17/remarkable-declines-in-global-poverty-but-major-challenges-remain.

Rich, Mokoto. "Fewer Top Graduates Want to Join Teach for America." *New York Times*, February 6, 2015. Online: http://www.nytimes.com/2015/02/06/education/fewer-top-graduates-want-to-join-teach-for-america.html.

Ripley, Amanda. "The U.S. Needs More Rigorous and Selective Teacher Colleges." *New York Times*, March 3, 2015. Online: http://www.nytimes.com/roomfordebate/2015/03/03/how-to-ensure-and-improve-teacher-quality/the-us-needs-more-rigoruous-and-selective-teacher-colleges.

Ritter, Nancy, Thomas Simon, and Reshma Mahendra. *Executive Summary: Changing Course: Preventing Gang Membership*. Online: http://permanent.access.gpo.gov/gpo41187/PDF%20version/239233.pdf.

Robinson, Keith, and Angel Harris. *The Broken Compass: Parental Involvement with Children's Education*. Cambridge, MA: Harvard University Press, 2014.

Robles, Frances, and Shaila Dewan. "Skip Child Support. Go to Jail. Lose Job. Repeat." *New York Times*, April 20, 2015. Online: http://www.nytimes.com/2015/04/20/us/skip-child-support-go-to-jail-lose-job-repeat.html?src=mv.

Rochkind, David. "Haiti Earthquake: Thanks to a CARE Microsavings Program, Mireille Is on the Road to Financial Stability." *Care*, January 11, 2013. Online: http://www.care.org/impact/stories/haiti-earthquake-thanks-cares-microsavings-program-mireille-road-financial-stability.

Roesch, Scott, et al. "Dispositional Hope and the Propensity to Cope: A Daily Diary Assessment of Minority Adolescents." *Cultural Diversity and Ethnic Minority Psychology* 16 (2010) 191–98.

Rogers, John, and Nicole Mirra. *It's About Time: Learning Time and Educational Opportunity in California High Schools*. Los Angeles: Institute for Democracy, Education, and Access, 2014.

Roling, Keum, and Charlotte Pritchard. "How Social Enterprise Can Reduce Gang Violence." *The Guardian*, January 28, 2013. Online: http://www.theguardian.com/social-enterprise-network/crime-and-justice-blog/2013/jan/28/social-enterprise-reduce-gang-violence.

Roodman, David. *Due Diligence: An Impertinent Inquiry into Microfinance*. Washington, DC: Center for Global Development, 2012.

Rose, Jeff. "Is College Overrated? The Top 21 Highest Paying Jobs with NO College Degree." *Good Financial Cents*, November 28, 2011. Online: http://www.goodfinancialcents.com/12-highest-paying-jobs-careers-without-no-college-degree-diploma/.

Rosenberg, Tina. "Escaping the Cycle of Scarcity." *New York Times*, September 25, 2013. Online: http://opinionator.blogs.nytimes.com/2013/09/25/escaping-the-cycle-of-scarcity/?hp.

———. A Green Revolution, This Time for Africa." *New York Times*, March 9, 2014. Online: http://opinionator.blogs.nytimes.com/2014/04/09/a-green-revolution-this-time-for-africa/?_r=1.

Roth, Genevieve. "What Would You Do With an Extra Hour Each Day? Here's Something You Can Do to Help Women around the World." *Glamour*, January 2015. Online: http://www.glamour.com/inspired/blogs/the-conversation/2015/01/clean-water-campaign.

Rothstein, Richard. "A Look at the Health-Related Causes of Low-Student Achievement." *EPI*, March 1, 2011. Online: http://www.epi.org/publication/a_look_at_the_health-related_causes_of_low_student_achievement/.

Rusaw, Rick, and Eric Swanson. *The Externally Focused Church*. Loveland, CO: Group, 2004.

Rutherford, Stuart. *The Poor and Their Money*. New York: Oxford University Press, 2000.

Sachs, Stefanie. *What the Fork Are You Eating?: An Action Plan for Your Pantry and Plate*. New York: Tarcher, 2014.

Sampson, Robert. *Great American City: Chicago and the Enduring Neighborhood Effect*. Chicago: University of Chicago Press, 2012.

Sanchez, Pedro. "En Route to Plentiful Food Production in Africa." Online: http://www.nature.com/articles/nplants201414.

Sawhill, Isabel. "Trends in Intergenerational Mobility." In *Getting Ahead or Losing Ground: Economic Mobility in America*, edited by Ron Hawkins, et al., 27–36. Washington, DC: Brookings, 2008.

Schapiro, Jeff. "Study: Christians Who Tithe Have Healthier Finances Than Those Who Don't." *Christian Post,* May 15, 2013. Online: http://www.christianpost.com/news/study-christians-who-tithe-have-healthier-finances-than-those-who-dont-95959/.

Schneider, John. *The Good of Affluence: Seeking God in a Culture of Wealth*. Grand Rapids: Eerdmans, 2002.

Schor, Juliet. *The Overspent American: Upscaling, Downshifting, and the New Consumer*. New York: Basic, 1998.

Schwartz, Carolyn, et al. "Altruistic Social Interest Behaviors Are Associated with Better Mental Health." *Psychosomatic Medicine* 65 (2003) 778–85.

"Scott Hillstrom: Entrepreneur of the Year." *Franchising World*, February 19, 2014 Online: http://franchisingworld.com/scott-hillstrom-entrepreneur-of-the-year-award-winner/.

Seabrook, John. "Don't Shoot: A Radical Approach to the Problem of Gang Violence." *New Yorker,* June 22, 2009. Online: http://www.newyorker.com/magazine/2009/06/22/dont-shoot-2.

Sedlak, Andrea, and Diane Broadhurst. *Third National Incidence Study of Child Abuse and Neglect, Final Report*. Washington, DC: Department of Health and Human Services, 1996.

Serpas, Ronal. "The Dangerous Contagion of Violent Crime." *Wall Street Journal*, April 5, 2015. Online: http://www.wsj.com/articles/ronal-serpas-the-dangerous-contagion-of-violent-crime-1428271115.

Shear, Robin. "Sharing the Secret to 'Results.'" University of Miami, January 21, 2015. Online: http://www.miami.edu/index.php/news/releases/sharing_the_secret_to_results/.

Shellnutt, Kate "The Toy Makers: Chris and Will Haughey." *Christianity Today,* June 23, 2016. Online: http://www.christianitytoday.com/ct/2016/julaug/chris-and-will-haughey.html

"Shelter Beds for Human Trafficking Survivors in the United States." Online: http://www.polarisproject.org/tools-for-service-providers-and-law-enforcement/shelter-bed-report.

Shemkus, Sarah. "In Poor Countries, Companies Step in to Fill Gaps Left by Agricultural Nonprofits." *The Guardian*, February 2, 2015. Online: http://www.theguardian.com/

sustainable-business/2015/feb/02/pioneer-firms-feed-world-agriculture-india-mozambique-profit.

Sher, Julian. *Somebody's Daughter: The Hidden Story of America's Prostituted Children and the Battle to Save Them.* Chicago: Chicago Review, 2011.

Sherman, Amy. *Restorers of Hope: Reaching the Poor in Your Community with Church-based Ministries that Work.* Wheaton, IL: Crossway, 1997.

Sherter, Alain. "Millions on Food Stamps Facing Benefit Cuts." *CBS News*, November 3, 2013. Online: http://www.cbsnews.com/news/millions-on-food-stamps-facing-benefits-cuts/.

Shi, David. *In Search of the Simple Life: American Voices, Past and Present.* Salt Lake City: Peregrine Smith, 1986.

Shifflett, Charlie. "Savings Groups Help Low-Income Families 'Put Their Money to Work.'" Online: http://fivetalents.org/media-center/blog/32-from-the-field/860-savings-groups-help-low-income-families-put-their-money-to-work#.VNTUSI1oxdg.

Shipler, David. *The Working Poor: Invisible in America.* New York: Vintage, 2011.

Shonkoff, Jack, and Deborah Phillips, *From Neurons to Neighborhoods: The Science of Early Childhood Development.* Washington, DC: National Academies, 2000.

Sider, Ronald. *Good News and Good Works: A Theology for the Whole Gospel.* Grand Rapids: Baker, 1999.

———. *Just Generosity.* Grand Rapids: Baker, 1999.

———. *Rich Christians in an Age of Hunger.* Downers Grove, IL: InterVarsity, 1977.

Sider, Ronald, and Heidi Unruh. "Why and How Christians Should Care for Poor Children." In *Hope for Children in Poverty: Profiles and Possibilities*, edited by Ronald Sider and Heidi Unruh, 128–37. Valley Forge, PA: Judson, 2007.

Sider, Ronald, Philip Olson, and Heidi Unruh. *Churches That Make a Difference: Reaching Your Community with Good News and Good Works.* Grand Rapids: Baker, 2002.

Sider, Ronald, et al. *Linking Arms, Linking Lives: How Urban-Suburban Partnerships Can Transform Communities.* Grand Rapids: Baker, 2008.

Simmons, Megan. "The Case for Conditional Cash Transfers in the United States." Online: http://www.ncpa.org/pub/the-case-for-conditional-cash-transfers-in-the-united-states.

Smith, Christian, and Hilary Davidson. *The Paradox of Generosity: Giving We Receive, Grasping We Lose.* New York: Oxford University Press, 2014.

Smith, Christian, Michael Emerson, and Patricia Snell. *Passing the Plate.* New York: Oxford University Press, 2008.

Smith, Warren Cole. "Frank Wolf Reflects on 34 years in Congress." *World*, December 4, 2014. Online: http://www.worldmag.com/2014/12/frank_wolf_reflects_on_34_years_in_congress.

Smolan, Rick, and Jennifer Erwitt. *Blue Planet Run: The Race to Provide Safe Drinking Water to the World.* San Rafael, CA: Earth Aware, 2007.

Smyth, John, and Terry Wrigley. *Living on the Edge: Rethinking Poverty, Class, and Schooling.* New York: Peter Lang 2013.

Snyder, C. R. *The Psychology of Hope: You Can Get There from Here.* New York: Free Press, 1994.

———, et al. "Hopeful Choices: A School Counselors' Guide to Hope Theory." *Journal of Personality and Social Psychology* 65 (2002) 1061–70.

Snyder, Howard and Melissa Sickmund. *Juvenile Offenders and Victims: 2006 National Report.* Washington, DC: U.S. Department of Justice, 2006.

Sohn, Emily. "Coke and Other Firms Make the Business Case for Aiding World's Poorest." *The Guardian*, November 14, 2014. Online: http://www.theguardian.com/sustainable-business/2014/nov/14/role-business-development-coke-cargill-cocoa-water-ghana-africa-asia.

Soronen, Rita. "We Are Abandoning Children in Foster Care." *CNN*, April 16, 2014. Online: http://www.cnn.com/2014/04/16/opinion/soronen-foster-children/.

Sparks, Sarah, and Caralee Adams. "High School Poverty Levels Tied to College-Going." *Education Week*, October 23, 2013. Online: http://www.edweek.org/ew/articles/2013/10/23/09college.h33.html.

Stafford, Tim. "Miracles in Mozambique: How Mama Heidi Reaches the Abandoned." *Christianity Today* 56 (2012). Online: https://www.irisglobal.org/relief-and-development/education; http://www.edunations.org/.

Stafford, Wess. *Too Small to Ignore: Why Children Are the Next Big Thing*. Colorado Springs: Waterbrook, 2005.

Stearns, Rich. *The Hole in Our Gospel*. Nashville: Thomas Nelson, 2009.

———. *Unfinished: Believing is Only the Beginning*. Nashville: Thomas Nelson, 2013.

Stiglitz, Joseph. "Inequality Is Not Inevitable." *New York Times*, June 27, 2014. Online: http://opinionator.blogs.nytimes.com/2014/06/27/inequality-is-not-inevitable/.

Subramanian, Courtney. "This Woman Fought the Tough Chicago Streets and Won." *Nation Swell*, July 21, 2014. Online: http://nationswell.com/crushers-club-gets-chicago-youth-off-streets-and-boxing/.

Sundararaman, T., and Anupama Hazarika. "Education, Hunger and Malnutrition in the Indian Context." In *Education, Poverty, Malnutrition and Famine*, edited by Lorraine Pe Symaco, 97–118. New York: Bloomsbury Academic, 2014.

"'Sundays Are the Worst' Website Urges Christians to Tip Better." *Huffington Post*, March 10, 2014. Online: http://www.huffingtonpost.com/2014/03/10/sundays-are-the-worst-christian-tipping_n_4934418.html.

Sweetland, Haley. "The War on Teacher Tenure." *Time*, October 30, 2014. Online: http://time.com/3533556/the-war-on-teacher-tenure/?pcd=pw-pas.

Szalavitz, Maria. "Helping Others Helps You to Live Longer." *Health Land*, August 23, 2013. Online: http://healthland.time.com/2013/08/23/helping-others-helps-you-to-live-longer/.

"'Take Care of the King,' Introduction & Interview by Lee Nentwig." *Paradigm Magazine*, February 20, 2014. Online: http://paradigmmagazine.com/2014/02/20/paradigm-magazine-eugene-brown-interview/.

Tanner, Lindsey. "Americans' Eating Habits Have Improved a Bit—Except Among Poor." *Huffington Post*, September 2, 2014. Online: http://www.huffingtonpost.com/2014/09/02/americans-eating-habits_n_5752498.html?utm_hp_ref=business&ir=Business.

"Teacher Tenure Rules Are in a State of Flux." *PBS News Hour*, November 29, 2014. Online: http://www.pbs.org/newshour/updates/teacher-tenure-rules-state-flux/.

"Tegu Is Growing." *Tegu*, February 26, 2015. Online: http://www.tegu.com/blog/2015/02/26/tegu-is-growing-now-hiring-in-tegucigalpa-and-nyc-area/.

Tembon, Mercy. "Overview." In *Girls' Education in the 21st Century: Equality, Empowerment, and Growth*, edited by Lucia Fort and Mercy Tembon, 3–21. Washington DC: World Bank, 2008.

Templeton, Beth Lindsay. *Understanding Poverty in the Classroom: Changing Perceptions for Student Success*. Lanham, MD: Rowman and Littlefield, 2011.

Thomas-Lester, Avis. "Kings of a Different Game." *Washington Post*, March 10, 2007. Online: http://www.washingtonpost.com/wp-dyn/content/article/2007/03/10/AR2007031001383.html?referrer=emailarticle.

Thorpe, Devin. "Why CSR? The Benefits of Corporate Social Responsibility Will Move You to Act." *Forbes*, May 18, 2013. Online: http://www.forbes.com/sites/devinthorpe/2013/05/18/why-csr-the-benefits-of-corporate-social-responsibility-will-move-you-to-act/3/.

Thurow, Roger and Scott Kilman. *Enough: Why the World's Poorest Starve in an Age of Plenty*. New York: PublicAffairs, 2009.

Timmer, C. Peter. *Food Security and Scarcity: Why Ending Hunger Is So Hard*. Philadelphia: University of Pennsylvania Press, 2015.

Tirado, Linda. "This Is Why Poor People's Bad Decisions Make Perfect Sense." *Huffington Post*, November 22, 2013. Online: http://www.huffingtonpost.com/linda-tirado/why-poor-peoples-bad-decisions-make-perfect-sense_b_4326233.html.

Todd, Scott. *Hope Rising: How Christians Can End Extreme Poverty in This Generation*. Nashville: Thomas Nelson, 2014.

Tortora, Bob. "Africans' Confidence in Institutions—Which Country Stands Out?" Online: http://www.gallup.com/poll/26176/africans-confidence-institutions-which-country-stands-out.aspx.

"Trafficking in Children on the Increase." UNODC, November 2014. Online: https://www.unodc.org/unodc/en/frontpage/2014/November/trafficking-in-children-on-the-increase—according-to-latest-unodc-report.html.

Trafficking in Persons Report. Online: http://www.state.gov/j/tip/rls/tiprpt/2014/.

Traub, James. "What No School Can Do." *NYT Magazine*, January 16, 2000, 52–57, 68, 81, 90–91.

Tudor, Martha Anne. "Rescued from Wealth." Online: http://www.compassion.com/magazine/rescued-from-wealth.htm.

Tufft, Ben. "Pope Francis Embraces Girl." *Independent*, January 18, 2015. Online: http://www.independent.co.uk/news/people/news/pope-francis-embraces-girl-after-she-asks-why-does-god-allow-children-to-become-prostitutes-9985855.html.

United Nations Office on Drugs and Crime. *Global Report on Trafficking in Persons 2014*. New York: United Nations, 2014.

United Nations Office of the High Commissioner for Human Rights. "Protocol to Prevent, Suppress, and Punish Trafficking in Persons, Especially Women and Children." November 15, 2000. Online: http://www.ohchr.org/EN/ProfessionalInterest/Pages/ProtocolTraffickingInPersons.aspx.

United Nations Settlement Programme. *The Challenge of the Slums: Global Report on Human Settlements, 2003*. Sterling, VA: Earthscan Publications, 2003.

US Department of Health and Human Services. "Head Start Impact Study, 2010." Online: http://www.acf.hhs.gov/programs/opre/resource/head-start-impact-study-final-report-executive-summary.

US Senate Committee on Foreign Relations. *International Trafficking of Women and Children: Statement of Inez, a Trafficking Survivor*, 106th Congress, 2nd session, February 22, 2000. Online: http://www.gpo.gov/fdsys/pkg/CHRG-106shrg63986/html/CHRG-106shrg63986.htm.

Vance, J. D. *Hillbilly Elegy: A Memoir of a Family and Culture in Crisis*. New York: Harper, 2016.

Velasquez-Manoff, Moises. "Status and Stress." *New York Times*, July 27, 2013. http://opinionator.blogs.nytimes.com/2013/07/27/status-and-stress/?src=me&ref=general.

Vincent, Roger. "Dream Center in L.A. Expects $49.7-Million Grant." *LA Times*, August 27, 2012. Online: http://articles.latimes.com/2012/aug/27/business/la-fi-property-report-20120827.

Waite, Linda, and Maggie Gallaher. *The Case for Marriage: Why Married People Are Happier, Healthier, and Better Off Financially*. New York: Doubleday, 2000.

Walker-Rodriguez, Amanda, and Rodney Hill. "Human Sex Trafficking." Online: https://leb.fbi.gov/2011/march/human-sex-trafficking.

Walters, Justin. "Why the New Research on Mobility Matters: An Economist's View." http://www.nytimes.com/2015/05/05/upshot/why-the-new-research-on-mobility-matters-an-economists-view.html.

Wang, Meme. "A Faith-Based Clinic in Chicago." http://journalofethics.ama-assn.org/2005/05/msoc1-0505.html.

Ward, Paula Reed. "Family Creates a Home for Ethiopian Adoptees Abused by Previous Parents." *Post Gazette*, March 8, 2015. Online: http://www.post-gazette.com/local/region/2015/03/08/Family-creates-a-home-for-Ethiopian-adoptees-abused-by-previous-parents/stories/201503220001.

"'Wealth Gap' Seen in American Diet." *NBC News*, September 1, 2014. Online: http://www.nbcnews.com/health/diet-fitness/wealth-gap-seen-american-diet-n193376.

"Web-based Injury Statistics Query and Reporting System." www.cdc.gov/injury/wisqars/index.html.

Webster, Daniel. "How to Close the Achievement Gap? Greater School Choice." *MPR News*, January 26, 2012. Online: http://www.mprnews.org/story/2012/01/26/webber.

Weinhold, Tim. "Why 'Overpaying' Workers Makes Biblical and Business Sense." *Christianity Today*, May 18, 2015. Online: http://www.christianitytoday.com/ct/2015/may-web-only/why-overpaying-workers-makes-biblical-and-business-sense.html.

Whaley, Floyd, and Austin Ramzy. "Outpouring for Francis in Poignant Manila Visit." *New York Times*, January 19, 2015. Online: http://www.nytimes.com/2015/01/19/world/asia/pope-in-the-philippines.html.

"'Where Am I? and What's the Best Move?': Eugene Brown Teaches Chess and Life Skills." *Education Town Hall Forum*, January 13, 2014. Online: http://educationtownhall.org/2014/01/13/chess-and-life/.

White, Howard. "Educating the World: How to Get Pupils in Developing Countries to Learn." *The Guardian*, September 26, 2013. Online: http://www.theguardian.com/global-development/poverty-matters/2013/sep/26/educating-world-children-developing-countries.

Wilson, Kim. "Thrift-Led Development." In *Savings Groups at the Frontier*, edited by Candace Nelson, 83–100. Rugby, UK: Practical Action, 2013.

Wilson, Kim, Malcolm Harper, and Matthew Griffith, eds. *Financial Promise for the Poor: How Groups Build Microsavings*. Sterling, VA: Kumarian, 2010.

Wilson, Marlene. *How to Mobilize Church Volunteers*. Minneapolis: Augsburg, 1983.

Wilson, William Julius. *The Truly Disadvantaged: The Inner City, the Underclass, and Public Policy*. Chicago: University of Chicago Press, 1987.

Wolf, Frank. "Virginia Can Do More to Combat Hunger." *Fairfax News*, October 25, 2013. Online: http://fairfaxnews.com/2013/10/op-ed-rep-wolf-says-virginia-can-combat-hunger/.

Wolf, Frank, and Anne Morse. *Prisoner of Conscience: One Man's Crusade for Global Human and Religious Rights*. Grand Rapids: Zondervan, 2011.

"World Can End Extreme Poverty and Increase Shared Prosperity." *World Bank*, April 2, 2013. Online: http://www.worldbank.org/en/news/video/2013/04/02/jim-kim-world-can-end-extreme-poverty.

"The World Only Needs 30 Billion Dollars to Eradicate the Scourge of Hunger." *FAO*, June 3, 2008. Online: http://www.fao.org/newsroom/en/news/2008/1000853/index.html.

"World Refugee Day: Global Forced Displacement Tops 50 Million for the First Time in Post-World War II Era." June 20, 2014. Online: http://www.unhcr.org/53a155bc6.html.

"World Report on Violence and Health: Summary 2015." Online: http://www.who.int/violence_injury_prevention/violence/world_report/en/summary_en.pdf.

WRAP, *The Food We Waste*. Online: http://www.ns.is/ns/upload/files/pdf-skrar/matarskyrsla1.pdf.

Wydick, Bruce. "The Best Ways to Help the Poor." *Christianity Today*, October 26, 2016. Online: http://www.christianitytoday.com/ct/2016/october-web-only/best-ways-to-help-poor.html?utm_source=ctweekly-html&utm_medium=Newsletter&utm_term=9581590&utm_content=474071919&utm_campaign=email.

———."Cost-Effective Compassion: The 10 Most Popular Strategies for Helping the Poor." *Christianity Today*, February 17, 2012. Online: http://www.christianitytoday.com/ct/2012/february/popular-strategies-helping-the-poor.html.

———. "The Key to Prosperity: It's Not Knowledge or Work Ethic, It Turns Out." *Christianity Today*, May 22, 2015. Online: http://www.christianitytoday.com/ct/2015/may-web-only/key-to-prosperity.html.

———. "Want to Change the World? Sponsor a Child" *Christianity Today*, June 14, 2013. Online: http://www.christianitytoday.com/ct/2013/june/want-to-change-world-sponsor-child.html?start=1.

Wydick, Bruce, Paul Glewwe, and Laine Rutledge. "Does International Sponsorship Work? A Six-Country Study on Impacts of Adult Life Outcomes." *Journal of Political Economy* 121 (2013) 393–436.

"Your Chicago: Crushers Club." *CBS News Chicago*, February 14, 2014. Online: http://chicago.cbslocal.com/2014/02/14/your-chicago-crushers-club/.

Yunus, Muhammad, with Alan Jolis, *Banker to the Poor: Micro-lending and the Battle against World Poverty*. New York: PublicAffairs, 1999.

Yunus, Muhammad, and Karl Webber. *Creating a World without Poverty: Social Business and the Future of Capitalism*. New York: PublicAffairs, 2009.

Zahn, Margaret, ed. *The Delinquent Girl*. Philadelphia: Temple University Press, 2009.

Zissis, Carin. "Learning from a Troubled Gang Truce." *US News*, June 27, 2014. Online: http://www.usnews.com/opinion/blogs/world-report/2014/06/27/el-salvador-gangs-provide-crime-reduction-lessons-in-latin-america.

CPSIA information can be obtained
at www.ICGtesting.com
Printed in the USA
BVHW041952260722
643004BV00005B/7

9 781532 600715